DUKE·UNIVERSITY·PUBLICATIONS

THE GREAT AWAKENING
IN VIRGINIA, 1740-1790

LONDON:

CAMBRIDGE UNIVERSITY PRESS

———

NEW YORK:

G. E. STECHERT & CO.

TOKYO:

MARUZEN AND COMPANY, LTD.

SHANGHAI:

EDWARD EVANS & SONS, LTD.

BUENOS AIRES:

J. LAJOUANE & CO.

GEORGE WHITEFIELD

The Great Awakening in Virginia, 1740-1790

BY

WESLEY M. GEWEHR

DUKE UNIVERSITY PRESS
DURHAM, N. C.
1930

PRINTED BY THE SEEMAN PRESS
DURHAM, NORTH CAROLINA, U.S.A.

TO

My Mother

WHOSE UNSHAKEN CHRISTIAN FAITH
THROUGH MANY TRIALS HAS BEEN A NOBLE
EXAMPLE TO HER CHILDREN

PREFACE

In this study of the Great Awakening in Virginia, the author endeavors to show the far-reaching effects of the series of evangelical revivals which swept the colony in wave after wave during the thirty or forty years preceding the American Revolution, and then again after the war. He believes that he has proven that the rise of the popular churches, which resulted from the Great Awakening, contributed very definitely, not only to the religious life of Virginia, but also to the rise of political democracy, and to the social revolution which had transformed the Old Dominion by the end of the eighteenth century. Furthermore, he shows that the Great Awakening set in motion certain humanitarian and educational forces which left their permanent impress upon the life of Virginia. These changes are designated the internal revolution, and the writer is firmly convinced that not enough attention has been paid to the part played by the churches in bringing about this transformation.

Many libraries have been visited in the preparation of this study, but especially useful were materials found in the Virginia State Library, the Virginia Baptist Historical Society, the Union Theological Seminary (Presbyterian) of Richmond, Virginia, the Library of Congress, and the Presbyterian Historical Society at Philadelphia. The sources, both printed and manuscript, appear in the documentation and in the bibliography at the end of the book. The location of some of the more valuable and rare materials is indicated from time to time in the notes.

I am much indebted to my teachers at the University of Chicago, particularly to Professors William E. Dodd and Marcus W. Jernegan, under whose encouragement and guidance this work was first undertaken as a doctoral dissertation. They offered many helpful suggestions and criticisms in the course of its preparation.

I can offer only a general word of appreciation to the librarians and archivists who assisted me in locating materials. I should, however, be ungrateful not to mention the name of Dr. Garnett Ryland, of the University of Richmond, who gave me freedom of access to the valuable materials in the Virginia Baptist Historical Society, and more than once called my attention to sources which I might have overlooked. To Mr. G. M. Peck, curator of special collections at Princeton University, I am indebted for engravings of the Presbyterian leaders. Dr. Ryland loaned me likenesses of Robert B. Semple and of John Leland. The New York Public Library kindly did much indispensable photostatic work. My wife rendered indispensable assistance in the reading of proof and the preparation of the index. Finally, I am under great obligations to the Duke University Press for its interest in publishing this study which otherwise might never have seen the light of day.

W. M. Gewehr.

Washington, D. C.,
October 3, 1929.

TABLE OF CONTENTS

LIST OF ILLUSTRATIONS AND MAPS

THE GREAT AWAKENING
IN VIRGINIA, 1740-1790

CHAPTER I

The Great Awakening Comes to America

The eighteenth century was an epoch of vital importance in the history of religious movements. It was the period of a great evangelical revival which was international and interdenominational in its scope. In Germany this was manifested in Pietism, associated particularly with the names of Spener and Francke. In the British Isles it became identified with the great Methodist revival of the Wesleys and Whitefield, in which a number of subsidiary streams combined.[1] In America, under the name of the Great Awakening, it swept as a tidal wave of religious fervor over the colonies from New England to Georgia. Wherever it penetrated, the evangelical movement brought with it a revival of personal religion and was concerned little, if at all, with a reformation of doctrine. It represented an effort to establish piety and to awaken a spiritual life in believers everywhere. It found churches dying under the burden of cold formalism; it left them reinvigorated and glowing with a fresh spiritual zeal.

In the American colonies the Awakening was preceded by a lamentable absence in religious zeal.[2] The Congregationalists of New England had declined very rapidly from their Puritan standards in the generations following the first settlement of New England.[3] The Half-way Covenant which permitted

[1] A. W. Nagler, *Pietism and Methodism* (Nashville, 1918), ably treats the whole question of the relation between these two movements.

[2] Joseph Tracy, *The Great Awakening*, deals especially with New England; C. H. Maxson, *The Great Awakening in the Middle Colonies*, with that region; Charles Hodge, *Constitutional History of the Presbyterian Church*, Vol. II, has a chapter on the Great Awakening; Thomas Prince (ed) *The Christian History* for the years 1743 and 1744 (Boston), and John Gillies, *Historical Collections Relating to the Success of the Gospel* (London, 1845, first published in 1754, are the great source books. See also F. L. Chapell, *The Great Awakening of 1740;* J. A. Smucker, "The Great Awakening," *Proc. American Antiquarian Soc.,* 1874; T. S. Capers, "The Great Awakening in the Middle Colonies," *Journal of the Presbyterian Historical Society,* VIII, 296-315.

[3] Prince, *The Christian History,* contains many testimonials as to this fact.

morally respectable persons to enter the church although they had not experienced conversion, opened the doors to laxity and worldliness. There also seems to have been no little defection from sound doctrine. Among the Presbyterians, too, little was known of vital experimental religion, and there was much complaint of lack of zeal and fidelity in the preaching of the gospel, to say nothing of the conviction that many members of the Synod of Philadelphia were in an unconverted state.[4] The Anglicans were no better off, indifference, coldness, formality and lack of spirituality characterizing both clergy and laity.[5] Religious destitution was also great among the Lutheran and Dutch Reformed churches of New York, New Jersey and Pennsylvania.[6] In a word, prior to the Great Awakening the evangelical doctrines were obscured by the externals, and religion had become a matter of dead formality in churches everywhere throughout the colonies.

Such were the conditions when, during the second quarter of the eighteenth century, sporadic revivals began to break out under the preaching of a number of evangelical pastors in various parts of the colonies. Theodorus Frelinghuysen, of the Dutch Reformed connection, landed in New York in January, 1720, and became the apostle of revivalism to that sect, which like every other had fallen into formalism.[7] The field of his labors was among the Dutch settlements of the Raritan Valley in New Jersey. The earnestness and passion with which Frelinghuysen preached resulted in many conversions as well as much opposition. By 1726 the revival had not only gripped the Dutch churches of the Raritan region, but was spreading to the newly organized Presbyterian congregations in the valley. Significantly enough Frelinghuysen, the originator of the movement, was not a Hollander but a German who had come under pietistic influences in the fatherland.

[4] Hodge, *Constitutional History of the Presbyterian Church*, II, 15-20, 22; Prince, *passim*.

[5] See below, Chap. II, where conditions in Virginia are discussed.

[6] Maxson, *The Great Awakening in the Middle Colonies*, Chap. I.

[7] *Ibid.*, p. 13.

Frelinghuysen worked hand in hand with the young Gilbert Tennent, who was ordained at New Brunswick in the fall of 1726 and who became one of the principal promoters of the revival among the Presbyterians.[8] In fact, the earliest beginnings of the Great Awakening in that denomination were evidenced at New Brunswick under Gilbert Tennent's preaching in 1727.[9] That the latter was greatly impressed and influenced by Frelinghuysen's evangelical zeal is unquestioned. In 1730 John Tennent, brother of Gilbert, became pastor at Freehold, New Jersey.[10] He served only eighteen months but during this time a remarkable revival occurred, albeit the congregation was in a most distracted condition at the time of his arrival. He preached with great emotion, frequently moving his hearers to tears, and before his death, in April, 1732, there had been many conversions. The work went on with even greater results under the ministry of his brother William, who filled the Freehold pulpit during the last six months of John Tennent's life and continued the work after the latter died.[11]

In 1734 the Awakening was given fresh impetus by the outbreak of Edwards' revival in Northampton, Massachusetts.[12] In the midst of spiritual deadness Edwards began to proclaim anew the evangelical doctrines. Remarkable conversions followed and Edwards soon had the entire community under the spell of his preaching. People became deeply concerned about eternal things and came in great throngs to hear him. They even met in private houses day and night to talk religion and to pray for pardon. In six months more than three hundred, or practically the entire population above sixteen years, were converted in Northampton. The revival spread from town to town through the whole Connecticut valley until one hundred and fifty com-

[8] *Ibid.,* pp. 16-17.

[9] Capers, "The Great Awakening in the Middle Colonies," *Journal of the Presbyterian Historical Society,* Vol. VIII, p. 299.

[10] Ingram, "Erection of the Presbytery of New Brunswick," *Journal of the Presbyterian Historical Society,* Vol. VI, 212-233, at p. 226.

[11] Maxson, pp. 31-33.

[12] See Tracy, *The Great Awakening,* Chapter I.

munities in Massachusetts and Connecticut were visited with scenes similar to those which took place at Northampton.[13]

Through reports which were given to the public the Edwardian revival had widespread influence in America and gave fresh impetus to the work. Over in England the *Narrative of Surprising Conversions* was read with deep feeling by John Wesley, and it encouraged him to work zealously for like results.[14] This was in October, 1738, a few months after Wesley's conversion, shortly after he had returned greatly depressed from America, and just before the beginning of his remarkable work in England. Wesley had Edwards' "Narrative" reprinted and gave it wide circulation. It was very influential in the spread of the revival spirit in the mother country.[15]

John Wesley had been in Georgia in 1736-7 at the very time that Edwards' revival was in progress in New England. The work of the young missionary in the colony is often spoken of disparagingly and Wesley himself could not, at the time, see any particular results. He left Georgia depressed and discouraged. In the light of later events, however, we can see that his efforts contributed to the Great Awakening. Whitefield found that Wesley had accomplished much good during his short stay in America and had laid foundations which could not be destroyed.[16] In his maturer judgment Wesley saw in his Georgia sojourn a period full of fruit both for himself and the people. "All in Georgia have heard the Word of God, and some have believed and begun to run well," was his later verdict. In his *Account of the Late Work of God in North America,*

---

[13] J. E. McCulloch, "The Place of Revivals in American History," *Meth. Rev.* (So.), Vol. XXI (1902), pp. 681-697; F. H. Foster, "Revivals of Religion" in *New Schaff Herzog Rel. Enc.*, X, 11-12. Foster places the number of conversions in New England at 50,000 out of a population of 250,000. Many new Congregational and Separatist churches sprang up.

[14] E. R. Hendrix, "Jonathan Edwards and John Wesley," *Meth. Rev. Quar.*, Vol. LXII, pp. 28-29.

[15] Hendrix, *loc. cit.;* Luke Tyerman, *Life and Times of John Wesley,* I, 397; *Maxson,* p. 2.

[16] G. Alexander, "Two Chapters from the Early History of Methodism in the South," *Meth. Rev.* (So.), Vol. XLVI, pp. 3-20, at pp. 7-8; the same article is in *Meth. Quar. Rev.*, Vol. LXIII; see also Tyerman, I, 170.

published in 1778, Wesley mentions his work in Georgia as one of the main sources of the Great Awakening.[17] His carefully kept *Journal* for these months, in which items are recorded meticulously, shows that he was an indefatigable worker. On Sabbaths he held services through the day, beginning at five A.M. Here, too, the first classes and bands appeared in which the more seriously minded persons met once or twice a week to reprove, instruct and exhort one another, while from these a smaller number was chosen for more intensive spiritual cultivation. Significantly, too, while in Georgia Wesley was accustomed to attend the services of the Moravians "not as a teacher, but as a learner." While much of Wesley's usefulness in Georgia was destroyed by his rigid conformity to the ritual and narrow sacramentarian views, still his stay was an epoch of vital importance in the life of the man, and in the moulding of the rudiments of Methodism. For the colonies we may regard the Georgia sojourn as supplying one of the contributory elements in the Great Awakening. When Whitefield came he found the people in Savannah eager to hear him.

When Whitefield arrived at Lewes, Delaware, on October 30, 1739, Edwards' revival had generally subsided and reaction had set in.[18] The evangelical spirit had been aroused in New England, the Middle Colonies, and in Georgia but some one was needed to restore and unify the work. This was Whitefield's great service. People were in an expectant attitude, for they had been reading of his notable work in the colonial newspapers.[19] In 1739 Whitefield preached with remarkable success

[17] Alexander, *loc. cit.,* pp. 5-6.

[18] Abel Stevens, *Centenary History of American Methodism,* p. 56; McCulloch, *loc. cit.,* p. 688. Under Aaron Burr a local revival had started at Newark which, in a sense, was a renewal of Edwards' work. See Maxson, pp. 41, 54.

[19] *Virginia Gazette,* July 27, 1739, for example, contains quotations from the London papers telling of the vast crowds which ran as high as 10,000 and 20,000, to whom Whitefield preached. See Maxson, pp. 41-42 for other examples.

in the Middle and Southern Colonies and in the fall of 1740 he made his tour through New England.[20]

It was in this year that the Great Awakening reached its high tide in the North. Edwards' revival was renewed on a much grander scale, being augmented by the ministrations of Whitefield. Fifteen thousand in New England are said to have "experienced religion" under his influence within a few weeks.[21] Edwards, too, preached with effect, and so vividly did he picture the torments of hell that people shrieked, cried, moaned and groveled on the floor or fell prostrate into a state of coma. In the Middle Colonies the revival broke out afresh among the Presbyterians, headed by the Tennents and the Log College group.[22] Samuel Blair's congregation at New Londonderry became the center of an extended awakening in Pennsylvania, and Samuel Davies, its greatest apostle in Virginia, received his training in Blair's school at Fagg's Manor.[23] The Dutch of New Jersey and New York and the pietists of Pennsylvania were also stirred by the visits of Whitefield in 1739 and 1740.[24] This was the time of Frelinghuysen's greatest revival, and thousands of Germans flocked to hear Whitefield although they could not understand English.[25]

Whitefield was the greatest single factor in the Awakening of 1740. He zealously carried the work up and down the colonies from New England to Georgia. Among the revivalists, his influence alone touched every section of the country and every denomination. Everywhere he supplemented and augmented the work with his wonderful eloquence. He literally preached to thousands and thousands as he passed from place

[20] The details are given in Joseph Belcher's *George Whitefield,* Chap. VI. See also Tracy, *op. cit., passim.*

[21] Channing, *History of the United States,* II, 441. See also Tracy, Chap. VII.

[22] See Maxson, Chap. V.

[23] Blair's narrative in W. H. Foote, *Sketches of Virginia,* First Series, pp. 107 ff., and in other places.

[24] Maxson, p. 59; Tracy, Chaps. IV, VIII.

[25] Oscar Kuhns, *The German and Swiss Settlements of Colonial Pennsylvania,* p. 156.

to place.[26] He was the one preacher to whom people everywhere listened—the great unifying agency in the Awakening, the great moulding force among the denominations.

One of the outstanding features of the great revivals which we have traced to their climax was that they increased dissent from the regular churches and either brought on or hastened many schisms and controversies. "Separatist" or Strict Congregational churches appeared in New England, the Baptists split into Regular and Separate, while the Old Side-New Side schism in the Presbyterian church lasted from 1741 to 1758. The Methodists, too, were the revivalist wing of the Anglican Church, and while they were not strong in the colonies before the Revolution, they represent a later phase of the Great Awakening which will demand our attention.

At this point we must take notice of the Presbyterian controversy, for the revival in Virginia cannot be understood apart from it. It was the New Side Presbyterian missionaries who followed upon the trail of Whitefield and whose work constituted the first phase of the Awakening in that colony.

We need not in this study discuss all the points of discipline and practice which led to the Presbyterian schism of 1741.[27] It is sufficient to note that for some years differences in certain views between two groups in the Synod of Philadelphia had been growing more pronounced.[28] One element which has been called the "strict Presbyterian," was desirous of rigidly adhering to all the rigours of the Scottish Presbyterian system.[29]

[26] E.g., *Virginia Gazette,* December 7-14, 1739, notices that Whitefield had preached nineteen times in Philadelphia and eight times in New York to such large crowds that the churches could not contain them. He resorted to the open fields where his hearers numbered from 5,000 to 10,000. People even stood in the rain to hear him. See *ibid.,* January 11-18, 1739/40. See Tracy for many estimates for New England.

[27] This schism forms a part of Maxson's study. The official documents are gathered in convenient form in S. J. Baird, *Collection of the Acts . . . of the Supreme Judicatory of the Presbyterian Church in America.* We shall hereafter refer to this valuable compilation as Assembly's *Digest.* It is organized topically and is indispensable.

[28] See Thomas Murphy, *The Presbytery of the Log College,* p. 158 ff.; Maxson, p. 69 ff.

[29] Samuel Miller, *Life of the Reverend John Rodgers,* pp. 73-74.

They were the Scotch-Irish group, trained in the old-world universities and zealous for all the Westminster standards. As a class they attached much importance to academic learning and were opposed to too close an examination of candidates for holy orders on the score of personal piety and experimental religion. The other faction in the Synod which, after the schism of 1741, became known as the New Side group, desired many modifications of the strict presbyterial order. While they believed thoroughly in an educated ministry, they did not set so high a value on human learning, provided the candidate satisfactorily met their requirement in personal piety.[30] They placed much emphasis on the matter of conversion and one's religious experience. In short, they were the evangelical wing of the Synod. The outstanding men in it were the Tennents, the Blairs, Samuel Finley, and others in sympathy with the Log College principles. In 1738 they had secured the erection of the New Brunswick Presbytery.

Each of the rival groups in the Synod was strong enough to secure the adoption of its favorite measure. In 1729, after long debate, the "Adopting Act" was passed by which assent to the Westminster Confession of Faith was required of all members of the Synod, and of all candidates for admission to the presbyteries.[31] This was a victory for the conservatives. In 1734 the New Side gained its main point by securing the adoption of an overture concerning the trials of candidates for the ministry. It was brought in by Gilbert Tennent and directed that all candidates for the ministry be examined diligently as to "their experiences of a work of sanctifying grace in their hearts," and that none be admitted who are not, "in the eye of charity, serious Christians." Each Presbytery was ordered to examine each year into the preaching and conduct of its ministers and "to take effectual care that each of their ministers are faithful in the discharge of their awful trust."[32]

[30] Murphy, pp. 163-164.
[31] Wm. M. Engles (ed.), Records of the Presbyterian Church (hereafter designated Recs. Pres. Ch.), September 19, 1729; Hodge, I, 150 ff.
[32] Recs. Pres. Ch., September 24, 1734.

The acts of 1729 and 1734 embodied the principal objects of both the Old Side and the New Side. They were the source of much contention during the next few years and their enforcement depended upon the several Presbyteries that examined candidates. The one or the other was carried out diligently or indifferently, according to the party which happened to control the Presbytery, and the acts became the subject of heated debate when the Synod convened. Each found it easy to charge the other with some violation or other of its favorite rule.

Two things brought the dissensions to a climax, namely, rivalry over the matter of institutions of learning patronized by the two parties and, secondly, the coming of Whitefield. The Presbyterian church considered a liberal education as an indispensable qualification for its ministers. The usual evidence of the literary qualifications of a candidate for orders was the possession of a diploma or degree from some College or University in Europe or in America. Many of the first ministers in this country had received their education in Scotland or Ireland, and some in the New England colleges. As there was no institution of higher learning in the Middle Colonies, the Presbyterian Church depended upon emigration from the Old World or from New England for its supply of ministers. This condition had its drawbacks. The expense of acquiring an education in New England was very high, to say nothing of going to Ireland or Scotland. In addition, the ministers who came from New England were brought up under the Congregationalist system, and their training produced habits and customs not altogether congenial to those of the strict Scottish Presbyterians. The men who came from across the Atlantic were not always of the best character, we are told. It was, indeed, difficult to ascertain the truth concerning a minister from abroad, for testimonials might easily be, and sometimes were, forged by those who came to the New World to escape from censure incurred by their misconduct.[33] Furthermore, the supply of ministers from Europe and

[33] Archibald Alexander, *Biographical Sketches of the Founder and Alumni of the Log College*, pp. 41-43. The subject of education in the Presbyterian Church is treated in Chap. IX, below.

New England was insufficient to meet the growing demands of the increasing membership.[34]

From these facts it is seen that there was a real need for a seminary conveniently located in the colonies and under the auspices of the Presbyterian Church, where candidates might secure the proper training for the ministry. It was to meet this demand that the Reverend William Tennent set up a school in his log house about twenty miles north of Philadelphia, on Neshaminy Creek.[35] This school, designated the "Log College" by its opponents, has become famed in history as the forerunner of Princeton. It soon became "the most approved place of education, south of Yale College, and north of William and Mary; and with this last mentioned venerable institution, gave the youth of the middle and southern provinces their only chance for extensive and thorough training; and was the only one in all the South where Presbyterian discipline prevailed."[36]

The Log College turned out a school of preachers who became noted for the fervency of their piety, their glowing zeal, their plain, exhortatory and impassioned gospel, their evangelical faith.[37] Personal piety and experimental religion were nourished with exceeding care by the master of the Log College, and his students went out to become the great revivalists in the Presbyterian Church—the leaders in the Great Awakening. William Robinson, the younger Tennents, the Blairs and Samuel Finley, all received their training in the Neshaminy school. The preaching of the Log College men was well adapted to the demands of the time and they attained wide popularity. In this ardour for the great work which they set out to do, these men were apt to disregard the ecclesiastical rules and formal regulations of the Synod. No presbyterial boundaries

[34] Philadelphia Synod to President Clap of Yale, May 30, 1746, in *Recs. Pres. Ch.*, May 31, 1746.

[35] Alexander, *Log College*, pp. 42-43; Murphy, pp. 71-73; Whitefield's description of the Log College is given in Alexander, p. 11, and in Murphy, pp. 76-77. See also Foote, *Sketches of Virginia*, First Series, pp. 225-6, 390.

[36] Foote, p. 390. See also Murphy, p. 161.

[37] Murphy, pp. 78-121, discusses eminent alumni of the Log College as does also Alexander. Foote, p. 390, for characteristics of these preachers.

limited their labours; they would preach far and wide wherever the harvest was ready and wherever people would listen to them; in their minds the preaching of the gospel should be restricted by no arbitrary rules of man.

One of the greatest complaints against Gilbert Tennent and his "New Light" brethren was that they passed beyond the limits of their own Presbytery and intruded into congregations under the care of other ministers.[38] In the Minutes of the Synod of Philadelphia for the year 1738, we read concerning an overture of some members to the effect "that some order should be made to prevent irregularities that may arise in our churches, by some ministers and probationers preaching to vacant congregations without the bounds of their respective Presbyteries, without allowance from the Presbytery under whose care the said vacant congregations may be."[39] The Synod adopted a rule "that no minister belonging to this Synod shall have liberty to preach in any congregation belonging to another Presbytery whereof he is not a member, after he is advised by any minister of such Presbytery, that he thinks his preaching in that congregation will have a tendency to procure divisions and disorders, until he first obtain liberty from the Presbytery or Synod so to do."[40] The rule produced much dissatisfaction and misunderstanding and, although it was repealed in 1740, the question of itinerating was one of the troubles which brought on the schism of 1741. "Disorderly itinerations" and the making of "irregular irruptions upon the congregations to which they have no immediate relation . . . thereby sowing the seeds of division among people," are among the protests of the Old Side at the time of the separation.[41]

From the list of celebrated men which it counted among its alumni, beyond a doubt the Log College performed its task well enough. But in the minds of the strict Presbyterians who were

[38] Alexander, p. 39; Murphy, pp. 164-5.
[39] Recs. Pres. Ch., May 25, 1738.
[40] Ibid., and May 28, 1739, June 2, 1740; Assembly's Digest, pp. 592-598.
[41] Recs. Pres. Ch., June 1, 1741.

educated in the old universities it was preposterous to suppose that the paltry learning handed out in a log cabin, principally by one teacher, could be adequate preparation for the ministry. Although Mr. Tennent's classical scholarship was beyond question, his proficiency in the arts and sciences was considered inadequate. The Old Side party regarded a number from the Log College who had been examined and licensed by the Presbyteries as "without sufficient qualifications."[42]

In 1738 the Synod adopted a proposal which was considered a direct blow at the Log College by the friends of that institution. This rule required "that every student who has not studied with approbation, passing the usual courses in some of the New England or European Colleges, approved by public authority, shall, before he be encouraged by any Presbytery for sacred work of the ministry, *apply himself to this Synod*, and that they appoint a committee of their members yearly, whom they know to be well skilled in the several branches of philosophy, and divinity, and the languages to examine such students in this place, and finding them well accomplished in those several parts of learning, shall allow them a public testimonial from the Synod, which, till better provision be made, will in some measure answer the design of taking a degree in the college."[43] This rule was passed in substantially the same form by the next Synod,[44] and meant that henceforth the examination of candidates for the ministry was to be in the hands of the Synod or its committee, rather than the Presbyteries. The Tennents and their friends regarded this as a measure for preventing the Presbyteries from admitting the graduates of the Log College into the ministry, and entered a protest against it.[45]

The rule of 1738 caused considerable exasperation. Alexander in his classic account of the Log College says: "The friends of the Log College saw that the act of the Synod was

[42] Phila. Synod to Clap, *Recs. Pres. Ch.*, May 31, 1746.
[43] *Ibid.*, and *Recs. Pres. Ch.*, May 29, 1738. Italics are mine.
[44] *Ibid.*, May 26, 1739.
[45] *Ibid.*, May 28; also Phila. Synod to Clap, *loc. cit.*

directed against that institution, for there was no other school at that time in the bounds of the Synod where young men were trained for the ministry. That was not all. The act implied a reflection on all those who had before entered the ministry from this school."[46]

It happened that in 1738 the supporters of the Log College had succeeded in getting the New Brunswick Presbytery established, which included most of their friends.[47] The principal object in getting this Presbytery erected was, "that they might license such young men as they deemed properly qualified for the office; and, in their opinion fervent piety was the first and principal qualification."[48] If the Synod deemed that the graduates of the elder Tennent's school lacked in some of the marks of deep learning, to the latter the Synod seemed to esteem too lightly the piety of the candidate. The New Brunswick Presbytery ignored the rule of 1738 from the very start. Instead of seeking to secure its repeal, the attitude was taken that the Synod had transcended its authority in taking away a right which belonged to the Presbytery.[49] In August 1738, therefore, the Presbytery admitted to trial, and later licensed and ordained, one of its scholars, Mr. John Rowland, without compelling him to submit to a preparatory examination by a committee of the Synod.[50] The Synod refused to admit Rowland to membership in their body, on the ground that it had the power to judge of the qualifications of its own members.[51] In 1739, the New Brunswick Presbytery licensed James McCrea and assigned him to supply five places that had asked for preachers.[52]

[46] Alexander, pp. 48-49.
[47] *Recs. Pres. Ch.*, May 26, 1738. Gilbert and William Tennent, Samuel Blair, Eleazer Wales, and John Cross are named as its ministers in 1739. In volumes VI, VII, VIII, of the *Journal of the Pres. Hist. Soc.*, Ingram tells the history and prints the early Minutes of this Presbytery.
[48] Alexander, p. 45.
[49] Ingram, *loc. cit.*, VI, 229; Murphy, pp. 169-170.
[50] Ingram, *ibid.*; *Recs. Pres. Ch.*, May 29, 1739; Alexander, p. 48.
[51] *Recs. Pres. Ch.*, May 31, 1740; Alexander, p. 48; Miller, p. 78.
[52] Ingram, *loc. cit.*, VI, 335, 338 ff. The revivals had caused a dearth of preachers.

It was in the midst of these contentions that Whitefield came on his second visit to America to preach the revival up and down the colonies. His coming only increased the animosities already existing between the two parties in the Synod. When the Great Revival broke out under his ministry the strict wing, or Old Side, was only too ready to condemn the work "as mere wild-fire and enthusiasm," while the New Side, or New Lights as they were called, warmly embraced his doctrines and became enthusiastic supporters of the movement he represented.[53] In the Old Side protest, read in the Synod of 1741, the New Side was charged with violating presbyterial practices, entertaining heterodox principles contrary to the Westminster Confession, and "preaching the terrors of the law in such a manner, and dialect as has no precedent in the Word of God, . . . and so industriously working on the passions and affections of weak minds, as to cause them to cry out in a hideous manner, and fall down in convulsion-like fits, to the marring of the profiting both of themselves and others, who are so taken up in seeing and hearing these odd symptoms, that they cannot attend to or hear what the preacher says; and then, after all, boasting of these things as the work of God, which we are persuaded do proceed from an inferior or worse cause."[54] The New Lights maintained, on the other hand, "that all true converts are as certain of their gracious state as a person can be of what he knows by his outward senses; and are able to give a narrative of the time and manner of their conversion. . . ."[55] In short, they were preaching the gospel of the Great Awakening, pure and simple, and in doing so took a position which the Synod considered as directly contrary to the Westminster Confession of Faith, the Catechism, and Directory, adopted in 1729. The strict wing regarded the followers of Whitefield "as a set of extravagant and ignorant enthusiasts," while the latter considered their con-

[53] Miller, *Life of Rodgers,* p. 79; *cf.* Murphy, pp. 163-4, and Maxson, p. 70.

[54] *Recs. Pres. Ch.,* June 1, 1741; Assembly's *Digest,* pp. 597-600.

[55] *Ibid.*

servative brethren of the Old Side "as a set of pharasaical formalists."[56]

Thus the coming of Whitefield furnished just the necessary fuel to precipitate the schism that had long been brewing. After the deliverance of the Old Side protest, the New Brunswick party withdrew, it being maintained by the majority of the Synod that they had no right to sit.[57] The four Tennents, William senior, and his three sons, William, Gilbert, and Charles, along with Samuel Blair, Richard Treat, and Eleazer Wales are named as the ring leaders of the group and all were excluded from the Synod.[58] Charles Tennent and Blair were from the New Castle Presbytery, the elder Tennent and Treat belonged to the Philadelphia Presbytery, while Wales and the other two Tennents are named as ministers of the recently formed New Brunswick Presbytery. These and others that had joined them "erected themselves into a separate body and licensed and ordained men for the work of the ministry that were generally ignorant and warm in the divisive scheme, and they have troubled Virginia and the New English government, and as we are informed, pretend that they belong to our body."[59] They found a strong ally in Whitefield.

After the exclusion of the New Brunswick Presbytery in 1741, the Synod of New York was formed by the union of the three Presbyteries of New York, New Brunswick, and New Castle. This took place in 1745, after several years of ineffectual efforts on the part of the New York Presbytery to procure a restoration of the excluded brethren.[60] This completed the schism which lasted until 1758 when, after nine years of negotiation, articles of union satisfactory to both wings were agreed

[56] Miller, p. 80.

[57] *Recs. Pres. Ch.*, June 1, 1741 and Phila. Synod to Clap in *ibid.*, May 31, 1746.

[58] Phila. Synod to Clap, *loc. cit.*

[59] Philadelphia Synod to Clap.

[60] *Recs. Pres. Ch.*, May 25, 1745; Assembly's *Digest*, pp. 600-608 for these negotiations pertaining to a restoration of the excluded brethren.

upon, and the Synods were united under the name of the Synod of New York and Philadelphia.[61]

That the disruption of 1741 came, was due to the presence of a pietistic group within the Presbyterian Church. These men were ready to break away from the formalism and rigidity that characterized the mode of worship in their denomination, and sought to substitute more of the devotional and emotional for the intellectual ideal in Christianity. Three issues caused by the Great Awakening brought on the schism. These were: (1) the revival and its method; (2) the evangelical training as given by the Log College; (3) the question of the right to itinerate.[62] A like movement occurred in other churches and led to similar divisions. Undoubtedly both sides were at fault in bringing on the schism, as some of the leaders were frank enough to acknowledge when union was restored. "The Old Side were wrong in opposing the revival of religion under Whitefield and his friends, and in contending against examinations on personal piety; while the New Side were wrong in violating Presbyterial order, in undervaluing literary qualifications for the ministry, and in giving countenance to some real extravagances which attended the revival of religion."[63]

If it can be said that the Great Awakening produced many extravagances and manifestations which were mistaken for true religion, and the results of which soon wore off, on the other hand, it cannot be denied that it kindled religious zeal and active missionary work which changed the complexion of the religious life of the colonies. In the Presbyterian Church it was the New Side that represented this movement, and it was their evangelistic activities that made Presbyterianism a dynamic force in Virginia. The pioneer in this missionary expansion was William Robinson.

[61] Assembly's *Digest,* pp. 612-617, for the steps towards union and the articles of agreement. *Cf.* Murphy, pp. 174-177.

[62] Ingram, *loc. cit.,* VI, 325.

[63] Miller, *Life of Rodgers,* p. 82. Even some of the New Side men later disapproved of some of the things they had countenanced in the revivals.

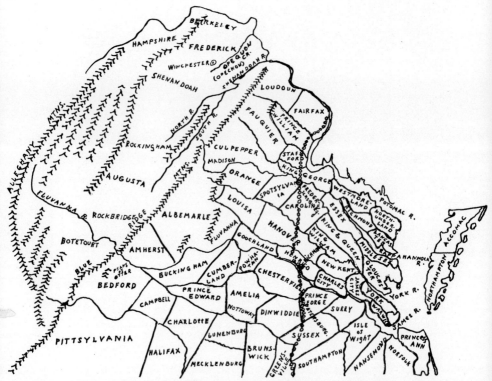

SKETCH MAP SHOWING THE PRINCIPAL COUNTIES OF VIRGINIA DURING THE PERIOD OF THE GREAT AWAKENING. ADAPTED FROM THE MAP BY JOHN HENRY

Fall Line Running Through Fredericksburg, Richmond, Petersburg, to East of Which is the Tidewater Section.

Chapter II

The Virginian Background

Prior to the Great Awakening, Virginia was a land in which privilege dominated in society, politics and the Church. The social fabric was stable, although it contained heterogeneous elements. The colony presented, in the main, a picture of two Virginias—the tidewater and the back country—between which there was little in common in manner of living, in political aspirations, or in spiritual desires.[1]

The Old Virginia was the Virginia of the tidewater section. It had the advantage over the upcountry in wealth, education and political power. Its dominant group was the planter aristocracy and, notwithstanding the existence of several social strata, the structure as a whole moved in harmony and good feeling.[2] Class lines were accentuated by the system of entails and primogeniture, which tended to preserve the groups intact.[3] To an astonishing degree a man's place in the social and political scale depended on the amount of property which he owned,[4] notwithstanding the fact that the suffrage was liberal and voting extended to nearly all free men.

The social organization of the tidewater was based on the plantation system with its large estates, staple crops and slave labor, and on the established Anglican church. The tobacco planters were the leaders in politics and society, and constituted the ruling group in the colony prior to the Revolution. Their great estates were extending up the rivers into the Piedmont section, but here they soon came into contact with democratic elements opposed to slavery and to the rule of the minority.[5]

[1] The standard histories of Virginia, as those of Burk, Campbell, Cooke, and Howison, all present substantially the same picture of society in the Old Dominion, but do not adequately portray the back-country society. The valuable studies of P. A. Bruce deal only with the seventeenth century.

[2] J. E. Cooke, *Virginia*, pp. 368-370; C. H. Ambler, *Sectionalism in Virginia*, p. 9.

[3] Ambler, p. 9.

[4] Philip Fithian, *Journal and Letters*, pp. 286-287.

[5] Ambler, pp. 7-8.

The middle of the eighteenth century passed, however, before
these inarticulate forces were marshalled under the leadership
of Patrick Henry to contest with the planters for supremacy.[6]
The Great Awakening, we shall see, brought them to a consciousness of their power.

In his manner of living the Virginia planter patterned after
the English country gentleman, whose habits he reproduced with
remarkable fidelity. There was this difference, however, that the
former was apt to live more luxuriously than his English coun-
terpart and too often he was ruined by his extravagances.[7] Perhaps the best portrayal of the social life of the Virginia aristocracy as it was established in the period preceding the Revolution is given by Philip Fithian who went from Princeton to
become tutor at Nomini Hall, the estate of Robert Carter, located in the Northern Neck.[8] Fithian became a frequent guest at
the homes of some of the best and most influential families of
the colony and his portrayals of the culture and refinements of
that class are delightful, although, perhaps, prejudiced by the
very environment in which Fithian found himself. Carter was
a member of the planter aristocracy. He possessed the title of
"Councillor", and owned about sixty thousand acres of land
scattered in different counties, and about six hundred slaves.
The Nomini Hall estate comprised twenty-five hundred acres
and a hundred and fifty slaves.[9] The Councillor was a man of
cultivated tastes and education, and quite a musician. He kept

[6] H. J. Eckenrode, *The Revolution in Virginia*, p. 7.

[7] Anon., *American Husbandry*, (London, 1775), I, 237-8, 242.

[8] *Journal and Letters* (1767-1774). Rich gentlemen maintained private
schools in their families. These were usually taught by unmarried clergymen or candidates for clerical orders, as Fithian, and constituted the most
approved method of education among the rich. Indeed, the tutorial system
became so well grounded as to prevent the development of Latin grammar
schools. The great distances between plantations also made the maintenance
of private teachers the most practical method of education for the gentry
class. The system "safeguarded the economic-social interests upon which the
plantation system was built." W. A. Maddox, *The Free School Idea in
Virginia*, p. 6. The *Virginia Gazette* contains frequent advertisements for
tutors.

[9] Fithian, *op. cit.*, p. 128 (1774).

a variety of fine instruments in the mansion house, and at Williamsburg he had an organ.[10] Music constituted an essential part of the education of the gentle folk and the "Music Master" was a frequent visitor at the Carter home. The Councillor was indefatigable in his practice and even tried his hand at transposing. Music was his "darling amusement."

The culture of the tidewater is evidenced by the numerous libraries which were owned by the leading planters.[11] The Byrd Library at Westover was advertised for sale in the *Virginia Gazette* of December 26, 1777, as "consisting of near 4000 Volumes, in all Languages and Faculties, contained in twenty-three double Presses of black Walnut. . . ." There were among others, books on the classics, history, law, voyages and travels, divinity, entertainment, poetry, and "physick."[12] The library at Nomini Hall contained a thousand or more volumes of a wide variety, in addition to which Councillor Carter had some four hundred and fifty at Williamsburg. In this library, as in others, were to be found the latest authors of note as Locke, Addison, Young, Pope, Swift and Dryden.[13] Works of Rousseau, Voltaire and the Encyclopædists figured prominently among the French publications found in these libraries of colonial Virginia.

Until the time of the Revolution tidewater Virginia enjoyed itself with its fêtes, balls, feasts, horse-races and cock fights. The two latter sports in particular were popular among the older generation. Horse-racing reached its height in the middle of the eighteenth century and attracted the attention of travellers like Burnaby and Smyth, who were struck by its widespread

[10] *Ibid.*, pp. 58, 67, 75, 76, 77 and *passim*.

[11] E. W. James, in *William and Mary College Quarterly*, II, III, IV, VI, and VIII, lists many libraries of colonial Virginia. The *Gazette* not infrequently advertises them for sale; *e.g.*, August 29, 1771 (Purdie and Dixon, eds.).

[12] "The Byrd Library at Westover," *Va. Mag. of Hist. and Biog.*, XII, 205-207.

[13] Fithian left a catalogue of the Nomini Hall library. It is printed in *W. and M. Quar.*, X, 232-241, XI, 21-28.

popularity in eastern Virginia.[14] Large stakes were involved in the races, and gambling on the favorites was, no doubt, a factor involved in the ruin of more than one wealthy planter.[15] The *Virginia Gazette* contains frequent announcements of the races.[16] Cock-fighting was also an established institution and the papers of the time show that much rivalry between gentlemen of different counties was settled by matches between their leading game cocks, on which they placed their stakes.[17] It is significant of the popularity of these sports that Devereux Jarratt, who became a leader in the Great Awakening, found much pleasure, when a youth of seventeen, in caring for and exercising horses for the turf, and in preparing game cocks for a match.[18]

Williamsburg, the colonial capital and seat of William and Mary College, became, on the gathering of the Burgesses, the scene of much that was brilliant and attractive in Virginia society.[19] At this season came the wealthy planter-politicians with their families to enjoy a winter of revelry and entertainments. The Governor's "Palace" rivalled in miniature brilliancy that of the King of England and the capitol became the seat of festivities. News items to the effect that "Last Night there was a Ball and elegant Entertainment at the Capitol, given by the Gentlemen of the Honourable the House of Burgesses, to his Excellency the Governor and the People of Rank in this City," appear regularly in the columns of the *Gazette*.[20] The anniver-

[14] See "Racing in Colonial Virginia," *Va. Mag. of Hist. and Biog.*, II, 293-305, which gathers much information from newspapers and other sources.
[15] *Ibid.*, p. 299.
[16] *Virginia Gazette*, February 17, 1774, October 20, 1774, October 27, 1774 (Purdie and Dixon), and many other places. The issues prior to 1770 are very fragmentary and scattered but the illustrations are typical, no doubt, of the middle decades of the eighteenth century. See also "Racing in Colonial Virginia," *loc. cit.*
[17] *Ibid.*, August 15, 1771 (P. & D.), April 29, 1773 (P. & D.), and many other dates.
[18] Jarratt, *Life of Devereux Jarratt*, p. 20. (Hereafter referred to as *Autobiography*.)
[19] See Cooke, *Virginia*, p. 398, for a quaint portrayal of the capital at this season.
[20] *Virginia Gazette*, March 19, 1772 (P. & D.), and other dates.

sary of the accession of the King was usually the occasion for a sumptuous ball given by the Governor, while other events as the birthdays of celebrities, were similarly observed.[21]

The hospitality and grand scale of living among the gentle society astonished Fithian.[22] From his *Journal* and from other contemporary sources we are impressed by the fact that the planter aristocracy constituted, on the whole, a polished, easy-going, pleasure loving group.[23] A social gulf existed between them and the plain folk who regarded their superiors with a certain feeling of awe which is perhaps best expressed by Devereux Jarratt, who says; "We were accustomed to look upon what were called gentle folks, as beings of a superior order. For my part I was quite shy of them, and kept off at a humble distance. A periwig in those days was a distinguishing badge of gentle folk and when I saw a man riding the road, near our house, with a wig on, it would so alarm my fears and give me such a disagreeable feeling that I dare say I would run off, as for my life. Such ideas of the difference between *gentle* and *simple* were, I believe, universal among all of my rank and age."[24] Fithian, too, emphasizes the fact of social alignments in Virginia and the great importance attached to property and wealth in contradistinction to virtue and genius.[25]

[21] *Virginia Gazette,* October 29, 1772 (P. & D.), October 28, 1773, etc.; on the birthday of Lady Dunmore, *Virginia Gazette,* January 21, 1775 (Dixon and Hunter).

[22] In 1774 Fithian wrote, "Mrs. Carter informed me that this family one year with another consumes 27,000 pounds of pork, and twenty beeves; 550 bushels of wheat, besides corn, four hogsheads of rum and 150 gallons of brandy" (p. 121). Again he writes (p. 262) that one hundred pounds of flour were consumed weekly by the great house. The negroes and labourers ate corn. "It is wonderful," he exclaims, "to consider the consumption of provisions in this family." Still he more than once commends the careful management and the economy of the master and mistress of Nomini Hall.

[23] The *Diary* of Landon Carter gives us many interesting glimpses to supplement Fithian and is better for the business side of the planter's life. Extracts in *W. and M. Quar.,* XIII-XVIII, XX-XXI. Of similar interest is Colonel James Gordon's *Journal* (*ibid.,* Vols. XI-XII), May 11, 1761, which records, "No company, *which is surprising.*" For a secondary account see Cooke, *op. cit.,* pp. 369-370.

[24] *Autobiography,* p. 14.

[25] Fithian, *Journal and Letters,* pp. 285-287.

The society which we have been describing comprised the leadership in the Old Dominion. The tobacco planter of the tidewater who wished to attain to a position of influence and distinction took to politics as his main avocation.[26] His chief ambition was to represent his constituents in the colonial assembly. Politics offered a respectable career to the man of means and leisure, and the freeholders in eastern Virginia accepted the leadership of the great planters without question.[27] The system of apportioning representatives unequally among the counties enabled the tidewater to control the legislature even in the face of a growing majority in the up-country.[28] The presence of this ruling aristocracy became firmly grounded in the traditions of the colony.[29]

We cannot well leave this description of the planter aristocracy without mention of the dark side. A ruinous system of credits under which the planters could obtain goods to the very limits of their resources from the English merchants brought disaster to many of them.[30] They borrowed heavily in anticipation of their incomes until their plantations were heavily mortgaged, and liens on practically everything raised from year to year were held by the English merchants.[31] Lack of foresight, lavish hospitality, reckless gambling, threw many an estate upon the market.[31a] The dependence on tobacco as a staple had its drawbacks, for the failure of a crop might bring serious embarrassments. Virginia offered splendid opportunities to the man of foresight. As a class the planters did not seem to possess this characteristic and the author of *American Husbandry* says that it is reported that fortunes were rarely made by them. He attributes this to a careless and extravagant economy.[32]

[26] Eckenrode, *The Revolution in Virginia,* pp. 6-7.
[27] Cooke, pp. 368-369.
[28] Jefferson, *Notes on Virginia* (1st ed.), pp. 308-309.
[29] See Jarratt, *Autobiography,* p. 15.
[30] *American Husbandry,* I, 227.
[31] *Ibid.,* pp. 227, 237; J. S. Bassett, "The Relations between the Virginia Planter and the London Merchant," *Am. Hist. Ass'n. Rep.,* 1901, pp. 551-575.
[31a] Eckenrode, *The Revolution in Virginia,* pp. 6, 39.
[32] *American Husbandry,* I, 237.

Opposed to the leadership of the planter group, in the middle of the eighteenth century, was the society of the Piedmont and of the Valley of Virginia. The country beyond the fall line of the rivers was not settled to any considerable extent until after the eighteenth century opened. During the early and middle decades of this century a double movement into the back country is clearly observable.[33] In the first place there were many small land holders, redemptioners, and newcomers who were pushed up the rivers in order to locate by reason of the engrossment of the desirable lands in the older area. Lands beyond the fall line were offered on attractive terms to settlers who would become defenders of the frontier. Much of it was acquired by speculative planters who agreed in turn to settle their grants. As settlement ascended the rivers, new frontier counties as Spotsylvania, Brunswick and Goochland were organized and towns were established, notably Richmond.[34]

Contemporaneous with this movement from the tidewater, though setting in a little later, was a steady stream of emigration from Pennsylvania into the Shenandoah Valley. Starting about 1732, this movement was geographically separated from the westward movement from the coast and by the middle of the century was not only filling up the Valley but was seeping through the gaps of the Blue Ridge into the Piedmont.[35]

The southwesterly migration from Pennsylvania was preponderantly one of Scotch-Irish and Germans. The first settlement in the Valley is placed on the Opeckon, south of Winchester, and the year, 1732.[36] At that time sixteen families from Pennsylvania crossed the Potomac to make their homes in the region indicated. They were the vanguard of group after group who passed on, some of whom, as we have observed, filtered

[33] F. J. Turner, "The Old West," in his *Frontier in American History,* pp. 84 ff.

[34] *Ibid.,* pp. 90 ff.; see also Morgan P. Robinson, *Virginia Counties,* a most convenient compilation.

[35] Turner, p. 99; Foote, *Sketches of Virginia,* First Series, p. 101.

[36] Foote, p. 101; Samuel Kercheval, *History of the Valley of Virginia,* p. 41; J. L. Peyton, *History of Augusta County,* p. 25.

through the Blue Ridge into the vacant backlands of the Piedmont.

The coming of the foreigners to the colonies is a significant fact, for everywhere they constituted most important elements in the Great Awakening. Pennsylvania was their chief haven and to it Scotch-Irish and Germans came by the thousands.[37] It is believed that the former constituted a third of the population of Pennsylvania by the time of the Revolution and the Germans probably another third.[38] Virginia received such a great accession of these two races that they practically possessed the Valley.[39]

Both the Scotch-Irish and Germans were very susceptible to religious influences. The former were devoted followers of John Knox, "brought up in the Old Testament, and in the doctrine of government by covenant or compact."[40] They were intensely individualistic and devoted to the principles of democracy in politics, and absolute liberty in religion. They were staunch Whigs, detesting both spiritual hierarchy and civil tyranny.[41] The Germans were deeply evangelical, earnest and pious. They belonged to many sects—Mennonites, Dunkers, Moravians, Schwenkfelders and others—and were fresh from

[37] On the former see H. J. Ford, *The Scotch-Irish in America;* C. A. Hanna, *The Scotch-Irish;* J. A. Waddell, *The Scotch-Irish of the Valley of Virginia.* On the Germans see J. W. Wayland, *The German Element of the Valley;* A. B. Faust, *German Element in the United States.* Kercheval, *op. cit.,* and Peyton, *op. cit.,* contain much information, as does also J. A. Waddell, *Annals of Augusta County.* See other county histories cited in the bibliography. Ford (p. 265) quotes James Logan, secretary of the province of Pennsylvania, as saying in 1729, "It looks as if Ireland is to send all its inhabitants hither, for last week not less than six ships arrived, and every day two or three arrive also." For a while these arrivals exceeded 10,000 a year.

[38] Turner, *op. cit.,* pp. 100, 103. The Germans numbered in Pennsylvania about 100,000, or half the total of that race in the colonies.

[39] *Cf.* Kercheval, *The Valley of Virginia.* The Germans settled in the northern part of the Valley in Frederick, Shenandoah and Rockingham counties, while Rockbridge and Augusta became the Scotch-Irish strongholds. Cf. also Henry Howe, *Historical Collections of Virginia,* pp. 451, 461 and Howison's *Virginia,* II, 171. The Germans were so numerous in the Valley that the laws had to be translated. Ambler, p. 13.

[40] Turner, *op. cit.,* p. 103.

[41] Howe, *Historical Collections of Virginia,* p. 453.

the influences of Pietism.[42] They formed plastic material for the revivalist who found them very receptive to a gospel which taught a direct personal relationship between Christ and the believer—the gospel of the Great Awakening. Probably no people in America were more subject to religious emotion than these Germans. In Virginia, however, the Scotch-Irish were to count as a more aggressive religious force than the Germans, and the first phase of the Awakening was their Presbyterian revival.

The great result of the migrations into the interior parts of Virginia was to arrest the westward march of tidewater institutions by the development of a society utterly out of sympathy with that section.[43] This new Virginia was heterogeneous in race and religion and it was susceptible to dissent and democracy. It was, in the main, a region of small farms, variety of crops and free labor. No dominant social caste existed, little accumulated wealth, and few refinements of life. The people were simple in habits, plain in manners and dress, and frugal in living.[44] If luxuries were practically unknown to them, at the same time there was plenty of wholesome food and each

[42] Kuhns, *German and Swiss Settlements of Colonial Pennsylvania,* Chap. VI, espec. pp. 155 ff.

[43] Ambler, *op. cit.,* pp. 4-5, 13; Eckenrode, *op. cit.,* p. 15.

[44] Jarratt, *Autobiography,* pp. 13-15, gives us a good glimpse of these plain folk. A similar and contemporaneous portrayal is in James Ireland, *Life.* Ireland became one of the earliest Baptist preachers. He was born in Edinburgh in 1748, came to America as a young man and began his career as a school teacher in Shenandoah County. See J. B. Taylor, *Virginia Baptist Ministers,* 2nd Series, p. 116. William Hickman, *Life and Travels,* gives another contemporary picture of the backcountry. As a young man he lived in Buckingham and Cumberland counties when the Baptist revival began. He joined the Baptists in 1773 and later moved to Kentucky. See *Kentucky Baptist Hist. Soc. Pubs.,* Vol. I. John Woolman, *Journal* has one or two glimpses of Virginia. The *Moravian Diaries,* published in the *Va. Mag. of Hist. and Biog.,* give interesting glimpses of the Germans in the Valley and Piedmont. These missionaries generally travelled afoot and were careful observers. Of value also is Joseph Doddridge, *Notes* (1763-83), published in Kercheval, *op. cit.,* pp. 164-263, and separately. Kercheval, *op. cit.,* and Peyton, *op. cit.,* and the county histories are valuable. Our account is based upon these sources and on standard secondary works. While one finds many variations in conditions, we have tried to bring together those facts which seem to be of general application to the region under discussion.

family provided its own homespuns.[45] Samuel Davies, writing
in 1755, notes that while few of the whites in the backcountry
were in abject poverty, many were very poor.[46] The pastimes,
the virtues and the vices of the people were those of a frontier
society.[47] We hear a good deal of various coarse amusements
and of much insobriety, but there were also many wholesome
diversions and recreations, all of which mark these people as
being just ordinary folks, neither perpetually degraded nor
debauched, and, on the whole, law abiding and respectful to
authority.[48] Some of them, notably the Germans of the Valley,
seem to have been exceptionally thrifty and industrious.[49] The
up-country was not entirely lacking in opportunities for education but, in the main, the people were unlettered.[50] It must not
be forgotten, however, that among some of the groups, as the
Scotch-Irish, there was a real taste for learning and literature,
and schools early appeared among them.[51]

[45] Jarratt says that they "always had plenty of plain food and raiment,
wholesome and good, suitable to their humble station and the times in which
they lived." Their food was the product of the farm and their shoes and
clothes homemade. Coffee and tea were luxuries. *Autobiography,* pp. 13-14.
[46] Letter to J. F., April 1, 1755; *cf.* Letter of Rev. John Todd to Mr. C.,
February 3, 1757. These are both in the little volume of Davies' *Letters,* cited
in the bibliography. See also Peyton, *op. cit.,* pp. 40-41; Woolman, *Journal*
(Harvard ed.), pp. 189-90; *Moravian Diaries, loc. cit.,* XI, 375-381.
[47] Doddridge's *Notes* is especially good on this phase as is also Jarratt.
[48] Ireland, pp. 49 ff.; Jarratt, p. 28; Hickman, *loc. cit.,* p. 8; Foote,
Sketches, Second Series, pp. 191-92. Ireland procured "profane and jest
books" so as to "improve me in vice," p. 51. Jarratt, pp. 42, 44; Peyton, pp.
58-59; Doddridge, *passim.*
[49] Kercheval, pp. 135, 136-137.
[50] English free schools or charity schools for the poor were established
by rich gentlemen. See Maddox, *Free School Idea in Virginia,* Chap. I. Jarratt was educated in such a school. At nineteen he became a tutor in Albemarle County but even then could scarcely read. *Autobiography,* pp. 28, 33-34.
[51] Peyton, *op. cit.,* pp. 34, 41, who thinks that "there was as much talent,
intelligence and spirit in the people of Augusta in 1732-50 as falls to the
lot of any equal number of people in the world." Jarratt's parents had as
their highest ambition to teach their children the rudiments of learning.
Autobiography, pp. 15-16. Ireland found the people of Shenandoah anxious
to start a school. *Life,* p. 44. Among the Scotch-Irish, the Presbyterian
preachers were also school teachers. Augusta Academy in the Valley was
started in 1749 near Lexington. It later became Liberty Hall and then a
College. See Peyton, pp. 42, 43 and below Chap. IX.

The political theories of interior Virginia and its attitude towards institutions were destined to raise certain issues. As a society, it was opposed to privilege and inequality whether in Church or State. These newcomers were individualistic and wanted not merely toleration in religion but absolute liberty, which meant that they were not to be compelled to contribute to any church unless they so desired, and then it must be the one of their choice. In politics they demanded a government based on the principle of the rule of the majority rather than of the property holders. Their idea of a constitution was one based on the natural equality of all men. If carried out, these ideas would involve a complete social, political, and religious revolution in the Old Dominion. Before such an upheaval could occur, these folk needed to be welded into a common consciousness of their grievances, a realization of their power, and must develop leadership. The Great Awakening furnished the needed impetus.[52] With it came the demand for a recognized social standing, the abolition of the Established Church, the recognition of the principle of religious freedom, and a democratic constitution.

In what manner did the Established Church minister to the needs of the two social groups that we have been surveying? A brief sketch of the organization of the Church will better enable us to approach this question. For ecclesiastical purposes Virginia was considered a part of the London diocese of the Anglican Church.[53] Since 1675 it had been under the jurisdiction of the Bishop of London, but as a matter of fact the Bishop made little effort to exercise any real authority in the colony until, near the end of the century, he appointed a deputy or Commissary to

[52] Cf. M. W. Jernegan, "Religious Toleration and Freedom in Virginia," in Harper's Source Problems in U. S. History, pp. 183-193.

[53] On the Anglican Church, W. S. Perry's monumental Historical Collections is the great source book. The transcripts of the Fulham MSS. in the Library of Congress, supplement Perry. The best history of the Anglican Church in Virginia is that by F. L. Hawks, referred to as Ecclesiastical Contributions, but on the institutional development Bruce is the leading authority in his Institutional History of Virginia in the Seventeenth Century, Vol. I.

represent him in that part of his jurisdiction.[54] The first Commissary of Virginia was the Reverend James Blair, a man of courage, broad vision and sincerity, who toiled for over a half century for the religious, educational and political welfare of the colony. Commissary for fifty-four years, a member of the Council for fifty years, founder of William and Mary College and its first President for over half a century, preaching all this while, his was a rare life of service for the Old Dominion.[55]

On the whole, the office of Commissary was burdensome and vexatious, and it was one which required rare talents for government. The Commissary's powers were few and he was but the shadow of a bishop. He had no real disciplinary authority over the clergy and thus was unable to remedy the most flagrant evils that existed within the Establishment. He did not even exercise the rites of ordination and confirmation,[56] while the right of inducting ministers presented by the vestries into their livings, and suspending or removing delinquent ones, lay in the hands of the secular authorities.[57] In spite of his few actual powers, the Commissary was often watched with a jealous and suspicious eye, for to many he was the symbol of prelatical tyranny.

The division of ecclesiastical authority between the Governor and Commissary, as well as the fact that the Commissary was a member of the Governor's Council and President of William and Mary College, led to many misunderstandings and disagreements between the two officials, which did not always redound to the uplift of the Church.[58] The real roots of these troubles lay in the confused relations between the ecclesiastical establishment and the State, and the frequent appeals of the less

[54] Bruce, *op. cit.,* p. 128; Eckenrode, *Separation of Church and State in Virginia,* p. 15.

[55] D. E. Motley, *Life of Commissary James Blair,* pp. 54-55. He became Commissary in 1690, according to Bruce.

[56] These belonged to the Bishop of London.

[57] Induction belonged to the Governor; the Governor and Council could suspend ministers but removals could be made only by the Assembly. Eckenrode, p. 10; Bruce, I, Chap. XIII.

[58] Perry, I, *passim;* Motley, *op. cit.,* Chap. III; Wm. Meade, *Old Churches, Ministers and Families of Virginia,* I, pp. 157 ff.

astute and influential Commissaries to the Bishop of London led to estrangements with the civil authorities. As the representatives of an outside authority, the deputies of the Bishop of London came to be regarded as a disturbing factor in the politics of the colony, and more and more their interference in Virginia affairs was received with ill grace.[59]

The real control over the Colonial Church, lay neither in the Governor, the Commissary, nor the more distant Bishop of London, but rather in the local vestries which managed the affairs of each parish.[60] Originally elective, these vestries had become self perpetuating and, therefore, irresponsible oligarchies.[61] Moreover the vestrymen were generally members of the County courts, the House of Burgesses or the Governor's Council, and thus were the depositories of power in the colony.[62] It is of no little significance that the same men who became the leaders in the struggle for independence were those who were most active in the proceedings of the vestries.[63] In the determined stand taken by the latter against Governors, Commissaries and Bishops, the historian Campbell sees the embryo of the Revolution; "political freedom," he says, "is the offspring of religious freedom; it takes its rise in the church."[64]

The welfare of the Establishment depended largely on the attitude of the vestries, for they presented ministers (and often did not present them) for induction, and also levied the parish rates for keeping up the churches, purchasing glebes, and paying the ministers.[65] Unfortunately for the Church, the attitude of the vestries was a most independent one and was too frequently dictated by selfish aims. We can only mention in a general way that during most of the eighteenth century the vestries were

[59] Eckenrode, *op. cit.*, pp. 20-21; Perry, I, 507, 517.

[60] Bruce, I, Chaps. VII-VIII.

[61] Hugh Jones, *Present State of Virginia* (1724), p. 66; Edward Ingle, *Local Institutions of Virginia*, p. 62; Eckenrode, *op. cit.*, p. 13.

[62] Bruce, I, 62; Perry, I, 407-408; Meade, I, 151; Eckenrode, pp. 20-21.

[63] Meade, I, 359-360; Perry, I, 349, 355-56. Meade claims that not more than three members of the Virginia Convention of 1776 were not vestrymen.

[64] *History of Virginia*, p. 44.

[65] Jones, *op. cit.*, pp. 66-67; Bruce, I, Chap. VIII, espec. pp. 74-78; Perry, I, 378, 390.

engaged in constant quarrels with the Governors on the one hand and the ministers on the other. The chief cause of difficulties was concerned with the matter of the presentation and induction of ministers. The latter power belonged to the Governor, but the simple fact is that the vestries were very jealous of their power to control the ministers and stoutly resisted any attempts of the former to break their independence. A favorite practice of the vestrymen was to hire the ministers by the year instead of having them inducted for life.[66] In this way they kept the ministers in a state of dependence and also minimized the Governor's position as Supreme Ordinary.[67] Their control over the clergy practically amounted to the power of appointment and removal, much to the detriment of the Establishment. Efforts of the Bishop of London to curb the independence of the vestries were no more successful than those of the Governors. Distant as they were from the colony, the Bishops had little real authority over the churches of the plantation and they realized it.[68] To remedy this condition they hoped to secure the establishment of one or two American Bishops, for, as we have seen, the Commissaries were quite helpless.[69]

It is generally admitted that the Virginia Establishment, as a spiritual factor in the life of the colony in the eighteenth century, was a failure. For one thing, it contented itself with serving only one social group, namely, the planter class. Even with them it had little influence in a spiritual way, and they had little respect for either the Sabbath or the Church. "A Sunday

[66] Perry, I, 390; Meade, I, 150; Campbell, p. 367; Bruce, I, 134 ff.

[67] The Governors claimed that if the vestries failed to present ministers within six months after a vacancy the power lapsed to the executive. They were unable to make good this claim, however, and a law of 1748 gave the vestries the right of presentation for a year after the occurrence of the vacancy. W. W. Hening, *Statutes,* IV, 440; Perry, I, 226-42, 321, 378, 393-396, 397, 400, 407-408. Queries sent out to the colony in 1724 showed that the practice of induction had all but fallen into disuse. Perry, I, 261 ff.,; 314-315, 400. Jones, *op. cit.,* p. 104.

[68] Dawson MSS., September 20, 1750, in which the Bishop writes the sentiment, "I am persuaded that no Bishop residing in England ought to have or willingly to undertake this province." See also Perry, I, *passim.* The Dawson MSS. are in the Library of Congress.

[69] See Commissary Dawson's pleading letter of 1753 in Perry, I, 407-8.

in Virginia don't seem to wear the same dress as our Sundays
to the Northward," wrote Fithian, even after the Great Awakening had made its inroads.[70] Virginia gentlemen too often went
to church not so much out of religious concern as to find an
occasion to talk over business affairs.[71] It was customary for
them to remain outside until the service had well begun and
occasionally the clerk had to come out to fetch them in to
prayers.[72] Returning for a visit to New Jersey after he had
been in the Old Dominion for six months, Fithian wrote: "I
went to meeting. How unlike Virginia, no rings of Beaux
chatting before and after Sermon on Gallantry; no assembling
in crowds after Service to dine and bargain, no cool spiritless
harangue from the Pulpit; Minister and people here seem in
some small measure to reverence the Day, there neither do the
one or the other."[73] The quaint portrayal of the historian Cooke
of this phase of the planter's life can easily be substantiated.
He tells us: "The planter and his family came in their coach,
and the parson read his homily; and then all went back to their
week-day pursuits but slightly edified. It was very much of a
Drowsyland, and a trumpet blast was necessary to arouse the
sleepers."[74] It was not that the gentry were not attached to the
Church as an institution, but the Establishment had become too
closely identified with the aristocratic society to be a factor in
its uplift.

If the Church meant little from the religious standpoint to
the social group to which it catered, it was next to nothing in
the lives of the common folk. Jarratt's experience is typical.
Until he came in touch with the Presbyterians in the backcountry, he says he does not remember "ever to have seen or
heard anything of a religious nature, or that tended to turn my
attention to the great concerns of eternity. I know not that I

---

[70] *Journal and Letters*, p. 202.

[71] *Ibid.*, pp. 202, 57-58, 296; also S. Davies in Foote, *Sketches of Virginia*, First Series, p. 203.

[72] Fithian, pp. 57-58.

[73] *Ibid.*, p. 156.

[74] Cooke, *Virginia*, p. 334; also *cf.* pp. 331 ff.

ever heard any serious conversation respecting God and Christ, Heaven and Hell. There was a church in the parish within three miles of me and a great many people attended it every Sunday. But I went not once in a year. And if I had gone ever so often I should not have been much the wiser for the parish minister was but a poor preacher—very unapt to teach or even to gain the attention of the audience."[75] When, in 1763, he became rector of Bath in Dinwiddie County, he found that but few of his parishioners were acquainted with the principles of the gospel. It was "as if the people had never a church or heard a sermon in their lives."[76] His plain, searching gospel was in strange contrast to the harangues on morality which they were accustomed to receive from their parsons. Jarratt was evangelical and an apostle of the Awakening.

In the backcountry the religious needs of the people were untouched until the Great Awakening. When Jarratt went to the frontier county of Albemarle about 1752, "there was no minister of any persuasion, or any public worship within many miles."[77] Such efforts as were made to minister to the inhabitants were under the auspices of dissenters. Thus Jarratt found that the Presbyterian missionaries were extending their activities into the region and a book of Whitefield's sermons had been left by some one at the house where he stayed. He was informed that the author was a "New Light" and had nothing good to say for Churchmen. It was not long before he went to live with a Presbyterian family, the mistress of which, he says, "was the first I had ever known to be truly and experimentally acquainted with vital religion." It was through her that the first permanent religious influences were brought into Jarratt's life. He soon embraced the Calvinistic tenets and even prepared to take orders in the Presbyterian ministry, when he saw a broader field of service open to him in the Establishment.[78]

Until the coming of the Baptists and Methodists about the beginning of the 'seventies, Presbyterianism was the greatest

<hr />

[75] Jarratt, *Autobiography*, p. 21.   [77] *Ibid.*, p. 28.
[76] *Ibid.*, p. 83.   [78] *Ibid.*, pp. 28, 35, 55-56, 59.

integrating factor among the dissenters, and, it is safe to say, represented the strongest group in the backcountry. Notwithstanding this, the Presbyterian ministers were too few for the work. Likewise they were a little too educated for the masses and, zealous as some of them were, it required the added stimulus of the Baptist and Methodist revivals adequately to meet the religious needs of the interior.[79]

The Presbyterians must share their pioneer missionary honors with the Moravian itinerants who, like them, visited Virginia even before the middle of the century.[80] Although the latter came as an off-shoot of the Great Awakening among the Germans of the Middle Colonies, they do not seem to have established themselves in Virginia as did their Presbyterian contemporaries and did not become an important factor in the colony. They were chiefly interested in their German brethren of the Valley and Piedmont, but frequently preached to the English and Scotch-Irish settlers.[81] To some regions on the extreme western frontier these Moravians were the very first to carry the gospel.[82] They mention many sects among the Germans, but on account of a dearth of preachers, religion was generally in a moribund state.[83] The Germans in the Valley had no settled pastor before 1749 and until then practically their only preaching came from the Moravians. There were periods and places when the people had no sermons for five years at a

[79] MS. Records of Hanover Presbytery (Va.) show that the Presbytery was organized in 1755 with six members, not including three Old Side ministers who did not join the Presbytery until the union of 1758. From 1760 to 1770 there were only about a dozen Presbyterian ministers in the colony. See James Ireland, *Life,* pp. 53, 68, 69, 70, 71, 96n., 111, 119, 120, for further evidence of the influence of the dissenters. William Hickman, *Life and Travels,* substantiates Jarratt and Ireland for Buckingham and Cumberland counties. *Ky. Bap. Hist. Soc. Pubs.,* I.

[80] "Moravian Diaries of Travel," *Va. Mag. of Hist. and Biog.,* Vols. XI-XIII.

[81] *Ibid., Diary of Spangenberg and Reutz* (1748), *loc. cit.,* XI, 238; of Gottschalk, XII, 66-67, and others.

[82] Spangenberg and Reutz (1748), *loc. cit.,* p. 237.

[83] Schnell and Hussey (1743-44), *loc. cit.,* XI, 376-377; Brandmueller and Schnell (1749), XI, 117, 119, and others.

time.[84] There were some German churches and pastors east of the Blue Ridge prior to this, but they do not seem to have taken an aggressive part in the great revivals as did their Scotch-Irish contemporaries.[85] Although in some places the Moravians met with no little opposition,[86] on the whole they found the Germans in a receptive attitude. We mention these missionaries because their efforts help to understand why the spiritual needs of the up-country and the Valley were supplied by dissenters, in so far as they were met at all.

In conclusion, it is well to recapitulate some of the reasons why the Established Church in Virginia failed. Lack of any effective control over the clergy by the proper ecclesiastical authorities has already been pointed out as a grave defect in the Colonial Church. More serious than this, however, was the character of the parsons themselves. The evidence is overwhelming that, as a class, the Virginia clergy were sadly deficient in the attributes of sound morals and good character.[87] The shining lights, like Jarratt and Bartholomew Yates, are few and far between.[88] Had there been more of them we surely should have heard of them before this. Too many of the clergy were not only a reflection on their own order but on religion in general. Immorality, card playing, drunkenness, profanity, avariciousness, quarrelsomeness were common enough among the eighteenth century parsons to bring almost the entire body into disrepute. James Craig, who was a sort of Jarratt in his efforts to save the Establishment, found that his predecessors had been shame-

[84] Brandmueller and Schnell, loc. cit., p. 117; Schnell and Handrup (1747), XII, 57-58 ff.

[85] My evidence for this is wholly negative. Neither Davies nor Jarratt mentions revivals among the Germans and above all one does not find the evidence in the Moravian Diaries where, it seems reasonable to assume, it would be recorded if anywhere.

[86] This was due to the Lutheran proclivities and also to Gooch's proclamation of 1745 against Moravians and other itinerants. Gottschalk, XI, 227-229; Schnell and Handrup, XII, 60.

[87] Fulham Transcripts, Dawson MSS., Perry, Meade, Jarratt, the Virginia Gazette, Gordon's Journal are some of the principal sources of evidence.

[88] On Yates see Fulham Transcripts (Va.), Box 1, no. 63; Perry, I, 349, 355, 356, 362. His death in 1734 was a real loss.

fully negligent in the care of the flock so that many "had never, or seldom, been at Church since they were baptized," and great numbers who did attend "were ignorant in the very first principles of Christianity."[89] He refers to two neighboring parishes which he says would be "much better without ministers, than . . . the two Brutes in that character."[90] Jarratt, as we know, had practically no friends among the Established Clergy. Indeed, they even sought to obstruct his work. The clergy were often guilty of gross delinquencies in conducting divine worship and performing sacraments.[91] There was good reason for the Presbyterian-inclined Colonel Gordon to frequently vent his disgust with the parsons of the Northern Neck.[92]

This condition in the Anglican Church did not improve even under the onslaughts of the Great Awakening. A writer in the *Virginia Gazette* in 1774 enumerated eight particulars in which the clergy fell short of their duties and concluded that every good person "who reads his bible, and inquires into the laws of the church," must become an adversary of the clergy.[93] It was becoming impossible, he felt, for a true Christian to remain in the Established Church, and he placed upon the clergy the blame for the rise of dissent.

The local conditions in Virginia, the lack of any authority there with power to examine candidates, and the necessity of the latter going to England for ordination made it difficult to obtain suitable men for the colonial pulpits. Frequent complaint was made of this by the Commissaries. Thus Horrock writes to his superior that candidates secured the support of some principal gentlemen, who in turn used their influence on the Governor, and the Commissary must either give offence to these gentlemen by not recommending the candidate "or be guilty of an

---

[89] Dawson MSS., September 8, 1759.
[90] *Ibid.*
[91] Fulham Transcripts, Box 2, nos. 125, 126, 127. October 25, 1772. Landon Carter wrote in his *Diary,* "God knows I went to commemorate the love and Passion of my divine redeemer, and if his servant was otherwise disposed, I hope it is to be imputed to some other cause than my neglect."
[92] *Journal, loc. cit.,* XI, 105, 108, 109, 110, 200, etc.
[93] *Virginia Gazette* (Rinds ed.), September 8, 15, 1774.

impropriety" to the Church.[94] Many who came over from England to fill colonial pulpits were incompetent castoffs, and the Bishop of London found great difficulty in ascertaining the true character of applicants.[95] Owing to the scarcity of the latter he sometimes had to accept candidates who had been educated as Presbyterians in Scotland and Ireland.[96] Clergymen of reputation, who had comfortable livings in England, were not inclined to go to the colony where, at best, ministers were on a precarious footing.[97]

There was nothing in the doctrines or the constitution of the Establishment to hinder its success, but defective preaching was one of the serious causes for its failure. There was almost a total lack of evangelical preaching even by men who were pious and probably interested in the salvation of men's souls.[98] Sermons were generally read in a cold, unanimated manner that was little adapted to awakening the convictions of sinners.[99] Nor did the contents of the sermons deal with the fundamental doctrines of the gospel, but rather consisted of "fine paintings of moral virtue" and "insipid speculations."[100] Jarratt despised the constant harangues on "moral virtue" which, he says, was "the cant term of all our velvet-mouthed preachers . . . a very pretty word and sounds soft and smooth."[101] Jarratt's great success was due to his evangelical preaching which appealed directly to the hearts of his hearers and made them sensible of

[94] Fulham Transcripts, Box 1, no. 32 (1768).
[95] *Virginia Gazette* (Rinds), September 22, 1774; Dawson MSS., December 25, 1750; Meade, *op. cit.*, I, 16.
[96] *Virginia Gazette* (Rinds), September 22, 1774, showing that the condition was a permanent one.
[97] Hawks, *op. cit.*, pp. 88-89.
[98] See Davies to Bishop of London (1752), in Foote, *op. cit.*, I, p. 202.
[99] Jarratt, *Sermons,* I, 27; Meade, I, 399, who says that the Anglican pulpits were so deep that the minister could see only a small part of his congregation. Colonel Gordon complains of the Anglican preaching as dry, formal or tedious, and more than once found more profit in staying home reading than attending church. *Cf. Journal,* June 17, 1759, October 7, 29, 1759, June 8, 1760.
[100] Jarratt, p. 88; Davies to Bishop of London (1752), in Foote, pp. 195-196.
[101] *Autobiography,* p. 88.

their sinful state. However, he was a great exception in his Church; on the whole neither the doctrines delivered from its pulpits nor the manner of delivery were likely to be of service to the souls of men in an age of evangelical Christianity.

There was a great work to be done in Virginia in the middle of the eighteenth century. The upper classes were indifferent, if not skeptical; the middle and lower classes were irreligious and unchurched because the Establishment failed to serve them. Had her formularies been used devoutly, had her doctrines been faithfully preached, had her clergy been consistently pious, had she proven susceptible to the Great Awakening, there is no reason why the Anglican Church should not have led in rebuilding the religious life of the Old Dominion. Since she met none of these conditions, that work had to be done by the popular churches which brought with them the gospel of evangelicalism.

The first deep inroads were made by the New Side wing of the Presbyterians. Their great revival constituted the first phase of the Great Awakening in Virginia, and to the rise and progress of that movement we now turn.

CHAPTER III

THE MILITANT PRESBYTERIANS

Presbyterianism as a vital force in the Old Dominion had its rise from two sources, namely, the Scotch-Irish migration into western Virginia and the spontaneous revival in Hanover County in eastern Virginia which began about 1740, and which the Presbyterians made their own. It is true that Francis Makemie had served several congregations on the Eastern Shore in Accomac County before the close of the seventeenth century, and in a certain sense he is to be regarded as the pioneer of the denomination in the colony. However, Makemie did not give the real impetus to its growth, for at his death in 1708, the congregation collected by him in Virginia ceased to exist and for about thirty years longer, or until the Scotch-Irish migration set in, the number and influence of the Presbyterians in the colony was small.[1] "Not one flourishing congregation could be found, nor one active minister lived in her borders."[2]

We have already taken account of the Scotch-Irish migration into the Valley and the Piedmont. The coming of these people was encouraged by Governor Gooch who saw in such sturdy pioneers a bulwark for the frontier, and he therefore granted them religious toleration. In 1738 the Synod of Philadelphia took upon itself the responsibility of looking after the religious needs of the growing number of Presbyterians in the backcountry of Virginia. A committee of two was named "to go and wait upon the Governor and Council of Virginia, with suitable instructions in order to procure the favour and coun-

[1] H. R. McIlwaine, *Struggle of the Protestant Dissenters for Religious Toleration in Virginia,* p. 31. Foote, *Sketches of Virginia,* pp. 40 ff. on Makemie's pioneer labors. The references to Foote are for the First Series unless otherwise indicated.

[2] Foote, *Sketches of Virginia,* p. 84; but there were Presbyterians in Virginia, as is evidenced from requests that were sent in to the Philadelphia Synod for preachers from the year 1719 on. The location of these groups is a matter of dispute. See *Records of the Presbyterian Church* for the years 1719, 1722, 1723, 1724; Foote, pp. 355-357; Ford, *Scotch-Irish in America,* p. 386; Miller, *Life of Reverend John Rodgers,* pp. 29-30.

tenance of the Government of that province, to the laying a foundation of our interest in the back parts thereof, where considerable numbers of families of our persuasion are settling. . . ."[3] The committee carried an address to Governor Gooch in behalf of the brethren in western Virginia, praying that they be allowed the "liberty of their consciences, and of worshipping God in a way agreeable to the principles of their education."[4] The Synod called attention to the loyalty of the Presbyterians in the Old World to the House of Hanover and concluded, "we doubt not but these our brethren will carry the same loyal principles to the most distant settlements where their lot may be cast, which will ever influence them to the most dutiful submission to the government which is placed over them."

In response to the request of the Synod Gooch sent the following favorable reply: "And as I have been always inclined to favour the people who have lately removed from other provinces, to settle on the western side of our great mountains; so you may be assured, that no interruption shall be given to any minister of your profession who shall come among them, so as they conform themselves to the rules prescribed by the Act of Toleration in England, by taking the oaths enjoined thereby and registering the places of their meeting, and behave themselves peaceably towards the government."[5] The reasons which animated Gooch in this grant of toleration were two: first, he desired to secure a frontier line further distant from the capital, —if possible, west of the mountains; secondly, he knew the Scotch-Irish to be hardy and brave soldiers and enterprising

[3] Minutes of the Philadelphia Synod, May 26, 1738, in *Records of the Presby. Church.* Also given in Foote, p. 103.

[4] *Ibid.,* May 30, 1738, and Foote, p. 104.

[5] *Recs. of Pres. Ch.,* May 28, 1739, and Foote, p. 104. While Gooch says nothing about the Presbyterian settlers to the east of the mountains, they were evidently to be included in those to whom toleration was to be extended, for the Synod made the petition in special behalf of a number of families who established themselves in Charlotte, Prince Edward and Campbell counties, all east of the Blue Ridge. These counties were, however, remote from the centers of civilization, for tidewater Virginia did not extend over sixty or seventy miles west of Richmond. See McIlwaine, p. 43. Gooch was a Scotchman himself.

citizens. At so great a distance from the older settlements he anticipated no collision between the Presbyterians and the Establishment.[6] This attitude continued as long as the Presbyterians confined themselves to the western regions remote from the seat of the Established Church. However, when their itinerant revivalist preachers came into the eastern section and threatened to undermine the Anglican order, the ruling class began to demand a rigid enforcement of the law, which required that nonconformist places of worship should be registered and their ministers licensed.[7] The whole social fabric of tidewater Virginia was bound up with the maintenance of the Established Church and to that end the parish form of church organization had to be preserved at all costs.

In 1738 Frederick and Augusta counties were authorized by act of the legislature to cover the entire area west of the Blue Ridge and to give the inhabitants the benefits of civil government as soon as they should be numerous enough.[8] The act also defined Augusta and Frederick parishes as coterminous with the counties of the same name, and provided for the election of vestries by the "freeholders and housekeepers."[9] The Established Church was always feeble in these western regions, and in Augusta at least it did not appear until fifteen years after the foundation of the county, when the ground was already occupied by the Presbyterians and other dissenters. The first vestry, however, was chosen in 1746.[10] Naturally, it was composed largely, if not entirely, of dissenters who, after conforming to the letter of the law which required the taking of oaths, managed the affairs of the parish to suit themselves.[11] When, finally, the first Anglican minister came to Augusta, he found himself sad-

---

[6] Foote, p. 105; Peyton, *Augusta County*, p. 80.
[7] *Cf.* Channing, *History of the United States,* II, 447.
[8] These counties were not actually organized until 1743 and 1745, respectively, until which dates they remained a part of Orange County. Robinson, *Virginia Counties,* pp. 43, 50; L. P. Summers, *History of Southwest Virginia,* p. 42; Samuel Kercheval, *A History of the Valley of Virginia,* p. 153.
[9] The act is given in Peyton, *op. cit.,* pp. 1-3.
[10] *Ibid.,* pp. 95, 96.
[11] *Ibid.,* p. 97; McIlwaine, *op. cit.,* pp. 40-41.

ly out of place, for the offshoot of the Establishment never flourished in the Valley. As soon as enough dissenting ministers arrived to satisfy the needs of the people, the congregation dwindled away, while Nonconformists even preached from the Anglican pulpit.[12] What happened in Augusta is probably typical of the course of events in other western counties on both sides of the Blue Ridge. In fact, liberty of worship was the rule in these far western counties, not because of the leniency of the laws or the tolerant temper of the clergy, but because of the secluded situation and the remoteness from the seat of government.

For many years the Presbyterians were the only denomination in western Virginia which was at all adequately supplied with ministers and churches. In fact, no other denomination seriously competed with them in the entire backcountry until the Baptists and Methodists appeared, after which their chief stronghold was in the Valley.[13] From about 1736 on, itinerant missionaries regularly visited the Presbyterian congregations on both sides of the Blue Ridge, the first being a Mr. Samuel Gelston, who came to the region around Opeckon.[14] He was followed by James Anderson[15] who carried the petition of the Synod to Governor Gooch in 1738 and visited congregations in the Valley during his journey. In the next year probably came John Thomson[16] and John Craig.[17] In 1740, under the auspices of Donegal Presbytery, Craig accepted a call from the

[12] *Ibid.*

[13] A good example of Presbyterian influence is seen in the case of Albemarle County. When the Baptists appeared about 1773 and gained converts, so many of them had grown up under Presbyterian influence that their first church was organized on the Presbyterian model. Edgar Woods, *Albemarle County in Virginia,* pp. 132-133.

[14] Foote, *Sketches of Virginia,* Second Series, p. 21; R. Webster, *History of the Presbyterian Church in America,* p. 362; "Tinkling Spring Church, Augusta County, Virginia," *Presby. Mag.,* II, 462-70.

[15] Foote, Second Series, p. 27.

[16] *Ibid.,* p. 28; Webster, pp. 355-356; Peyton, p. 34. There seems to be an uncertainty as to Thomson's visit. See "Tinkling Spring Church," *loc. cit.,* p. 463.

[17] Foote, Second Series, p. 28; Webster, p. 463. See also E. H. Gillett, *History of the Presbyterian Church in the United States,* I, p. 108; "Tinkling Spring Church," *loc. cit.*

congregation of Triple Forks of Shenandoah, in Augusta County, and became the first settled pastor of his denomination west of the Blue Ridge.[18] He spent the rest of his days serving the Presbyterians of the Valley. He was a good organizer and displayed to a remarkable degree "the adaptability and resourcefulness of a pioneer." Owing to the size of the county his congregation had to be accommodated with two churches, Augusta church[19] near Staunton, dedicated in 1749, and Tinkling Spring to the south,[20] near the present Fishersville.[21] In 1754 Craig resigned the latter charge and confined his labours to the Old Stone or Augusta church.[22] His death occurred in 1774.[23]

Other preachers followed Craig into these western regions. The Reverend Samuel Black settled in Albemarle County, near Rockfish Gap, just east of the Blue Ridge,[24] and Alexander Miller came to share the work in Augusta County.[25] About 1744 John Thomson removed to the Valley for a few years and carried on an extensive missionary work.[26] In 1748, when Samuel Davies settled in Hanover under the auspices of the New Side Synod, Craig, Black, Miller and Thomson were the only other representatives of the denomination in Virginia.

[18] Peyton, *Augusta County*, p. 80; Ford, *Scotch-Irish*, p. 381. Craig was a native of northern Ireland but had received his education in America.

[19] See J. N. Van Devanter, *History of the Augusta Church, 1737-1900*, espec. pp. 15 ff.

[20] See "Sketch of Tinkling Spring Church," *loc. cit.,* p. 465. Another special account of an early church is J. A. Trostle, *Timber Ridge Presbyterian Church, Rockbridge County, Virginia.* Timber Ridge Church was completed in 1756. Peyton, Chap. V, has a general account of the early churches. He says the very first one was erected near Opeckon about 1736. The Augusta was next. Some of these churches constructed of stone, like Augusta and Timber Ridge, have survived the storms of centuries. They were built with great labour, sand and stone having to be hauled from long distances in a day when there were neither wheeled vehicles nor roads.

[21] So located by Peyton, *op. cit.,* p. 81.

[22] Tinkling Spring Church, *loc. cit.,* 467.

[23] Extracts from his Memoir are printed in Foote, Second Series, pp. 28-33.

[24] Woods, *Albermarle County*, p. 130, says that this was about 1747. Black remained until his death in 1770.

[25] Foote, p. 166.

[26] Webster, *op. cit.,* pp. 355-356. In 1749 Thomson was living in Amelia County.

Missionaries sent out by both the Old Side Synod of Philadelphia and the New Side Synod of New York, from time to
time visited the congregations which were rapidly increasing on
both sides of the Blue Ridge.[27]

The four settled ministers in the western counties belonged
to the Old Side Presbytery of Donegal in Pennsylvania, and they
were not apostles of the Great Awakening which was extending
over the colonies in the decade of the 'forties. As we have seen,
their group represented the strict wing of the Church and was
opposed to many features of the great religious revival. It remained, therefore, for others to carry into the Old Dominion
those ideas which were to make Presbyterianism an evangelical
force. These were the New Light[28] missionaries of the school of
the Tennents and Whitefield. Their chief successes were in
eastern Virginia, which they made the real center of the Great
Awakening in the South. They introduce us to quite another
source of Presbyterianism in Virginia, namely, the revival in
Hanover County.[29]

Even before the coming of William Robinson and the New
Light missionaries, eastern Virginia was beginning to be stirred
by the reports of the remarkable outbursts of religion in the
North. In the *Virginia Gazette* people read of Whitefield's
effective preaching and were no doubt awaiting his arrival in

[27] Foote, p. 102.
[28] So called because the doctrine of the "new birth" which they preached
so earnestly and powerfully had so long been obscured by formalism that it
was really novel to its hearers. See discussion of the origin of the term by
A. Alexander in the *Watchman and Observer,* March 18, 1847. *Cf.* Murphy,
The Presbytery of the Log College, pp. 163-164; Howison, *History of Virginia,* II, 163.
[29] There are three accounts of the Hanover revival which may be classed
as sources. Foremost is that of Samuel Morris as he related it to Davies
and as the latter retold it in his letter to Bellamy, June 28, 1751. David
Rice's *Memoirs* contains an account written many years after the event. Of a
similar nature is the account of Reverend James Hunt as he secured it from
his father, one of the leaders of the revival. The account was originally
written in 1792 and was given to the *Literary and Evangelical Magazine* in
1819. It is found on pp. 346-353. Davies also wrote an account of the Hanover revival to Dr. Doddridge, October 2, 1750. See Perry, *Historical Collections,* I, 368-371.

Virginia with keen anticipation.[30] It was Friday, December 14, 1739 when Whitefield reached Williamsburg, "the metropolis of Virginia," as he called it.[31] Saturday, December 15, he records: "Dined with the Governor, who rec'd me most courteously. Paid my respects to the Rev. Mr. Blair, the Commissary of Virginia. He received me with joy and asked me to preach."[32] On Sunday Whitefield preached from the text, "What think ye of Christ?" The *Gazette* reports "There was a numerous Congregation, and 'tis thought there would have been many more, if timely Notice had been given of his Preaching. His extraordinary Manner of Preaching, gains him the Admiration and Applause of most of his Hearers."[33] Following Whitefield's visit the *Gazette* printed a eulogistic poem on the man which it copied from the *New York Gazette*,[34] while William Parks at Williamsburg printed and offered for sale two of Whitefield's sermons.[35]

Whitefield's brief stay in Williamsburg undoubtedly increased interest in the profound work of God that was prevailing very generally all over the North. However, the real awakening in the Old Dominion is not to be attributed to his preaching but to a spontaneous revival which began in Hanover County a year or two later among people who had probably never heard Whitefield.[36] However, on his second visit to Virginia Whitefield had a direct part in the movement.

[30] December 7-14, 1739, for examples; July 27, 1739, for quotations from the London papers regarding his work in the Old World.

[31] Whitefield's *Journal*, December 14, 1739, in Tyerman's *Life of Whitefield*, I, 343; *Virginia Gazette*, December 7-14, 1739. Tyerman prints the parts of Whitefield's *Journal* which refer to his Virginia visits, as well as much more.

[32] *Journal*, in Tyerman, I, 343.

[33] *Virginia Gazette*, December 7-14, 1739.

[34] *Virginia Gazette*, January 11-18, 1739/40. The same number contains notices of his successful preaching in New York, New Jersey and Pennsylvania to great crowds of from 5,000 to 10,000 who even stood in the rain to listen to him.

[35] See W. C. Torrence, *Trial Bibliography of Colonial Virginia*, Part I, pp. 128-129.

[36] "The Presbyterian Church in Hanover Previous to Mr. Davies," in *Watchman of the South*, June 15, 1843. The account contains nothing new.

A certain Samuel Morris seems to have been the leading figure in the Hanover revival.[37] He and a few other individuals[38] became interested in certain religious books which fell into their hands and began to hold meetings in each other's houses.[39] They spent the time in reading passages from Luther's *Commentary on Galatians,* from some of Whitefield's sermons which fell into their hands, and from Boston's *Fourfold State.*[40] The news of these gatherings spread abroad and it was not long before others began to attend them. Morris tells us that "the plainness and fervency of these discourses being attended with the power of the Lord, many were convinced of their undone situation, and constrained to seek deliverance with the greatest solicitude."[41] Some became so affected "that they could not avoid crying out, weeping bitterly, etc." As these manifestations were very unusual and appeared ridiculous among a people hitherto quite indifferent in matters of religion, Morris insists that they could not have been prompted by affectations, but were due solely to deep spiritual concern.[42] At first no other

[37] I have been unable to find anything definite concerning Morris prior to the revival. Hunt gives him the rank of "gentleman." Miller in his *Life of Rodgers* calls him a wealthy planter which Howison accepts in his *History of Virginia.* George G. Smith, in *Meth. Quar. Rev.* (So.), N.S. XIV, 46, says that he was a brick mason but gives no authority for the statement. Charles Campbell in his *History of Virginia* (Philadelphia, 1860) on p. 439, classifies Morris as "an obscure man, a bricklayer, of simplicity of character, sincere, devout, earnest. . . ."

[38] Hunt says four gentlemen of whom his father was one, but does not mention Morris by name. *Loc. cit.,* p. 346. See also Rice's *Memoir of Davies,* in *Evan. and Lit. Mag.,* II, 115.

[39] The accounts agree in this but Hunt adds that, unknown to each other, the four gentlemen began to absent themselves from church for the same reason. They found this out when they were summoned to appear before the magistrate for non-attendance at church. It was then that they resolved to hold the private meetings. *Loc. cit.,* pp. 346-347.

[40] Morris's account in Foote, First Series, p. 122; Rice says, "A few leaves of Boston's Fourfold State fell into the hands of a wealthy planter and made so deep an impression on his mind that he never rested until he obtained a copy of the work." *Evan. and Lit. Mag.,* II, 115. Smith, *loc. cit.,* says that Morris got Whitefield's sermons from a Scotchman who had taken notes when he heard the great divine in Glasgow.

[41] In Foote, p. 122. Morris's account is also in Alexander's *Log College,* pp. 221 ff. [42] *Ibid.*

exercise than reading was attempted at these gatherings. Such a thing as extempore praying was utterly foreign to the experience of all, and probably owing to the prejudice against reading prayers, which was done with levity and carelessness in the parish churches, this, too, was omitted.[43] There was no singing, doubtless because of sheer ignorance of church music.[44] Not until the coming of William Robinson were these features added to the exercises.[45]

David Rice, in his *Memoirs*, also tells how the soil was prepared for the awakening in Hanover. His uncle, like Morris and like James Hunt's father, was instrumental in arousing his neighbors. He obtained possession of a copy of Luther's *Commentary on Galatians* and of books written by certain great divines. "From these old books he made large extracts and by frequently reading them over, his memory being good, he could give a pretty good account of the whole of them. When his neighbors came to see him, he would commonly introduce religious conversation, and often repeat whole pages from these extracts. His conversation at length began to make some serious impression on his neighbors.[46] As a result, one man who was a good reader began to hold regular meetings on the Sabbath for his neighbors. Whether or not the details have come to us with exactness, we can well believe that in such ways as this the revival gradually spread.

The reading of religious books was soon attended by such numbers that it became necessary to build regular houses for the meetings. Says Morris: "My dwelling house was at length too small to contain the people, whereupon we determined to build a meeting house for reading."[47] The name "Morris's Reading House" was given to this building and it was given to others which were erected for the same purpose as the needs of the people demanded.[48] When the report of the remarkable

[43] *Ibid.;* David Rice's *Memoirs,* in R. H. Bishop, *History of the Church in Kentucky,* p. 34; Miller, *Life of Rodgers,* p. 34.
[44] Rice, p. 34.   [45] *Ibid.,* p. 36.   [46] *Ibid.,* p. 33.
[47] In Foote, p. 122 and Alexander, p. 222.
[48] Hunt's narrative, *loc. cit.,* p. 347.

awakenings spread abroad, Morris was invited to travel long
distances in order to read to congregations who desired his services. In this way the movement extended and the number of
reading societies increased.[49]

For a time little or no attention was paid the movement by
the governmental authorities. As the new opinions gained adherents, and the gatherings in the Reading Houses caused the parish
churches to become deserted, the leaders in the propaganda came
to the notice of the law. Several of them were arrested and fined
for not attending their parish church as often as was required
by statute.[50] Being informed of the English Act of Toleration,
which allowed liberty of worship to Nonconformists, their plea
was that they were Protestant dissenters.[51] When finally the
leaders were summoned to appear before the Governor's Council at Williamsburg "to declare their creed and name," they
were at a loss what to say, but suddenly hit upon the name of
Lutheran, as they remembered that Luther was a great reformer
and had been of special help to them through his books.[52]
They were thereupon allowed to return home in peace and continued thus until the coming of Robinson in 1743.[53] Until that
time the people of Hanover had not listened to a single dis-

[49] Morris, in Foote, p. 122 and Alexander, p. 222; Miller, *op. cit.*, p. 36.
[50] According to Dr. John Rice, Morris was fined at least twenty times
for non-attendance at church. *Evan. and Lit. Mag.*, II, 115. See also Foote,
p. 123; Miller, pp. 36-37 n.; Rice's *Memoirs*, p. 35, and Howison's *History of
Virginia*, II, 175.
[51] Rice's *Memoirs*, p. 35.
[52] Morris in Foote, p. 124 and Alexander, p. 222.
[53] According to Morris's narrative. Hunt's later account (1819) states
that on the way to Williamsburg one of the four principals took shelter in
the house of a poor man on the road and found a copy of the Presbyterian Confession of Faith. Meeting at Williamsburg, they found that the
book was more in harmony with their beliefs than Luther and they presented it to the Council as their own Confession. Gooch, who was a
Scotchman, saw immediately that they were Presbyterians and, therefore,
came under the Toleration Act. The Council was not satisfied but during
the session a tremendous storm came on. All being seized with awe, the
four gentlemen were dismissed. Hunt, in *Evan. and Lit. Mag.*, II, 348-349.
Rice's *Memoirs*, p. 35, agrees with Morris's account.

senting minister. Far from assuming the name of Presbyterian, they were probably wholly ignorant of that church.[54]

In the winter of 1742-1743 the Reverend William Robinson[55] was sent out by the New Light Presbytery of New Brunswick[56] to visit the Presbyterian settlements in the western parts of Virginia and North Carolina. Thus far the work of the Presbyterian ministers had been confined mainly to supplying the congregations formed by the Scotch-Irish settlers, but with Robinson's tour a period of active missionary and evangelistic work began.[57] Robinson had studied at the Log College and in his piety, zeal, and devotion to his work, he possessed the characteristics of the New Side school. About all that we know of his personal appearance is that small pox had robbed him of an eye and that a rather rough exterior clothed a warm heart and a passion to serve men.[58]

Travelling southward, Robinson preached to the congregations in the Valley of Virginia, while on the eastern side of the Blue Ridge his evangelistic labours met with much success in what were then Lunenberg and Amelia counties.[59] Meantime his fame had reached Hanover, where Morris's awakening was in full progress.[60] Anxious to hear this unknown man whose

[54] Morris says that the only denomination of dissenters of which they knew anything prior to Robinson's coming was the Quaker. Foote, p. 124; see also Davies' statement, p. 121.

[55] See *Watchman of the South*, June 15, 1843, article on "The Presbyterian Church in Hanover Previous to Mr. Davies"; Ford, *Scotch-Irish*, pp. 383-384; Alexander, *The Log College*, pp. 217 ff.; Murphy, *Presbytery of the Log College*, pp. 101-105.

[56] The Minutes of New Brunswick Presbytery show that he was licensed as probationer on May 27, 1740, and ordained August 4, 1741. *Jour. Pres. Hist. Soc.*, VII, 145, 153.

[57] Ford, *op. cit.*, pp. 383-4; Murphy, pp. 101-102.

[58] A very interesting account is in George Morgan's *The True Patrick Henry*, pp. 51-52; Alexander, p. 233.

[59] Davies to Bellamy, in Alexander, p. 222 and Foote, p. 128; Alexander, pp. 217-220; Foote, pp. 126 ff.; Ford, pp. 383-384.

[60] David Rice says that the news of Robinson's preaching was brought to Hanover by an Augusta man who had come down into "Old Virginia" to purchase supplies. Falling in with some of the Hanover "Lutherans" and learning their views, he told them of Robinson. *Memoirs*, pp. 35-36. *Cf.* Howison, II, 175-6.

preaching, they were told, accorded with their views of religion, commissioners were dispatched in quest of Robinson who, it seems, was overtaken just as he was about to leave for other parts.[61] Upon earnest request that he visit the people of Hanover County, he turned his horse eastward, arriving at his destination in July, 1743.

According to Morris, Robinson remained with them for four days. He was the first Presbyterian minister that preached in Hanover County, and the people attended his preaching in considerable numbers. Concerning the missionary's effectiveness, Morris says: "Such of us as had been hungering for the word before, were lost in agreeable surprise and astonishment, and some could not refrain from publicly declaring their transports. . . . Many that came through curiosity were pricked to the heart, and but few in the numerous assemblies on those four days appeared unaffected. They returned alarmed with apprehensions of their dangerous condition, convinced of their former ignorance of religion and anxiously inquiring what they should do to be saved."[62] The sermons were of the awakening type, and people throughout the county were affected.[63] The Reading House could not contain all that came, so meetings were held out of doors.[64] Morris refers to Robinson's stay "as the glorious days of the Son of Man."[65]

Robinson's advent marks the revival of Presbyterianism in eastern Virginia. Finding themselves in perfect accord with his views, the Hanover dissenters adopted the name Presbyterian and attached themselves to the Presbytery of New Castle at the first opportunity.[66] The evangelist corrected some of the defects

[61] Rice's *Memoirs,* p. 36; Alexander, pp. 217-220; also Hunt's account, *loc. cit.,* p. 351.

[62] In Foote, p. 128 and Alexander, pp. 222-223. The statement of Morris was made in 1750.

[63] Hunt's account, *loc. cit.,* p. 351.

[64] *Ibid.*

[65] Robinson died in 1746. He spent his last days in Delaware. Ford, p. 383, says he bequeathed his books to Samuel Davies with the injunction that the latter take up the work in Virginia.

[66] Miller, *Life of Rodgers,* p. 42.

in their services and taught them to add prayer and the singing of Psalms to their worship.[67] He also left them a volume or two of Erskine's sermons which constituted a valuable addition to their stock of literature and was carefully read.[68] "With these improvements," says David Rice, "their meetings were greatly enlarged, and excited considerable attention." The Reading Houses flourished and some, like Morris, were called upon to go fifteen, twenty, and even thirty miles to read Erskine to the eager congregations.[69] These laymen were much more highly esteemed than the parish parsons and the effects of their work were considerable. New meeting-houses were erected and people chose regular readers to carry on the work which became more extensive than ever when other New Light revivalists followed in the wake of Robinson. From this time on Hanover County became the center of the Great Awakening in the South,[70] and was "the cradle of Presbyterianism" in eastern Virginia. From it emanated the first dissenting movement which seriously impaired the supremacy of the Established Church.

Following the departure of Robinson, Hanover County was visited by a succession of Log College itinerants who kept up the work until Samuel Davies accepted the pastoral charge of the congregations there and in adjacent counties in 1748. The first of these missionaries was John Blair. Born in Ireland in 1720, trained in Tennent's school at Neshaminy, licensed by the New Side Presbytery of New Castle, Blair visited Virginia soon after Robinson and, like him, organized congregations east and west of the Blue Ridge.[71] He came fresh from the regions of revival in Pennsylvania where, in 1740, as we have seen, a very notable awakening had commenced in his brother Samuel's congregation at New Londonderry, in Chester County, and

---

[67] Rice's *Memoirs*, p. 36; Morris, in Foote, p. 128, and Alexander, p. 223; Hunt, *loc. cit.*, p. 351, who says that Robinson "brought them into some kind of church order on the Presbyterian model."

[68] Rice, p. 36.

[69] *Ibid.*, pp. 36-37; also Morris in Foote, p. 128, and Alexander, p. 223.

[70] *I.e.*, in its first or Presbyterian phase.

[71] Ford, *op. cit.*, pp. 383-384.

spread considerably through the province.[72] This revival had a very intimate connection with the Virginia awakening, inasmuch as the great Davies himself was educated in the school established by Samuel Blair at New Londonderry, otherwise called Fagg's Manor, during his ministry there.[73]

John Blair came with all the enthusiasm of the revivalist or, as Morris says, "in the fulness of the gospel." Once more were the congregations of Hanover stirred to the very depths and new impressions were made upon many. "One night in particular a whole house full of people was quite overcome with power of the word, particularly of one pungent sentence and they could hardly sit or stand or keep their passions under proper restraint."[74] During Blair's stay there was a general deepening of concern among the people and the results of his preaching strengthened them in their Presbyterian views. In 1746 he visited Virginia a second time, and organized several more congregations.[75]

In the winter of 1744-45, the Reverend John Roan was dispatched by the New Castle Presbytery as a supply to the people of Hanover.[76] Roan, like Blair, was of Irish nativity and a product of the Log College. He appears to have been a more extreme type of revivalist than either of his two predecessors and his zeal led him into many vigorous attacks upon the Established Church and clergy. He "spoke freely of the parish ministers, publicly and privately inveighed against their delinquency in morals, and their public ministrations; and turned the ridicule and scorn of his hearers against the teachers appointed and supported by law. The parish clergy and their friends were excited.

[72] Blair's narrative is printed in Prince, *The Christian History*, in Tracy, *The Great Awakening*, pp. 24-33, and in Alexander, pp. 173-192; extracts in Foote, pp. 109-115.

[73] Foote, pp. 107-108.

[74] Morris, in Alexander, p. 223, as contained in the letter from Davies to Bellamy, 1751.

[75] Ford, p. 384. He succeeded his brother in the church and school at Fagg's Manor and later became Professor of Divinity at Princeton and for a time acted as President. He died in 1771. Murphy, *op. cit.*, pp. 92 ff.

[76] Foote, p. 134; Howison, II, 177.

Unable to refute the allegations, they appealed to the strong arm of the law to protect their privileges and restrain both the speech and actions of their adversaries."[77]

Until this time the dissenters of Hanover had not met with any serious opposition from the governmental authorities. Aside from an occasional arrest for remaining away from the parish church, they had been left pretty much to worship as they pleased, although their meeting houses were not registered according to law.[78] But the coming of the itinerant revivalist preachers soon changed this attitude of leniency and the authorities began to take extreme measures to curb them. Under Roan's vigorous preaching the number of converts rapidly multiplied and the revival was carried into places where there had been little appearance of it before.[79] Neighborhood after neighborhood, in Hanover and adjacent counties, called upon the fiery evangelist to declare the Word, and numbers responded to his earnest appeals.[80] This, together with his free remarks about the degeneracy of the clergy and his denunciatory harangues in unlicensed meeting houses, aroused the government, and Williamsburg became alarmed. Roan himself had not obtained a license according to the Toleration Act and was regarded by the authorities as "an itinerant come to stir up discord and schism."[81] To make matters worse, says Morris, "a perfidious wretch deposed he heard Mr. Roan utter blasphemous expressions in his sermons."[82]

In 1738 Governor Gooch had promised the Synod of Philadelphia that he would extend the terms of the Toleration Act to their ministers who should visit the Scotch-Irish settlements on the frontiers.[83] This act required the taking of the oath of allegiance and the declaration against transubstantiation and "that Nonconformist places of worship should be registered and

[77] Foote, p. 134.
[78] McIlwaine, op. cit., p. 46.
[79] Morris, in Foote, p. 134, and in Alexander, p. 224.
[80] Foote, p. 134.   [81] McIlwaine, p. 46.
[82] In Foote, p. 134, and Alexander, p. 224.
[83] See above, pp. 40-42; Records of Pres. Church, May 28, 1739.

those who ministered in them be licensed."[84] The enforcement of the act, as Channing points out, would destroy the efficiency of itinerant missionaries and also work a hardship upon many of the regular Nonconforming clergy who confined themselves to no particular meeting house but preached in a half dozen churches in the course of a month. In the opinion of Gooch, the terms of the Toleration Act did not extend to such as Roan for, in the first place, he was neither licensed according to the statute nor were his meeting houses registered. Furthermore, he had come into the settled parts of Virginia, a region not included in Gooch's promise to the Synod, for the principal reason in his extending his protection to the Presbyterians was to settle the frontier, and that beyond the Blue Ridge, if possible. Finally, Roan had not come under the auspices of the Synod of Philadelphia, if a strict interpretation of the Governor's promise were necessary, and had not heeded the admonition of the latter that the ministers must "behave themselves peaceably towards the government."[85]

Gooch's attitude towards Roan and his like is seen in his charge to the grand jury delivered at the meeting of the Colonial Court on April 25, 1745.[86] In this he calls attention to the "unusual" information he had received "of certain *false teachers* that are lately crept into this government; who, without orders or licenses, or producing any testimonial of their education or sect, professing themselves ministers under the pretended influence of *new light, extraordinary impulse,* and *such like* fanatical and enthusiastic knowledge, lead the innocent and ignorant people into all kinds of delusion; . . ." Contrary to what he at first thought would be the result, these deceivers were drawing large numbers of disciples after them to the danger of the estab-

[84] Channing, *History of the U. S.,* II, 448; for the oaths and the declaration, see p. 455.

[85] Gooch to the Synod of Philadelphia, reported by Mr. Anderson on May 28, 1739. Also quoted in Foote, p. 104.

[86] Burk, *History of Virginia,* III, 119-121; Foote, pp. 135-137; *Records of Pres. Church,* May 27, 1745 n. Burk copied this charge from a Williamsburg paper and Foote took it from him. We are told by Foote that it does not appear in the court records. We quote from *Records of Pres. Church.*

lished institutions, and the Governor advised the jury to use all lawful measures to suppress them.[87]

Meantime, on April 19, the grand jury had presented Roan "for reflecting upon and vilifying the Established Religion in divers sermons, which he preached at the house of Joshua Morris in the parish and county of James City on the 7th, 8th and 9th of January last, before a numerous audience in the words following, to wit,—'*At church you pray to the Devil*'—and '*That your good works damn you, and carry you to hell*',—'*That all your ministers preach false doctrine, and that they, and all who follow them, are going to hell*'—and '*The church is the house of the Devil,—that when your ministers receive their orders they swear that it is the spirit of God that moves them to it, but it is the spirit of the Devil, and no good can proceed out of their mouths.*'"[88] At the same time Thomas Watkins, of Henrico County, was presented for saying "your churches and chappels are no better than the synagogues of Satan," while Joshua Morris was indicted for permitting his house to be used by Roan for these unlawful meetings.[89] Roan had already left the colony before his indictment[90] and the cases were continued until the October session of the court.

The news of the conduct of Roan and the New Side preachers, together with the Governor's charge, soon reached the Synod of Philadelphia. That body was quick to make clear its position by denying any connection with these schismatics. It assured Gooch that those who were carrying on the unchristian practices "and perhaps assume the name of Presbyterians . . . never belonged to our body, but are missionaries sent out by some, who by reason of their divisive and uncharitable doctrines and practices, were in May, 1741, excluded from our Synod, upon

[87] A. Alexander, in *Watchman and Observer*, March 18, 1847, who contends that Gooch feared the formation of a powerful party opposed to the Established Church but also regarded their fanaticism as dangerous.

[88] Foote, p. 138, who quotes from the court records.

[89] *Ibid.* See also Morris's account in Alexander, p. 224.

[90] Morris, *loc. cit.* The latter says that Roan remained longer than any of his predecessors.

which they erected themselves into a separate society, and have industriously sent abroad persons whom we judge ill qualified for the character they assume, to divide and trouble the churches."[91] The Synod thereupon requested the continued protection of the government for their ministers who should "produce proper testimonials" and "behave themselves suitably."

In reply, the Governor assured them of his continued good will towards all their missionaries "producing proper testimonials, complying with the laws, and performing divine service in some certain place appropriated for that purpose, without disturbing the quiet and unity of our sacred and civil establishments. . . ."[92] He was quite willing to extend the protection of the law to all those entitled to it, but would have no more of "the wicked and destructive doctrines and practices of itinerant preachers."

The records of the Colonial Court held in Williamsburg on October 19, 1745 show that the cases of Roan, Watkins, Joshua Morris and Samuel Morris of Reading House fame were all brought up for trial. Of Roan's case we are told: "Six witnesses were cited to prove the charge against Mr. Roan, but their depositions were in his favor; and the witness who accused him of blasphemy, when he heard of the arrival of Messrs. Tennent and Finley, fled, and has not returned since, so that the indictment was dropped."[93]

Shortly after the charges were made against Roan, Watkins and Morris, Gilbert Tennent and Samuel Finley, two of

[91] Philadelphia Synod to Gooch, May 28, 1745, in *Recs. of Pres. Church* for that date; also given in Foote, p. 139.

[92] *Recs. of Pres. Church,* May 29, 1746; the letter is dated June 20, 1745, and is also found in Foote, pp. 139-140.

[93] Morris, quoted in Foote, p. 142, and in Alexander, p. 224. Of a number of cases that came up convictions were secured in only two and these were not decided until 1748. Samuel Morris and Isaac Winston were the ones who were fined. McIlwaine says, "Throughout these cases the sympathies of the petit juries seem to have been decidedly with the defendants." *Op. cit.* p. 50. The fact that juries even at Williamsburg were not hostile to dissenters shows what progress liberal ideas in religion were making among the people. Until 1747 the Presbyterians were subject to fines for nonattendance at church, for not until then were their meeting-houses licensed.

the most prominent leaders of the New Side, were sent by the
Presbyteries of New Brunswick and New Castle with an address to Governor Gooch in behalf of the Presbyterians in
Hanover.[94] They were given a respectful reception and seem
to have had no trouble in making the situation in the church
clear to the Governor, for they were given license to preach in
Hanover. Their stay was limited to only a week, however,
after which the regular meetings for the reading and prayer
were resumed. Morris was again presented and was repeatedly
fined in court for non-attendance at church and "keeping up
unlawful meetings." But this did not check the good work and,
says Morris, "the bush flourished in the flames."[95]

Sometime after the departure of Gilbert Tennent and Samuel Finley, the people of Hanover were visited by the Rever-
ends William Tennent and Samuel Blair, who continued the succession of Log College evangelists.[96] "After Mr. Tennent and
Blair were gone," says Morris, "Mr. Whitefield came and
preached four or five days, which was the happy means of
giving us further encouragement, and of engaging others to
the Lord, especially amongst the church people, who received
the gospel more readily from him than from ministers of the
Presbyterian denomination. After his departure we were desti-
tute of a minister, and followed our usual method of reading
and prayer at our meetings, till the Reverend Mr. Davies, our
present pastor, was sent us by the Presbytery to supply a few
Sabbaths in the spring of 1747, when our discouragements from
the government were renewed and multiplied."[97]

We are fortunate in having from the hand of Parson
Henry, of St. Paul's Parish, Hanover, uncle of the famed Patrick, a few letters to Commissary Dawson which give us the

[94] Morris, quoted in Foote, pp. 140-141, and Alexander, pp. 224-225.
[95] *Ibid.*
[96] *Ibid.,* in Foote, p. 144, and Alexander, p. 225. See above, pp. 12-13.
[97] *Ibid.,* in Foote, pp. 145-146, and Alexander, p. 225. Contrary to his
usual custom, Whitefield failed to record in his *Journal* anything he saw or
did on the occasion of this visit to Hanover. See Tyerman, *Whitefield,* II,
167, who places the date of this visit as November, 1746, but the letter of
Parson Henry referring to it is dated October 14, 1745. See below, pp. 61-62.

views of a representative Churchman towards the New Light dissenters, and whether they be right or wrong, help us to understand the attitude of mind of his class. In a long epistle of February 13, 1744/5[98] Henry tells his superior of the principles and practices of these "new Preachers that have lately seduc'd some unwary people in this Parish." He speaks of the emphasis which they placed upon conviction as a necessary preparation for the work of grace—a conviction which must be so deep as to bring the sinner to the point of despair. Conversion, reports Henry, is a very definite experience with the New Lights, the exact time and manner of which are known, so that "every converted person is as assuredly sensible of the Spirit of God working in him, as he would be of a wound or stab, or anything else that he knows by his outward senses." Not only this, but all who have had this experience, especially ministers, "have the spirit of discerning," so that they can tell whether or not a man is truly converted or is merely playing the hypocrite.[99] Samuel Morris and a certain Thomas Green in particular are mentioned as claiming this power. It is also held that a true Christian may know whether a minister has experienced sound religion merely by hearing him preach or pray. Since the call to preach is inward and comes from God alone, an unconverted minister can have no real authority among Christians, even though after trial and examination he has been regularly ordained and preaches sound doctrines.[100] It follows, then, that Christians are not obliged to adhere to pastors who they think are not in a state of grace, and have the right to go where they think they receive the most benefit. Finally, concludes Henry: "Both Preachers and people are great boasters of their assurance of salvation. They are so full of it here, that the greatest

[98] Dawson MSS. in Library of Congress. All following quotations are from this letter unless otherwise designated. We preserve the spelling and punctuation of the parson. A few of the Dawson MSS. are printed in *William and Mary College Quarterly*, Vol. I, series 2, pp. 261-281.

[99] We find that this is a common allegation against the denominations that represent the Great Awakening. See especially John Thomson's *Doctrine of Conviction set in a Clear Light*, for the opinion of the Old Side.

[100] Another opinion commonly said to have been held by the New Lights.

number of those who have lately left the Church, and followed those Enthusiastick Preachers, do confidently assert that they are as sure of going to Heaven at last, as if they were there already:[101] Nay, some people here who have always been justly reputed guilty of several immoralities, such as cheating, lying and even theft, and whose practices (I well know) are the same now as before, these very men do boast as much of their assurance, as others who are reckond blameless in their conversation. . . ." Such conduct the parson brands as impudent.

In regard to the methods of the New Lights, Henry says that Robinson, Roan and Blair "as well as their brethren elsewhere, strive with all their might, to raise in their hearers, what they call convictions, which is thus performd. They thunder out in awful words, and new coin'd phrases, what they call the terrors of the law, cursing & scolding, calling the old people, Grey-headed Devils, and all promiscuously, Damn'd double damn'd, whose (souls?)[102] are in hell though they are alive on earth, Lumps of hell-fire, incarnate Devils, 1000 times worse than Devils &c and all the while the Preacher exalts his voice puts himself into a violent agitation, stamping and beating his Desk unmercifully until the weaker sort of his hearers being scar'd, cry out, fall down & work like people in convulsion fits, to the amazement of spectators, and if a few only are thus brought down, the Preacher gets into a violent passion again, Calling out Will no more of you come to Christ? thundering out as before, till he has brought a quantum sufficit of his congregation to this condition, and these things are extoll'd by the Preachers as the mighty power of God's grace in their hearts, and they who thus cry out and fall down are caress'd and commended as the only penitent Souls who come to Christ, whilst they who don't are often condemn'd by the lump as hardened wretches almost beyond the reach of mercy in so much that some are not

---

[101] John Thomson criticised the New Side brethren for this attitude. See his *Government of the Church,* p. 50. We shall see it in connection with the Separate Baptists.

[102] MS. mutilated.

so season'd, impute it to the hardness of their own heart, and wish and pray to be in the like condition."

Henry was much aroused because the New Lights "have been at great pains to vilifie the Clergy of this Colony and have told their followers, both in public & private that they can never reap any benefit by going to hear them, because they are not the Servants of God, and have no authority to meddle with Holy things; They endeavor to give them a mean opinion of our Liturgy, but this I believe they have done chiefly in private for I did not hear that they spoke against it in their Sermons, however I know, that their adherents generally despise it, and one of them (Thomas Green) told one of his neighbors that it containd abundance of lies, and mention'd that sentence in the Te Deum (All the earth doth worship thee) as one."[102a]

What was probably more galling to the parson was the fact that some of the New Light converts regarded him as "a stranger to the true religion." One Roger Shackleford in particular, he says, accused him of preaching "Damnable doctrine" and pitied him "as being an unconverted graceless man." The same individual, claims Henry, was even sure that the Bishop of London lacked true religion. The fearlessness with which these dissenters "publickly tell their hearers, that they shall stand at the right hand of Christ in the day of Judgment, and condemn all of them who do not come to him at their call," is also mentioned by Henry.

Regardless of the fact that Whitefield was considered a New Light, Parson Henry thought it advisable to permit him to preach from his pulpit. This was done, however, on condition that the great evangelist read from the Book of Common Prayer before the sermon, which he did. That this action was a matter of policy on Henry's part is seen in the reasons he wrote to Dawson. He says: "If I had refus'd him access to the Church, he would have preach'd in the Church yard, or

---

[102a] In another letter of November 21, 1747, Henry wrote that the New Lights "were very industrious in casting all the reflections they could, upon the established church and its ministers." Dawson MSS.

very near it, and then the whole congregation would have gone over to him, this was what I plainly foresaw as did also my Friends; for tho the number of his followers there were but few, yet all the people to a man had a great desire to hear the famous Whitefield."[103] The parson also hoped that Whitefield's use of the Prayer Book would refute the condemnations of the Anglican liturgy by the New Lights.[104] He claims that Whitefield advised the dissenters to return within the folds of the Church.

If there was little sympathy between the supporters of the Establishment and the New Lights, there was just as little between the Old Side wing of the Presbyterian church and the revivalists. The Reverend John Thomson was a missionary of the Philadelphia Synod who was sent to Virginia on several occasions and finally settled there.[105] In 1738 or 1739 it appears that he visited congregations in the Valley and the western counties. Later on he removed to the Valley and finally to Amelia County, where he was living when he published his *Explication of the Shorter Catechism* in 1749.[106] Thomson visited Hanover at the time of Morris's revival and, we are told, the followers of Robinson, Blair and Roan "shut the doors against him, alledging he was an opposer of these three, the last of whom had wrote to some of them, requesting them in the name of the Lord, and for the Sake of Christ Jesus, not to allow Mr. Thomson to preach in their house, because he is an enemy to Christ & true religion."[107] Parson Henry invited Thomson to his home and obtained from him an account of the origin of the New Side movement in the Presbyterian Church which he included in his letter to the Commissary.

[103] Henry to Dawson, October 14, 1745. Dawson MSS.   [104] *Ibid.*

[105] See sketch in Webster's *History of the Presbyterian Church,* pp. 355-356.

[106] See Torrence, *Trial Bibliography of Colonial Virginia,* for the year 1749. Also Webster, *loc. cit.* When Thomson lived in Amelia Davies knew him as a neighbor and in his letter to Bellamy speaks highly of his judgment and piety and says, "He acknowledged the Revival had done much good in Hanover and rejoiced in seeing the prosperity of religion." Quoted by Webster, p. 357.

[107] Henry to Dawson, February 13, 1744/45, Dawson MSS.

In 1741 Thomson published two little works. One of these[108] examines the causes and nature of the schism in the Presbyterian church and the other,[109] the tenets of the New Side brethren. Concerning these works Webster says that they "are as able, learned, judicious and evangelical as any of the writings of Dickinson and Blair."[110] Probably in no other books can one find a better statement of the position of the Old Side, or rather their views of the New Side. As Thomson saw them, the principal tenets of the revivalists were: (1) deep and definite convictions which must fill the heart with terror; (2) definite experience of conversion without which one remains "in a damnable unconverted state;" (3) the ability of a truly converted person to determine whether or not another is converted; (4) that an unconverted minister has not been called by God and cannot be the means of conversion.[111]

Thomson examined each one of these "errors" and in a very able manner attacked them "as tending to corrupt the great Fundamental Doctrine of Conversion or Regeneration. . . ." He maintained that the work of grace did not come in successive stages but was a process complete in itself.[112] Therefore conviction, if it came from God, was in itself evidence that a person was in a converted state. Not all the other spiritual graces as faith, love, repentance may be apparent, but nevertheless they exist just as breathing may be the only evident sign of life in a body. Thomson criticized severely the emphasis placed upon the terrors or fears of the law by the New Lights.[113] These manifestations of fear, he explained, are not necessarily signs of pardoning grace in the sinner, but might, on the contrary, be evidences of the lack of it and of the presence of a guilty conscience. Thus what the New Lights called convic-

---

[108] *The Government of the Church of Christ.*
[109] *Doctrine of Conviction Set in a Clear Light.*
[110] *Op. cit.,* p. 356.
[111] *Doctrine of Conviction,* pp. 12-15. These are precisely the things that Henry mentions in his letter to the Commissary but whether he got them from observation or from Thomson, who visited him in Hanover, we do not know.
[112] *Ibid.,* pp. 15 ff.   [113] *Ibid.,* pp. 32 ff.

tions might really be false displays occasioned by the terrors of the law. It follows, then, that inward exercises are not the true criteria of one's spiritual estate, as the revivalists maintained, so much as one's future conduct and his desires. Thomson pointed to many instances in the Bible to prove that the preparatory convictions so emphasized by the New Lights were entirely unnecessary, and also to the fact that Christ and the Apostles emphasized primarily the "still Gospel Grace." In fact, he pointed out certain absolute evils apt to result from preaching the terrors of hell.[114]

As to the definite assurance of conversion, Thomson believed it to be attainable but also presented reasons why it might not be evidenced by many. He furthermore asserted that everyone set apart for the work of the ministry is called of God.[115] It is the external call alone which is visible and which "Authoriseth the Minister to officiate, and the People to receive and submit to their Ministry."[116] While true grace is desirable in a minister, still if Providence permits a graceless person to be ordained, then even such an one is called and it is his duty to officiate. His sin is not in answering God's call but in neglecting the grace which should be in him. God may even use a hypocrite to preach his word successfully. The ill success of the gospel rests not with the preacher so much as with the hearers, otherwise people could not profitably listen to a preacher unless they were sure of his conversion. How could the unconverted ones, then, judge of the competency of the ministers?

Even from this brief statement we see that a real gulf existed between the conservative and revivalist wings of the Presbyterian Church. Unquestionably the former regarded the latter as vainglorious boasters,[117] while the revivalists considered their Old Side brethren as lacking in the essential Christian graces. The disagreement over church government grew out of other more deep-seated differences which Thomson expresses as the "low and bad Opinion" held by the New Side "of the generality

[114] *Doctrine of Conviction,* pp. 46-47.
[115] *Ibid.,* pp. 68 ff.   [116] *Ibid.,* p. 71.
[117] See Thomson, *Government of the Church,* preface, p. v, p. 50.

of their Brethren, judging them to be quite void of Grace yea and Worse, even designed Enemies to the Life of Religion. . . ."[118] Something of the temper of the Old Side is seen in Thomson's being "almost fully persuaded" that Whitefield was "a downright Deceiver, or else under a dreadful Delusion," while he considered the latter's autobiography and journals as "nothing but mere confused inconsistent religious Jargon, contrived to amuse and delude the simple; and perhaps a little Time may discover more of the Mystery of Iniquity than the World is aware of as yet."[119] Thomson pitied the "Folly" of the New Side brethren in their admiration for Whitefield and wished "freedom to them from their captivating Delusion."

As both Old and New Side missionaries visited Virginia, the echo of the schism was felt there. We have noted Thomson's reception in Hanover and can sympathize with him in his statement that the more "forward and faithful" he was in warning the people of the dangers of the new doctrines and notions in religion, "the more I was maligned, despised, hated and forsaken by my own People: So that as the great Apostle says I was counted their enemy because I told them the Truth."[120]

Over in the Valley John Craig's adherence to the Old Side gave offence to some of his congregation "who then," he says, "looked upon me as an opposer of the work of God, as they called it, an enemy to religion, and applied with all keenness to their holy and spiritual teachers, to come and preach, and convert the people of my charge, and free them from sin and Satan, and from me, a carnal wretch on whom they unhappily depended for instruction, to their souls' utter destruction. They flying speedily came and thundered their new gospel through every corner of my congregation; and some of them had the assurance to come to my house, and demand a dismission of some of my subscribers who had invited them, being tainted with these notions formerly."[121]

[118] *Ibid.*, pp. 2, 8 ff.   [119] *Ibid.*, preface, pp. VII ff., X-XI.   [120] *Ibid.*, p. IV.
[121] Craig's *Memoir*, in Foote, Second Series, p. 31.

Like Thomson, Craig found himself much maligned by the revivalists who, he says, "freely loaded me with these and such like (appelations), poor, blind, carnal, hypocritical, damned wretch; and this given to my face by some of their ministers. And when I administered the Lord's Supper to my people, they mockingly said to their neighbors going to it, what, are you going to Craig's frolic? I thought God had given me a difficult plot to labor in, but I ever called upon him in trouble, and he never failed to help."[122]

Such was the situation in the Old Dominion when Davies settled in Hanover. With his coming Presbyterianism enters upon a new period in eastern Virginia—the period of consolidation and expansion. The Log College missionaries had done their work in laying the foundations well, and now the master builder was at hand to complete the structure. The work of this great divine, the chief instrument in the Presbyterian revival in Virginia, is well worthy of careful examination.

We have thus far seen that the permanent introduction of Presbyterian doctrine and discipline into Virginia came from two sources, namely, with the great Scotch-Irish migration into the western parts of the colony, and with the coming of the New Light revivalists into eastern Virginia where the spontaneous awakening in Hanover had prepared the soil. William Robinson and his sucessors made this revival the work of their own hands, but they were able to do it only because they themselves were products of the Great Awakening. In the Valley of Virginia and in the western counties it was the Old Side wing of the Church that gained the first foot-hold and settled the first pastors, but the New Light missionaries carried the spark of the revival into those regions also. Just before the coming of Davies to Hanover, in fact, a considerable awakening occurred in Augusta and Frederick counties under the preaching of William Dean, a graduate of the Log College, and Eliab Byram,

[122] Craig's *Memoir,* in Foote, Second Series, p. 31.

who belonged to the New Side Presbytery of New York.[123]
However, it was in Hanover and adjacent counties that the New
Side accomplished its great work, and when Davies came in
1747, it had no settled pastor in the colony. On the other hand,
four ministers were established in western Virginia under the
care of the Old Side Synod of Philadelphia.[124]

[123] John Leland's "Virginia Chronicle," in *Works*, p. 100; Webster, *op. cit.*,
pp. 491-492, 526, where will be found sketches of these men. John Leland
was a Baptist observer.

[124] Just how long Thomson was in the Valley and when he removed to
Amelia does not seem clear. We know he was a resident of the latter county
in 1749 as he tells us in the title page of the Catechism which he published
in that year. Attached to his name were the titles M.A. and V.D.M.

CHAPTER IV

SAMUEL DAVIES AND THE CONSOLIDATION OF PRESBYTERIANISM IN EASTERN VIRGINIA

Samuel Davies was born on November 3, 1723, in the county of New Castle, then a part of Pennsylvania, but which has since been included in the State of Delaware. He obtained the principal part of his education at Samuel Blair's school at Fagg's Manor, Pennsylvania, there being no college nearer than New Haven or Williamsburg. Entering the Presbyterian ministry, he was licensed by the New Side Presbytery of New Castle on July 30, 1746, at the age of twenty-three and in the following February he was ordained evangelist.[1]

At the time Davies completed his studies and entered upon his career in the church, he was in a very delicate state of health, supposedly in the earlier stages of consumption. With few hopes of more than a very short time in which to labour on this earth, he entered upon his work with all the vigour that his feeble body would allow. From the time of his licensure until his permanent settlement in Virginia in the spring of 1748, Davies visited many vacancies, some in Pennsylvania, some in New Jersey, but chiefly in Maryland, where a remarkable revival had been started by William Robinson about the year 1745, which was at its height when Davies visited Somerset County.[2]

In the spring of 1747 Davies was dispatched on his first visit to Hanover, whither he was sent to supply the congregations for six weeks. He at once secured from the Colonial Court

[1] Memoir of S. Davies in Rice's *Evangelical and Literary Magazine*, II (1819), 112, 186, 201, 329, 353, 474, 560 ff. This Memoir was published anonymously in 1832 in a small volume. Sketches of Davies in various magazines contain nothing new. Foote, *Sketches of Virginia*, First Series, pp. 159 ff. has much material. Of interest is J. G. Hughes' sketch of Davies in the *J. P. Branch Papers of Randolph-Macon College*, IV, no. 2 (June, 1914). See also Ford, *The Scotch-Irish*, and Alexander, *The Log College*.

[2] Davies to Bellamy, June 28, 1751, in Alexander, *op. cit.*, p. 231; Albert Barnes, Introductory Essay in Davies' *Sermons*, p. xv. In this essay Barnes quotes largely from William Hill, prominent in the Presbyterian revival of 1787, whose stepfather was a member of Davies' congregation.

Samuel Davies

license[3] to preach at four meeting houses in and about Hanover, a thing which, according to Morris, had never been done before.[4] Indeed, just before Davies' coming a proclamation from the Governor had been set up at the meeting houses "strictly requiring all magistrates to suppress and prohibit, as far as they lawfully could, all itinerant preachers etc."[5] The fact that Davies secured his license shows that Governor Gooch was not opposed to Non-Conforming ministers who properly qualified themselves and preached at specified places, but only to "itinerants who went from place to place scattering the seeds of religious disorder."[6]

Upon this first mission to Hanover, Davies remained only about six weeks.[7] He soon, however, received a call signed by about a hundred and fifty heads of families begging him to return and settle as a regular pastor for the congregations of Hanover and adjacent counties.[8] Davies accepted and in May, 1748 began his permanent pastorate in the Old Dominion.[9] From this time on he began to recover his health, but for a while he looked upon these signs of improvement "only as an intermission of a disorder that would finally prove mortal."

When he arrived in Virginia the second time, Davies was accompanied by the Reverend John Rodgers, who came for the purpose of assisting in the evangelistical work.[10] The two had been fellow students at Blair's seminary when they were preparing for the ministry. They preached one Sabbath in a

[3] He took the usual oath of fidelity to the government and subscribed to the Thirty-Nine Articles of the Anglican Church with four exceptions. Howison, *History of Virginia*, II, 179. Davies' MS. containing his position on the Thirty-Nine Articles is in the Dawson papers, under date of April 21, 1747.

[4] Davies to Bellamy, in Alexander, p. 226, quoting Morris.

[5] *Ibid.*

[6] H. R. McIlwaine, *Struggle of Protestant Dissenters for Religious Toleration in Virginia*, p. 52.

[7] After his first brief stay, during which his wife died, Davies' health became greatly impaired and the next year was spent "under melancholy and consumptive languishments." He re-married on October 4, 1748. Hughes, *loc. cit.*, pp. 68, 70.

[8] *Ibid.*, p. 68.

[9] Davies to the Bishop of London, January 10, 1752, in Foote, p. 192.

[10] Miller, *Life of the Reverend John Rodgers*, p. 25.

licensed house in Hanover and then journeyed on to Williamsburg so that Rodgers might qualify under the Toleration Act.[11]
Governor Gooch was favorable towards granting Rodgers' petition and made overtures in his behalf, but the Court absolutely
refused to license him. Rodgers was out and the Court was
"determined to keep him out," to use the words of his principal
opponent.[12] He was forbidden to preach within the colony under
penalty of a fine of five hundred pounds and a year's imprisonment. So determined, indeed, was the attitude of some of the
members of the Court that there was even talk of prosecuting
Rodgers for having already preached without license and of
revoking the license granted to Davies the preceding year. There
was nothing for Rodgers to do except to leave Virginia without
fulfilling his mission, and Davies returned to Hanover without
him.[13]

It was just forty years since Makemie's death in 1708, and
not a single organized Presbyterian church was to be found in
the older settled parts of Virginia, nor was there any other minister of his denomination within two hundred miles of Davies.[14]
No help could be expected from the three or four Old Side
ministers, far off in Albemarle and Augusta counties, for they
were under the jurisdiction of the Philadelphia Synod and, so
far from rendering Davies any assistance, they must be counted
among his detractors. Only incipient steps had been taken by
the New Side Synod of New York to form congregations in
Frederick County and a few other places.[15] In addition, there
was little intercourse between the Scotch-Irish of the western
counties and the people of the eastern parts of Virginia—their

[11] The power to grant licenses had been taken away from the County
Courts and was now exercised by the Colonial Court at Williamsburg. This
consisted of the Governor and his Council. We use the expression Colonial
Court in preference to General Court so as to avoid possible confusion with
a legislative body.

[12] Miller, p. 51.

[13] Rodgers was an animated and popular preacher and the success of
Davies was causing the Court to take alarm. See Hughes, loc. cit., p. 69;
Howison, II, 181.

[14] Davies to the Bishop of London, January 10, 1752, in Foote, p. 192;
also Hill, quoted in Barnes, op. cit., XVIII.

[15] Barnes, "Introductory Essay," pp. xviii-xix, quoting Hill.

interests, social, economic and religious, were of an altogether different character.[16]

While Davies' success, then, depended wholly on his own efforts, the times favored him. The Established Church had reached a low ebb and occupied the very precarious position which we have described in the second chapter of our study. As a body the clergy had lost all influence over the mass of the people and were considered as the mere parasites of the rich and the great.[17] The Hanover revival showed how eager people were to hear the gospel, whether read from pious books or preached by the itinerant revivalists. It was Davies' good fortune to come into a community where the soil had already been prepared and where a large number of the people were open to conviction and easily impressed by evangelical preaching.

Davies' license to preach in Virginia gave him permission "to assemble and meet any congregations of Dissenters at the several meeting houses, on the lands of Samuel Morris, David Rice, and Stephen Leacy in Hanover County and on the lands of Thomas Watkins in Henrico County, without molestation, they behaving in a peaceable manner and conforming themselves according to the directions of the acts of parliament in that behalf made."[18] In these four meeting houses, scattered in two counties, the great man began his pastorate. He had not been in Virginia many months before the zeal and effectiveness of his preaching led people who travelled great distances to his services to petition the Colonial Court for the licensing of additional houses in new neighborhoods.[19] Davies went to Williamsburg to plead his cause in person and that he did so effectively is evidenced by the fact that on November 1, 1748, just six months after the refusal of the Court to license Rodgers, he obtained the right to minister in three additional houses, one each in Louisa, Goochland, and Caroline counties.[20]

[16] *Ibid.*, p. xix.

[17] *Ibid.*, p. xxii, and Chapter II, *supra*.

[18] License given in Foote, p. 160, dated April 14, 1747; also in Fulham MSS. transcripts, Box II, number 128 (Va.).

[19] McIlwaine, pp. 53-54.

[20] Foote, p. 168, gives the license; also in Fulham transcripts, *loc. cit. Cf.* Davies to Bellamy, in Alexander, p. 227.

This made seven places in five different counties between which the indefatigable Davies divided his time. Two years later, in 1750, the County Court of New Kent granted him a license for an additional house in that county, but the action was immediately revoked by the Colonial Court, which claimed that the matter was beyond the jurisdiction of the county justices.[21] Davies' itinerary was extensive. In the five counties in which he laboured there were eight ministers of the Established Church.[22] To the Bishop of London he wrote in 1751: "the extremes of my congregation lie eighty or ninety miles apart and the dissenters under my care are scattered through six or seven different counties."[23] He estimates that under his charge were one hundred families in Hanover County, twenty or thirty in Henrico, ten or twelve in Caroline, fifteen or twenty in Goochland, and about the same number in Louisa. These were the counties in which the licensed meeting houses were located. In addition there were fifteen or twenty families in Cumberland where there was no licensed place of preaching and about the same number in New Kent where the license had been revoked.[24] The nearest meeting houses were twelve or fifteen miles apart, while some of the members lived twenty, thirty, and in some instances forty miles away from where they attended. "Were they all compactly situated in one county," says Davies, "they would be sufficient to form three distinct congregations."[25] In 1751 he placed the number of his communicants at about three hundred, including a considerable number of Negroes, although the number that came to hear him ran into the thousands.[26] To Bellamy he wrote: "Were you, sir, a narrow bigot, you would, no doubt, rejoice to hear that there are now some hundreds of dissenters in a place where, a few years ago, there were not ten. . . ."[27]

[21] Commissary Dawson to the Bishop of London, in Perry's *Historical Collections,* I, 366, 407; Fulham transcripts, Box I, number 184 (Va.). Peyton Randolph's opinion in MS. Virginia Religious Papers, Library of Congress.
    [22] Fulham Transcripts, *ibid.*   [23] Quoted in Foote, pp. 183-184.   [24] *Ibid.*
    [25] Davies to Bellamy, in Alexander, p. 227.
    [26] *Ibid.* Four or five hundred and sometimes twice that number came to hear him in his smallest houses.   [27] *Ibid.*

Many "church people" were among those who responded to Davies' ministry. It was his custom to preach frequently at his various chapels on week days, which was the cause of strenuous opposition from the established clergymen because many Anglicans who did not dare absent themselves from their own parish church on the Sabbath were willing enough to hear Davies on another day. Davies at first regarded their presence as due to curiosity, but he soon saw that many were by this means led to forsake the Establishment and become Presbyterians.[28]

The spread of this schism soon became a source of great concern to the Commissary. In 1752 that official informed the Bishop of London that until Davies came the people "quietly conformed to the doctrine and discipline of our church, constantly frequented the public worship of God, and the Christian sacrifice," but since he "has been allowed to officiate in so many places, . . . there has been a great defection from our religious assemblies. The generality of his followers, I believe, were born and bred in our Communion."[29] Governor Dinwiddie, too, was alarmed by the rapid spread of dissent since the arrival of Davies in the colony,[30] while from the body of the clergy an "Address to the House of Burgesses," drawn up in 1751, complained of the activities of the Presbyterians in the counties of Hanover, Henrico, Goochland, Amelia and Albemarle.[31] They called the attention of the Assembly to the fact that Davies and his followers had no right to the title of Presbyterians because they had been excluded from the Synod of Philadelphia in 1741 "for their erroneous doctrines and practices," and had not yet recanted or been readmitted. By no law of the colony, they claimed, were Davies and the New Light ministers entitled to preach, far less, to practice itinerating and gain converts by inveigling "ignorant and unwary people with

[28] *Ibid.;* see also Barnes, "Introductory Essay," p. xxvi, quoting Hill.

[29] Perry, I, 384-386; Dawson MSS.; Fulham transcripts, Box I, number 11 (Va.). The letter is dated June 17, 1752.

[30] Dinwiddie to the Bishop of London, 1752, in Perry, I, 395-396; *Parallel Source Problems in United States History,* pp. 219-221. M. W. Jernegan prints many extracts bearing on the struggle for religious freedom in Virginia in this book. Hereafter we shall refer to it simply as *Source Problems.*

[31] Perry, I, 381-383 and *Source Problems,* pp. 221-223.

their sophistry." In their petition the clergy prayed that these dissenters "be suitably checked and discouraged."

The opposition to Davies was based, it seems, on three grounds: first, whether or not the Toleration Act extended to Virginia; secondly, if it did, did the Act grant the right to itinerate; and lastly, it was even questioned whether the New Lights came within the recognition of the law, even if the first two points were conceded. Although much was made of the last of these contentions, it was the first two which involved the legal status of all dissenters in the colony and in fighting for them Davies was doing a service to all non-conforming denominations.

The English Toleration Act of 1689 exempted dissenters from attendance at the parish churches provided they took the oath of allegiance to the Crown, continued to pay their tithes, and attended their religious services with the regularity provided by the law.[32] Furthermore, their ministers must be regularly ordained, must accept certain articles of the Church of England, subscribe to the oaths and preach only in registered places of meeting. Ten years later an act was passed by the Virginia legislature applying the Toleration Act to the colony in so far as it concerned exemption from penalties to dissenters who attended their worship "once in two months," but the act does not specifically mention dissenting ministers.[33] In 1711 Parliament passed a supplementary act which allowed properly qualified dissenting ministers "to officiate in any congregation in any county" provided the meeting place was duly certified and registered.[34]

It was not until the return of Davies from England in 1755 with an opinion from the Attorney General, Sir Dudley Rider, that the legal status of the dissenters in Virginia was finally determined under the above laws. Until that time the action of the government towards the Presbyterians was not always consistent.[35] At times there was a disposition to be lenient and then

---

[32] *Source Problems,* pp. 202-203.
[33] *Ibid.,* p. 204 and note 2; W. W. Hening's *Statutes at Large,* III, 171.
[34] *Source Problems,* pp. 204-205; McIlwaine, *op. cit.,* p. 55.
[35] We shall see that years later the government was loath to concede to the Separate Baptists what the Presbyterians had really gained for all

again the Council questioned whether the Toleration Act even extended to Virgina at all.[36] Davies persistently claimed that dissenters in the colony were on the same footing as those in England and that all of the exemptions of the Toleration Act respecting both preachers and congregations applied to Virginia, "not as *an English law,* for we are convinced that it does not extend hither by virtue of its primitive enaction, but as *received into the body of the Virginia laws* by our Legislature."[37] The great point at issue was whether or not English *practice* extended to the colony, or whether the interpretation of the Council in each individual case should prevail. On one occasion soon after the exclusion of Rodgers, Davies was permitted to argue this point before Peyton Randolph, Attorney General of the colony, and in an able and clear speech showed that if the English Act of Toleration did not extend to the colony neither did the Act of Uniformity, for the one was intended to mitigate the other.[38] In view of the law of 1699 it could hardly be maintained, nor was it successfully done, that the Act of Toleration did not extend to Virginia. Davies was always able to support his claims "with great learning and eloquence" and eventually he was sustained by the British authorities.[39]

Probably the best statement of Davies's position is found his *Appendix Proving the Right of the Synod of New York to the Religious Liberties and Immunities allowed to the Protestant Dissenters.*[40] In this little pamphlet Davies points out that it cannot be maintained that the Act of Toleration does not extend to the colony since Quakers, "Presbyterians that see

Protestant dissenters, although the Baptists were not inclined to keep within the provisions of the Toleration Act at all.

[36] F. L. Hawks, *Protestant Episcopal Church in Virginia,* p. 109; Foote, p. 170.

[37] Davies to Dr. Benjamin Avery, May 21, 1752, in Foote, pp. 208-209, and *Source Problems,* pp. 223-224.

[38] Hawks, p. 109; *Evan. and Lit. Mag.,* II, 118; Miller, *Life of Rodgers,* p. 53 note.

[39] Hawks, p. 109.

[40] Published in Williamsburg in 1748 as an appendix to his *Impartial Trial.* It is to be found in the Library of Congress. The copy of the *Impartial Trial* in the Pennsylvania Historical Society lacks this appendix.

fit to oppose us," and other sects are given legal toleration. Secondly, Davies held that if the law did not extend to the colony, then dissenters could not be held culpable under it. How, too, could it be maintained that the Act did not exist in Virginia when Presbyterian ministers were compelled to qualify under its terms? There was no colonial statute requiring Protestant dissenting ministers to take oaths, record their meeting houses and subscribe to the Articles of Faith.[41] Thus Davies showed how inconsistent the position was that the Toleration Act did not extend to the colony when ministers were made to conform to it and were punished under its provisions. Had not Gooch also promised protection to Presbyterian ministers as long as they conformed themselves to the rules prescribed by the Act of Toleration in England? It was obviously impossible to restrict the interpretation of the Virginia law of 1699 to its letter.

It was not long before the ground of discussion shifted to the question of itinerating and the number of preaching places a dissenter might have. The English act of 1711, allowing dissenters to preach in more than one county, had never been enacted in Virginia,[42] but Davies held that "the reason of the law is at least as strong here as in England, and consequently it extends hither. . . ."[43] He even claimed the right to preach to Presbyterians *anywhere*,[44] an interpretation which carried with it the unrestricted right to itinerate and the duty of the Colonial Court to license houses for preaching whenever they were applied for.

The action of the Court in granting Davies licenses in five counties and in registering several houses that were "to be erected"[45] would seem to favor the latter's interpretation of the Toleration Act, although the Court did refuse the same privilege in a sixth county. There were many, however, who be-

[41] *Impartial Trial*, appendix. The act of 1699 did not specifically mention ministers.

[42] H. J. Eckenrode, *Separation of Church and State in Virginia*, pp. 33-34.

[43] To the Bishop of London, January 10, 1752. See *Source Problems*, pp. 224-230, at 228 and 230, note 1; Foote, pp. 184-195, 206. *Cf.* below note 51.

[44] Letter of January 4, 1749/50 to Rector of St. Margaret's Parish, Caroline, whom he even invited to go to law on the matter. Dawson MSS. (somewhat mutilated).

[45] Bishop of London (to Commissary Dawson?), December 25, 1750, in Foote, p. 177 and *Source Problems*, pp. 217-18.

lieved that the Court had gone too far and that dissenting ministers could qualify only in the county where they lived "and how Davies can be said to live in five different counties, they who granted the license must explain."[46] At the very most the Anglican conception of a "legal indulgence" was that a minister should be confined in his labours to a definite and limited parish, although several meeting houses might be necessary to the convenience of the people, as was the case in some of the Anglican parishes.[47] Any concession beyond this they might well regard as a favour which even the ministers of the Established Church did not enjoy. This is what Commissary Dawson had in mind when, in 1752, he complained to his superior that the dissenters "not satisfied with our licensing so many, now most unreasonably apply for more. I think it is high time for the Government to interpose, to give their immodesty a check and to restrain their teachers within the bounds of a parish, lest their insolence should grow to a dangerous height. In the meantime, till they can have teachers settled within such bounds, let the people go to Church, whither they contentedly would have gone, if Mr. Davies had never come among them."[48] It was not surprising, therefore, that Davies' claims were considered unreasonable, and it was felt that he already had more than "either the king's instructions or the Act of Toleration intended."[49] The latter, it was contended, "was never meant to permit . . . itinerant preachers to gather congregations where there was none before."[50]

In a long thirty-nine page indictment of Davies much was made of the point that by the Toleration Act "a dissenting congregation may be allowed a dissenting teacher; but if there be not one to be had, . . . the Act of Toleration cannot give them one."[51] The writer contends that no such thing as "occasional

[46] *Ibid.*

[47] Dawson to the Bishop of London, June 17, 1752, in Fulham transcripts and Dawson MSS.

[48] *Ibid.,* and Perry, I, pp. 384-386.

[49] Dawson to the Bishop of London, July 27, 1750, in Perry, I, 366; also Fulham transcripts, June 17, 1752.

[50] Bishop of London (to Dawson?), December 25, 1750, in Foote, p. 177 and *Source Problems,* pp. 217-18.

[51] This is in the form of an unsigned and undated MS. booklet in the Virginia Religious Papers of the Library of Congress. It answers about

ministrations" are known to that law and that "to erect congregations and meeting houses purely that they may be vacant, and visited once in a twelvemonth by an occasional ministrator, who must hereby much neglect his particular congregation is not agreeable to the Act of Toleration, which obliges people to go to some place of public worship every Lord's day. The style of the act is not *a* teacher and *fifty* congregations, but *a* teacher and *a* congregation, as may be seen in the eleventh paragraph." Davies' interpretation of the law, it was held, was a new one and one which never would have been granted in England, even though conditions had been the same as in Virginia. It was no fault of the law that there were not enough ministers so that each congregation might have one; at the same time the fact that there were not enough was no justification for every family or two to have a licensed meeting house solely "that they may remain a little vacant congregation, to invite an occasional ministrator to give them a lecture, when he happens to come their way." "Vicinity of residence," it was pointed out, "is a necessary prerequisite for the erection of a parish in this country from the very nature of the thing; for how could a pastor attend one part of his parish at Williamsburg, and another at the Mountains? If two such distant places should petition to be erected into one parish, or consolidated, would not the petition be deservedly laughed at?" What more could one ask than to have a parish which extended into five different counties "at least in extent upwards of 200 miles"?[52] Surely the motives of such a man could not be confined to making converts to Christianity but extended rather to the building up of Presbyterianism.

Davies, on his part, resented the epithet "itinerant" as a stigma which he did not deserve.[53] He argued that ministers of the Establishment, on account of the extent of the parishes and the scattered population frequently had two or three meeting

every argument presented by Davies in his various letters to the Commissary and the Bishop of London. It is entitled Observations on Mr. Samuel Davies, his Letter, etc., and may well be a reply to the letter of January 10, 1752, referred to above.

[52] Dinwiddie to the Bishop of London, in Perry, I, 395-396 and *Source Problems*, pp. 220-221, June 5, 1752.

[53] *Ibid.*; also Davies to the Bishop of London, January 10, 1752, *loc. cit.*

places or chapels of ease. One of the ministers in Hanover County had three churches situated in two counties and his parish was probably sixty miles in circumference. Although he divided his labours in this way, he was not considered an itinerant but a settled pastor. Since for some years there was no other minister to assist him, Davies contended that the Toleration Act permitted the Presbyterians to obtain as many licensed houses as would make worship accessible to them all. They might have as many as Davies chose to serve and yet be regarded as one congregation. In fact, was it not the intention of the Toleration Act to make worship accessible to dissenters and to permit them to worship in their own way? How else can they have toleration? Having a widely scattered congregation which necessitated many meeting houses, Davies claimed, did not make him less a settled pastor than if he officiated to one congregation in Hanover. If there was reason for the Established Clergy to have several meeting houses, there was even more reason for his having a number, for the dissenters were fewer in number and more widely scattered than the Church people. If Davies were not allowed to "itinerate" and if the number of his meeting places were reduced, many of his people would either be deprived of the gospel or be compelled to attend the Established Church. Surely, he maintained, if the spirit of the Toleration Act was to allow nonconformists to worship in a lawful way, they were entitled to a sufficient number of houses to accommodate them. The law, he claimed, presumed this for it compelled dissenters to attend the Anglican Church, *unless they attended some dissenting congregation.* The Toleration Act did not "particularize the number of houses to be licensed for the use of one congregation," but merely required that they be properly registered. Until a sufficient number of ministers could be secured so that he could divide his congregation, Davies contended that the precedent of the Establishment permitted him to take care of all the dissenters under his charge.

Whatever Davies' argument might be, the Anglicans could point out that the Act of Toleration "was not designed to introduce separate congregations but to give them a permission to continue, after they were unfortunately formed." Governments provided for established churches because they believed that uniformity in religion was best for the state. Dissenters from it are tolerated merely "as an evil which cannot wholly be prevented."[54] Surely no law providing for exemption from attending the state church was ever intended to permit nonconformists to spread promiscuously and thus undermine it.[55] If anything, it is the Establishment which is entitled to privileges and yet its ministers are not allowed to run off for occasional ministration, nor are parishes erected when there is no prospect of a settled minister.[56] Davies' interpretation, it was pointed out, was absolutely opposed to the purpose of the Toleration Act, which was "to unite their Majesties Protestant subjects in interest and affection." Furthermore, it was stated, had there been no more dissenters in England at the time of the act of William and Mary than there appears to be now in Virginia, it never would have been passed at all. Was not Virginia founded as a retreat for Churchmen as other colonies were for dissenters? Why should the latter expect special privilege any more than Anglicans could expect such in Massachusetts or Rhode Island?

In support of the position of the Anglicans was the opinion of Peyton Randolph, who believed that no more than one house should be licensed for one preacher in a county, for "if they are permitted to range and raise contributions over the whole country, when our clergy are confined to a single parish," it will encourage many to fall away from the Establishment and will tend "to sow dissension and confusion among the people."[57]

Notwithstanding the influences brought to bear against Davies and the apparent reasonableness of the Anglican position, the authorities in England sustained the former. Involved in the opinion of Attorney General Rider was the principle that under the Toleration Act the Colonial Court "had no right to limit the number of houses for public worship to be allowed Dissenters," and "no right to specify the persons to speak in

---

[54] MS. Observations on Mr. Davies, his Letter, etc.
[55] Ibid. See also Bishop of London to Dr. Doddridge, May 11, 1751, in Perry, I, 372 and Source Problems, pp. 218-219.
[56] MS. Observations.
[57] MS. undated, in Virginia Religious Papers, Library of Congress.

particular meeting-houses."[58] By this time (1755), however, the increase in the number of ministers in Virginia had largely removed the objection to the granting of more licenses, namely, the granting of them to the same man. The healing of the schism three years later bettered the situation still more.

We have thus far traced the opposition to the New Side Presbyterians in two of its aspects, namely, the contention that the Toleration Act did not extend to dissenting ministers in the colony at all—an argment which could hardly have much weight —and, secondly, the much more serious one that it did not entitle a minister to as many licenses as he saw fit to claim. A third kind of opposition which Davies had to meet was the charge that the New Lights were not Presbyterians at all, but had been excluded from that body because of their erroneous doctrines and false teachings and, therefore, they did not belong to any group of dissenters which came under the terms of the Toleration Act. This was the burden of the petition of the Virginia clergy to the Burgesses in 1751, while a few years previous to this Gooch had branded the New Side missionaries as *"false teachers* . . . professing themselves ministers under the pretended influence of *new light, extraordinary impulse,* and *such like* fanatical and and enthusiastical knowledge. . . ."[59] He also made out his case "that they have no manner of pretence to shelter under the acts of toleration. . . ."[60]

Probably the most serious effort of this sort to bring discredit upon the New Side Presbyterians was that made by the Reverend Patrick Henry of Hanover, who, in 1746, published a Virginia edition of John Caldwell's *Trial of the Spirit.*[61]

[58] T. C. Johnson, *Virginia Presbyterianism and Religious Liberty,* p. 40.
[59] Charge to Grand Jury, 1745, in *Source Problems,* pp. 206-210.
[60] *Ibid.*
[61] The full title is *An Impartial Trial of the Spirit operating in this part of the world; by comparing the nature, effects and evidences, of the present supposed conversion with the work of God.* It was published in Boston in 1742 and contains Caldwell's opinion of conversion and its effects as preached and practiced by the adherents of the Great Awakening. The book is by no means such a sane discussion as is Thomson's *Doctrine of Convictions,* and contains a good deal of raillery. It does, nevertheless, bring out certain characteristics of the New Lights—their preaching of terror, their emphasis on "experiences" and the accompanying physical manifestations, their doctrine of definite witness of the spirit to conversion, their seemingly boastful

In his preface the Virginia publisher tells that it is his purpose to open the eyes "of some deluded People among us, who are imposed upon by *Itinerants;*—and to let the World see, what the *Presbyterians* in the *Northern* Provinces think of these men, who, tho' they pass here for *Presbyterian* Ministers, are, in Reality a Set of Incendiaries; Enemies not only to the established church, but also common Disturbers of the Peace and Order of all religious societies wherever they come." He represents the New Side group as seceders who had been "judicially excluded" by the Philadelphia Synod "upon their refusing to submit to the Rules and Order of the Synod." This having been the case, they were no longer Presbyterians but imposters and schismatics who "have been more rampant in the Northern Provinces, than either their Missionaries or Mr. Whitefield have thought it for their Interest to be in this Colony. . . ." He reflects upon the educational standards of the New York Synod by saying, "In a short Time they ordain'd a great many young Men, of much Zeal for their newfangled Principles, but little Knowledge, some of whom were taken from the Plough, their pretended Conversion supplying the Place of Learning."

The publication of the *Trial of the Spirit* must have been damaging to the reputation of the New Side evangelists, for in the first year of his settlement in Hanover Davies saw fit to answer it. In 1748 he wrote *The impartial Trial, impartially Tried, and convicted of Partiality*. It consisted of a reply to both Henry's preface and Caldwell's sermon. For one thing, Davies showed that Caldwell was an imposter. He had been a minister in Ireland but was obliged to flee to the New World to escape conviction for theft. His real name was Thornton, but he changed it to Caldwell when he came to New England and posed as a Presbyterian minister. He distinguished himself for his virulent opposition to the revival, which found expression in his sermon on "The impartial Trial of the Spirit." Shortly after this, Davies shows, he was exposed by some former ac-

humility, their intolerance of non-evangelical sects, their disregard of Presbyterial order by itinerating, their assertions against unconverted ministers and the like. The identity of the Virginia publisher is given on the card in the catalogue of the Library of Congress.

quaintances from Ireland, was found guilty and apparently excluded from the ministry. From New England he went to Pennsylvania and practiced medicine. Here, says Davies, "He was oblig'd to renounce his New Name Cal'dwell, for really he was Call'd-ill; and to content himself with his old Name Thornton again."[62] Efforts to reassume his ministerial dignity in the Presbyterian Church failed, whereupon Thornton endeavored to get recommendations to the Bishop of London. The last Davies heard of him was that he was on his way to England.

In addition to exposing Caldwell, Davies replied to his sermon, defending on rational and scriptural grounds certain phenomena of the Awakening and upholding the evangelical preaching of the New Side school as productive of true results. He also pointed out that many irregularities in doctrine and practice had attended the revival in New England which did not exist in other places, so that Caldwell's sermon did not necessarily describe the work elsewhere.[63] On the whole, he viewed the publication as a monstrous and audacious misrepresentation both of the work of God and its promoters.

In answer to Henry's preface, Davies gave an account of the schism and of the doctrines and polity of the New Side in order to prove that the churches under the care of the latter were Presbyterian "except only the circumstance of meeting yearly in a Synodical Capacity in Philadelphia; the Want of which, I presume, he (the publisher) don't think sufficient to unpresbyterianize them; unless he look upon Philadelphia as sacred to Presbyterians; and New York and the Jersies uninhabitable and even inaccessible to such." He showed that the action of the Synod in not giving the excluded brethren a trial was unlawful and that the exclusion was not a "judicial" one. Furthermore, he offered plenty of proof in refutation of Henry's judgment of the educational standards of the New

[62] Davies, *Impartial Trial*, p. 34.
[63] Davies himself did not attach such significance to the physical evidences of conversion as did many other revivalists. At the same time he did not discountenance them altogether and saw how they might easily be the motor impulses attendant upon the state of mind of the sinner under conviction. See *Impartial Trial*, p. 40 and below, pp. 110-112.

Side. In many places he assailed Henry's logic and put him in a rather ridiculous dilemma for some of his statements. One feels in going through the controversy that Davies had decidedly the better of it and his publication must have more than offset the effects of Caldwell's sermon and the preface of the Virginia publisher.

In one other publication Davies took pains to dispel the misrepresentation of the New Side. In his *Appendix Proving the Right of the Synod of New York to the Religious Liberties and Immunities allowed to Protestant Dissenters,*[64] he pointed out the absurdity of the contention that the members of the New York Synod could not be classed as dissenters when they subscribed to the Test and to the Articles and took the Oaths. By these very acts they renounced Catholicism and disclaimed the jurisdiction of the Pope over civil princes. If these were not the earmarks of Protestant dissenters, asks Davies, what were? He also refutes the charge that the members of the New York Synod were "an upstart, New Sect, that were not in existence when said (Toleration) Act was enacted, and consequently no such Protestant Dissenters, as it refers to." If this were the case, Davies contends that all sects not in the Synod of Philadelphia must be novel. "Must the Synod of Philadelphia be the standard of Antiquity, Protestantism, Presbyterianism, Orthodoxy, etc.?" Was it not sufficient that the New Side observed all the standards of Presbyterianism such as the Bible, the Catechism and the Westminister Confession? Furthermore, Davies pointed out that the epithet New Lights, unjustly deserved by the New York Synod, did not make it a new sect.[65] He resents the attachment of that designation to the followers of the New Side group.

It is easy enough to see that the secret of all these efforts to restrict the sphere of New Side missionaries and to deprive them of the benefits of toleration was the fear of the eventual fate of the Established Church and of the welfare of the social

---

[64] See above, note 40.

[65] *Ibid.,* p. 11. He points out that the original New Light Presbyterians were an Irish sect that fell into many Arminian and Arian errors opposed by the orthodox Presbyterians.

group with which it was identified. The Churchmen did not, in the main, wish to deny the benefits of the Toleration Act to dissenters, but neither did they believe that the latter should be permitted to extend it to suit their conveniences. In their position against unrestricted itinerating, it is only fair to accept their word that they believed the law to be on their side. Let dissenting congregations have the protection of the Act as soon as they arrived at the proper state of maturity to be entitled to it, a state evidenced by settled pastors within the bounds of definite and reasonably restricted parishes. Any demands beyond this were considered as unreasonable and contrary to the law.[66]

Frequent charges were made that the New Lights preached down the Establishment, railed against the character of the clergy, blasphemed the sacraments and reviled the liturgy. So widespread was this impression that Gooch called it their *favourite theme*.[67] It is impossible to determine how much truth there is in these charges. Some of the ministers, notably Roan, no doubt spoke pretty freely about the degeneracy of the clergy and the uselessness of their preaching.[68] On the other hand, the indictment against Roan for "vilifying the Established Religion, in divers sermons" was dropped.[69] The Reverend Patrick Henry is careful to say that he never heard that the New Lights spoke against the Liturgy in their sermons, but he knew that their adherents "generally despise it."[70] The Presbyterians, however, were not spared by the Anglicans. Davies tells us that he was informed that the pulpits around him "ring with exclamatory Harangues, Accusations, Arguments, Railings, Warnings, etc. etc. etc. against New Lights, Methodists, Enthusiasts, Deceivers, Itinerants, Pretenders, etc. etc. etc. . . ."[71]

[66] MS. Observations on Mr. Davies.

[67] Charge to the Grand Jury, 1745, in *Source Problems*, pp. 206 ff.

[68] Patrick Henry writing to Dawson, February 13, 1744/45, mentions this especially. Dawson MSS.

[69] According to Morris, *Source Problems*, p. 212.

[70] To Dawson, February 13, 1744/45, Dawson MSS. In another letter of November 21, 1747, Henry says that a common complaint against the New Lights was that they were "very industrious in casting all the reflections they could upon the established church and its ministers." Dawson MSS.

[71] Davies, *Impartial Trial*, p. 26.

To Davies' credit it must be said that he did not win his converts by preaching against the Establishment. He saw nothing in its articles and constitution that would hinder the genuine piety of those who accepted them, although he himself was a nonconformist.[72] On the other hand, he was not blind to the irreligion that existed on every hand and he took every opportunity to preach against it.[73] He repeatedly asserted that he had come to Virginia not "to presbyterianize the colony," but to propagate Christianity regardless of what denomination its adherents assumed.[74] Indeed, he deplored the fact that so much was made of Presbyterianism as a party or faction rather than a form of Christianity. As a Presbyterian, he pretended "to no superior sanctity above the established clergy, who are piously aiming at the great end of their office. . . ."[75]

Davies did not need to make the Establishment an object of attack. He found the people eager for the evangelical doctrines and they were only too willing to receive them whether they came from Presbyterian, Anglican, Baptist or Methodist. The Great Awakening, we have seen, had brought about a revival of personal religion. It emphasized the new birth, placed much importance on the emotional manifestations, and appealed alike to all classes. The Virginia clergy as a body held aloof from the influences of the revival and even attempted to hinder its progress. By the test of the age the Establishment was doomed to failure, for the measure of strength was the degree of the acceptance of evangelical principles. The denominations which heartily accepted the Great Awakening became strong and popular. Those that opposed it suffered, and the Virginia Establishment was in this group.

Educated under the influence of the New Lights, Davies had imbibed their tenets and came to Virginia with the new

[72] Davies, *Impartial Trial,* pp. 26-27; see also his letter to Bishop of London, January 10, 1752, *loc. cit.*

[73] For instance, his *Two Discourses on Virginia's Danger and Remedy* inspired by Braddock's defeat and the severe drought.

[74] *Ibid.,* p. 37; *Impartial Trial,* p. 26; S. Finley, *Sermon on the Death of the Reverend Samuel Davies,* p. 23; "Letter to Mr. F.," February 7, 1757, in *Letters,* p. 27; *Sermon on the installation of Reverend John Todd,* January 9, 1753.

[75] To Dawson (cir. 1752), in *Memoir,* pp. 33-34.

gospel. The chief aim of his preaching was to promote genuine Christianity by changing the hearts and lives of men. He endeavored, he says, "to alarm secure impenitents; to reform the profligate; to undeceive the hypocrite; to raise the hands that hang down, and to strengthen the feeble knees. . . ."[76] His sermons were "plain and pungent, peculiarly adapted to pierce the conscience and affect the heart."[77] In common with the evangelicals everywhere he used the direct, hortatory appeal in the second person, wherever possible.[78] His sermons were prepared with great care and thought and their popularity is attested by the many editions in which they appeared in both England and America during the course of the next century.[79] We are told that he frequently read his sermons, but he could not have fallen into the dull routine of the Established clergy and accomplished what he did. It is probable that in the majority of cases he preached without the use of a manuscript.[80] His eloquence and his influence in developing a new type of oratory characterized alike by naturalness, warmth and directness of expression, and great dignity of style are too well known to need further comment here.[81] The fact that he was the "earliest hymn writer of Colonial Presbyterianism" and that some of his hymns continue in common use is, however, often overlooked.[82] Finally, what-

[76] To the Bishop of London, January 10, 1752, in Foote, p. 109 and *Source Problems,* p. 229.

[77] David Bostwick, "Character of Samuel Davies," in Davies' *Sermons,* N. Y., 3 vol. ed., I, p. 49; see also Finley, *loc. cit.,* p. 21.

[78] In his sermon before the New Castle Presbytery, October 11, 1752, he gives his views as to how ministers should preach. His sermon entitled "Vessels of Mercy and Vessels of Wrath" is a good example of the awakening appeal.

[79] Nine English editions appeared between 1761 and 1800 while Barnes' 4th American edition appeared in 1845. See *Princeton Sesquicentennial Celebration,* p. 371.

[80] Foote, First Series, p. 303.

[81] See Ford, *Scotch-Irish,* p. 390; *Evan. and Lit. Mag.,* II, 202, 360-361; *Watchman of the South,* January 6, 1842; Howison, II, 75; Cooke, *Virginia,* p. 338. His influence on Patrick Henry who as a young man from nineteen to twenty-two years was accustomed to listen to him is commented upon in these references. Cooke says that Henry declared Davies to be the greatest orator he had ever heard.

[82] L. F. Benson, "President Davies as a Hymn Writer," *Jour. Pres. Hist. Soc.,* II, 280 ff. His hymns, eighteen in number, are printed here also. A. MS. volume of Davies' poems is in possession of the Union Theological Seminary

ever may be said of the New Lights as a group, Davies never indulged in any wild reveries of enthusiasm of which so many of them were accused.

In spite of the sincerity of his motive and his professions of respect for the Establishment, Davies was regarded by many of his opponents as artful, crafty and subtle, "if such shallow sophistry deserves to be called by either of these names."[83] His plea that he had come not so much to preach Presbyterianism as "the catholic principles of Christianity" was considered a mere subterfuge. Could not these, it was pointed out, be better learned by a frequent attendance at the parish church than by a lecture once in a twelvemonth? "If Mr. Davies wants to make converts from Heathenism, his business lies rather among the Indians, or in North Carolina where there are few teachers under any denomination, than in a colony divided into parishes under a clergy who have been regularly ordained."[84]

In these indictments we see the attitude of a large group of people who, having no sympathy with the Great Awakening, naturally could not look upon any of its preachers with favour. Even conceding to Davies the honesty of every one of his professions, there was still the argument that others would follow him and that the meeting houses would become so many centers for the propagation of Presbyterianism. Moreover, if the colony could not be kept from wickedness and heathenism by all the clergy in it, how could one man alone undertake to do it, especially since he owned himself to be but weak and insignificant? Finally, the fact that the Presbyterians had more congregations than they could supply with ministers and yet kept accepting more groups of dissenters, seemed to prove that they would rather see the congregations without any ministrations at all than have the people attend some other church.[85]

of Richmond, Va. One of the hymns has been found in more than a hundred hymnals in England alone. Benson, p. 282.

[83] MS. Observations on Mr. Samuel Davies; see also Davies' letter to the Rector of St. Margaret's Parish, January 4, 1749/50, in which he answers some charges against him. Dawson MSS.

[84] MS. Observations on Mr. Samuel Davies.

[85] Ibid.

The opposition to the dissenters was based on more than religious grounds. One effect of the Great Awakening was that in bringing together large groups of dissenters under their own leaders, it produced in them a certain political solidarity that made them conscious of their power and led them to assert it. A few years after the coming of Davies the dissenters in Hanover had become strong enough to influence candidates for the legislature. The writer of the "Observations" remarks that it was a matter of public notoriety that they "exacted Bonds from candidates to serve and stand by their Interests, before they would suffer them to be elected Burgesses, a most unjustifiable and unprecedented thing." He considered this "party spirit" to be a most dangerous thing.[86] It augured ill not only for the religious Establishment, but for the whole social, political and economic fabric with which it was identified.

In 1751 Davies made an effort to persuade Jonathan Edwards to settle in Virginia, following the latter's dismissal from Northampton.[87] He secured pledges amounting to eighty pounds sterling for his support. It is very likely that Edwards would have accepted the offer, but he was already installed in Stockbridge before the messenger from Virginia arrived. It is certainly interesting to speculate what might have resulted had Edwards become Davies' colleague in the Old Dominion. No other colony, perhaps, could have boasted two such religious leaders. As it was, in 1752 the Reverend John Todd came instead of Edwards, to begin a long ministry of over forty years in eastern Virginia.[88] Since the purpose of Todd's coming was to relieve Davies of a part of his large circuit, the Colonial

---

[86] In a MS. petition to the Virginia Assembly from Lancaster County in 1758, we read: "The Dissenters in the County of Hanover, in 1751/2 (within five years after Mr. Davies settled there) had multiplied so, as to influence the candidates to give Bond, not to divide the parish, before they would agree to vote them Burgesses; who were Expel'd the House, for giving such bond." (Va. Religious Papers, Library of Congress.) It does not appear that this petition was ever presented. We shall see that the Baptists, too, endeavored to exercise political influence.

[87] Foote, *Sketches of Virginia,* Second Series, pp. 41-43, contains the correspondence.

[88] H. A. Edson, "John Todd of Virginia and John Todd of Indiana," *Pres. Rev.,* VII, pp. 16-26.

Court could not consistently refuse him a license, nor did it.[89] He was allowed "to officiate as an Assistant to Samuel Davies, a Dissenting Minister in such places as are already licensed by this court for the meeting of Dissenters."[90] He was installed as pastor of Providence church in Louisa County.[91]

Two other missionaries, Mr. Robert Henry and Mr. Greenman, were sent by the New York Synod to preach to the people in the back country about the same time that Todd came. The former of these preached for some months without license but was not molested by the authorities.[92] In 1755 he settled in Virginia, becoming pastor of two churches, one in Charlotte, and the other in Prince Edward County.[93] He also gave part of his time to Falling River Church in Pittsylvania County. A third minister, John Wright, settled in Cumberland County about the same time, making four ministers labouring in the territory formerly embraced in Davies' circuit when Hanover Presbytery was formed in December, 1755.[94] In addition, were two other ministers who had come to Virginia under the auspices of the New York Synod. These were John Brown and Alexander Craighead. They settled in the western counties and were included in the new Presbytery.[59] Black, Craig, and Miller, the

[89] Perry, I, pp. 393 ff.; *Evan. and Lit. Mag.*, II, 361.

[90] Todd's MS. license dated April 22, 1752, in Virginia religious Papers. (Library of Congress).

[91] R. Webster, *History of the Presbyterian Church in America*, pp. 608-609.   [92] *Ibid.*, pp. 650-652.

[93] McIlwaine, *op. cit.*, p. 58; Webster, pp. 650-652. His churches were Cub Creek and Briery, respectively.

[94] McIlwaine, p. 63; Webster, pp. 624 ff.

[95] MS. Records of Hanover Presbytery for 1755. These records have never been printed and are in the custody of the Union Theological Seminary of Richmond. The article entitled "Old Hanover Records" in the *Watchman and Observer* for November 6, 20, 27, December 4, 18, 1845, is in the nature of a running summary of the records. Foote, *Sketches*, Second Series, Chaps. IV, VI, and VIII contains an account of the Presbytery and its early members. The Presbytery was authorized by the Synod of New York on September 3, 1755, and held its first meeting on December 3, with Davies as moderator and Todd as clerk. Henry, Wright, Brown and Craighead were the other members. See Webster, pp. 434 ff. for sketch of Craighead, and pp. 656-7 for one of Brown. Webster tells us that Craighead is said to have settled in Augusta County in 1749 (p. 436), while Brown was called to Timber Ridge and Providence churches in 1753. In 1797 he removed to Kentucky.

Old Side ministers, did not come into the Presbytery until after the reunion of 1758.

Meantime, from the fall of 1753 until February 1755, Davies was absent from Virginia on a mission which took him and Gilbert Tennent to England for the purpose of raising funds for the College of New Jersey. Their success there was beyond expectation and assured the future of Nassau Hall.[96] It was during this visit to England that Davies secured from the Attorney General the opinion favourable to every one of his contentions regarding the application of the Toleration Act to Virginia. After this the only obstructions placed in the way of the Presbyterians were those imposed by the letter of the law. Davies' fame attracted great crowds in England and Whitefield invited him to make his home with him.[97] This Davies declined because not all dissenters liked Whitefield and he feared it would injure the success of his mission. He took advantage of his opportunity to visit John and Charles Wesley with whom he was greatly delighted. Later on John Wesley coöperated with Davies in the latter's efforts to propagate Christianity among the Negroes and keep them supplied with books.[98]

Commissary Dawson wrote to the Bishop of London that "the New Lights seemed to be in a declining condition during the absence of Mr. Davies, but upon his return they revived,— at least they make much noise."[99] It was not only the return of Davies that revived the work. In January, 1755, Whitefield made his third visit to Virginia and his presence gave fresh stimulus to the New Lights. Under date of January 14, he records: "In Virginia the prospect is very promising. I have preached in two churches and, this morning, am to preach in a third. Rich and poor seem quite ready to hear. Many have been truly awakened."[100] The following day he wrote; "I have not

[96] Davies MS. Journal which he kept on this trip is in possession of the Union Theological Seminary of Richmond. It is printed in Foote, First Series, pp. 228-281.

[97] See Hughes, *op. cit.*, p. 74.

[98] See below Chapter IX; *Journal of John Wesley*, IV, 125-6, 149-50, 194.

[99] Dawson MSS., August 13, 1755, and Fulham transcripts, Box I, number 176 (Va.).

[100] Quoted from Tyerman's *Whitefield*, II, 339.

been here a week, and have had the comfort of seeing many impressed under the word every day. Two churches have been opened, and a third (Richmond) I am to preach in to-morrow. I find prejudices subside, and some of the rich and the great begin to think favourably of the work of God. Several of the lower class have been with me, acknowledging what the Lord did for them when I was here before."[101] Whitefield was loath to leave the colony. Just before passing into North Carolina he remarked: "Had I not been detained so long northward, what a wide and effectual door might have been opened. Here, as well as elsewhere, rich and poor flock to hear the everlasting gospel. Many have come forty or fifty miles; and a spirit of conviction and consolation seemed to go through all the assemblies. Colonel R—, a person of distinction, opened one church for me, invited me to his house, and introduced me himself to the reading desk. Blessed be God, I see a vast alteration for the better."[102]

The period following Whitefield's visit and the return of Davies, until the latter left Hanover to accept the presidency of Princeton College, was one of expansion and consolidation in Virginia Presbyterianism. With the increase in the number of ministers, and with the status of the dissenters now determined, Davies and his colleagues were not hampered by the narrow interpretations of the Toleration Act that had hindered progress in the earlier years of his ministry. The years 1755 and 1756 in particular seem to have been marked by a considerable extension of the Awakening and a great increase in the number of Presbyterian communicants. The congregations, not only of Davies, but of Todd, Wright, and Henry were visited by pronounced revivals and the number of hearers sometimes ran as high as two thousand.[103] The fact that Davies

---

[101] Tyerman's *Whitefield*, II, 339.　　[102] *Ibid.*, January 17, 1755.
[103] Letter of Todd to Whitefield, June 26, 1755, in *Evan. and Lit. Mag.*, IV, 550-551, in which Todd writes: "The impressions of the day you preached last here at my meeting house, can, I believe, never wear out of my mind. . . ." Letter of Wright, August 18, 1755, in *ibid.*, p. 551, and of the same to Reverend Mr. ——— in Scotland, January 20, 1757, in *ibid.*, pp. 572-3; also to Mr. Peter Munford (Montford), 1761, in Webster, *op. cit.*, pp. 624 ff. Letter of Davies, July 14, 1756, in *Evan. and Lit. Mag.*, IV, 552. See also Gillies, *Historical Collections,* for which the above letters not

now had three assistants did not cause him to lessen his activities. In 1756 his parish was sixty miles in circumference, but his excursions carried him far and wide.[104] In the summer of 1757, in a period of about two months, he rode nearly five hundred miles and preached forty sermons.[105] He was much in demand in both Virginia and North Carolina and so great were the inroads on his time that his congregation requested the Presbytery of Hanover that their pastor "might be exempted from supplying any of the vacancies in their bounds, unless his congregation be provided for in his absence."[106] The Presbytery exempted him from half of his usual appointments, which was objectionable to his Elders.[107]

Beginning in 1757 Davies and Todd, sometimes singly and then again together, made frequent preaching tours into the Northern Neck, which were to result in the permanent establishment of Presbyterianism in that region.[108] The courts of

otherwise directed were written. In his letter Davies mentions that 2,000 attended the sacramental meeting in Henry's church in Lunenburg and of these two hundred communed. Wright mentions a congregation of 2,000 in July 1755. He added a hundred new communicants to his congregation in July, 1756, eighty or ninety in August, thirty or forty in November. Letter of January 20, 1757.

[104] Letter of Davies to R. E. Esq., March 2, 1756, in *Evan. and Lit. Mag.,* IV, 547.

[105] Thomas Gibbons, *Divine Conduct Vindicated,* p. 37. Gibbons was one of Davies' correspondents and the latter wrote this to him.

[106] MS. Records of Hanover Presbytery, April 26, 1758.

[107] Patrick Henry informed Dawson that the dissenters in Hanover "have erected a kind of spiritual court which they call a session, compos'd of the Preacher himself as Moderator, and twelve of his congregation who are dignified with the title of Elders." Also that no such courts are authorized by the Toleration Act. Dawson MSS., date mutilated.

[108] Dawson MSS., Letter of David Currie and John Leland, ministers of the Established Church, dated Lancaster County, April 12, 1758. They report that Davies preached in the open in Lancaster and Northumberland counties in June, 1757, and again in November. In April, 1758, Todd preached three days in each of the above counties. Colonel James Gordon records that Davies and Todd were in the Neck in March, 1759. He calls the former "dear Mr. Davies." Todd was there again in the fall and also in 1760 and 1761. "Journal of Col. James Gordon," in *William and Mary College Quarterly,* XI, pp. 102, 109, 199, 225. Gordon also refers to other Presbyterian ministers sent as supplies until Waddell settled there in 1762. The Colonel informs us that eight or nine hundred persons were present to hear Davies and Todd on March 25, 1759 (p. 102).

Northumberland and Lancaster counties granted Davies license to build a meeting house in each county,[109] but one is surprised to learn that the Court of Westmoreland refused, on the old ground that the Act of Toleration did not extend to America.[110] The Presbyterian missionaries were well received in the Neck and found a staunch ally in Colonel James Gordon, who did much to build up Presbyterian sentiments in the aristocratic circles.[111]

Probably in no section of Virginia was the Established Church in a more lamentable state of decline, or the faults of

[109] Dawson MSS., *ibid*. Following is a copy of the original petition for the meeting house in Lancaster which I found in the Virginia Baptist Historical Society. "We the Subscribers Inhabitants of Lancaster County do certifie the Worshipfull Court of the said County, that we intend to make use of a place on the Land of John Mitchell in this County, as a place for Public Worship of God, according to the practice of Protestant Dissenters of the Presbyterian Denomination. And we desier that this our certificate may be registered in the Records of the Court, according to the direction of an (act of) Parl. commonly called the act of Toleration.

John Mitchell
Thomas Carter."

The petition is endorsed: "At court held for Lancaster County on the 20th Day of May 1757. This Certificate was presented in Court and ordered to be recorded.

Test Thomas Edwards, Jun.
Clk."

On March 17th, 1758, however, the Court rescinded the above action on the grounds that it was taken "unadvisedly and by surprize" and that the Court "is now informed that no Act of Parliament relating thereto is binding in this Colony, and that there is an Act of Assembly now in force here w'ch forbids any person to preach, who has not rec'd. an Ordination from some Bishop in England, and subscribed to be conformable to the Orders and Constitutions of the Church of England. . . ." Original MS. in Va. Bap. Hist. Soc. In spite of prohibition, we know that the Presbyterians continued to preach in the Neck, especially in Lancaster, and the meeting house was built.

[110] Dawson MSS. Letter of Currie and Leland. I find no other statement of the action of Westmoreland County, nor does the letter mention the above action in Lancaster County although the letter was written nearly a month later and the prohibition of the Court was ordered to be posted on the court-house door.

[111] James Gordon and his brother John came to Lancaster County in 1738 from Ireland. They were Presbyterians and became wealthy and influential merchants. Colonel James Gordon was a man of excellent qualities. His daughter, Mary, married the noted Presbyterian minister, James Waddell. See *W. & M. Quar.*, XI, 98.

the clergy more apparent than in the Northern Neck.[112] The coming of Davies alarmed the parsons, two of whom reported of the Presbyterians in 1758, that "the progress of this new sect, as we may call them in this part of the country, has been so rapid, that in Lancaster County a meeting house is actually a building of 60 feet by 30. . . ."[113] They attributed the growth of the denomination to "the Arts and sly insinuations of some persons, who without any just ground, make it their business not only to malign the whole body of clergy here for the fault and miscarriages of a few of them, but also the rites and ceremonies of the best and purest church." Since the coming of Davies, they assert, more has been said against the bishops and clergy of the Church of England than had ever been said against the Bishop of Rome. "Could we persuade ourselves that nothing but the pure Glory of God, the advancement of true religion was intended by these gentlemen, or was the number of dissenters in these parts sufficient to support such an undertaking, we should not be alarmed; but when they have no other means to compass their designs than that of drawing off the people from their established church, who can forbear using their best endeavors to put a stop to such proceedings? When the people's affections are alienated from their teachers, they are likely to give but little heed to any advices they may offer, and then how soon may they be brought to the greatest contempt both of their persons and doctrine?"

Various endeavors were made to check the Presbyterians in the Northern Neck. Most significant, perhaps, was the use made of the social prestige of the Establishment. Colonel Gordon tells us that one of the parsons "endeavors to make it a scandalous thing" for gentlemen to attend Presbyterian meetings and that many who were inclined to come hesitated to do so for fear of being laughed at.[114] The Presbyterians had not yet quite outlived the social stigma attached to the name of New Lights.

[112] Foote, *Sketches,* p. 354; Gordon's *Journal* gives many glimpses.
[113] Dawson MSS. letter of Currie and Leland, April 12, 1758.
[114] *Journal,* May 26, 1760, loc. cit., p. 199.

One of the most persistent opponents of the Presbyterians in the Neck was Colonel Edwin Conway, who was at the same time a friend of Gordon.[115] He brought forward a new charge against Davies which was that the latter had sent a small pamphlet among the Negroes in which he "much Reproached Virginia. And informs the Negroes they are Stronger than the Whites being Equal in Number then, and having an Annual addition of thousands. I Can't See any Advantage to the Country to give this account to the Negroes."[116] Conway was also instrumental in drawing up a petition to the Assembly, "That, contrary to law, a Dissenter was admitted to preach, last year, in this old county, to the great grievance of us, his Majesty's Dutiful and Loyal subjects, for it hath occasion'd contention and great uneasiness among the people, and a talk against the Bishops of England, and Clergy of Virginia. Tho' the Inhabitants of this County have always been united in the Church; and but very few ever heard a Dissenter preach, before Last Summer; yet several of 'em Subscribed to Raise a Sum of Tobacco, to build a Meeting-House, and have agreed with an Undertaker for one, sixty feet by thirty. This Proceeding affrights our apprehension that Dissension may be the forerunner of Rebellion; a fatal Consequence!" The petition contains a latent note of fear of the political influence of the Dissenters,[117] and prays that "If Dissenters be admitted to Preach, . . . we Humbly Propose they may be Laid under Proper Restrictions; and Confin'd to their Meeting Houses.[118] And that none may have Power to give 'em License to Preach, but the Governor, with the advice of the Council."[119] From Gordon's *Journal* we learn that Conway did

---

[115] *Journal,* January 9, 1759, and passim.

[116] Conway to Dawson, March 3, 1758, Dawson MSS. Conway probably referred to Davies's pamphlet, *The Duty of Christians to propagate their religion among Heathens, Earnestly recommended to the Masters of Negroe Slaves in Virginia* (London, 1758). It was certainly not of an inflammatory nature.

[117] It is this petition which speaks of their influence in Hanover County. See above, note 86.

[118] It is to be remembered that Davies had been preaching in the open in Lancaster County and Northumberland.

[119] The petition was signed only by Conway and two others and does not seem to have been presented.

his utmost to prevent the building of the meeting house, but
without success. The Presbyterians had come to stay. Supplies
were regularly sent into the Neck by Hanover Presbytery[120] to
carry on the work commenced by Davies and in 1762 James
Waddell accepted a call to the churches of Lancaster and
Northumberland, much to the satisfaction of Colonel Gordon
and other Presbyterians.[121]

It must not be overlooked that the times were auspicious for
this expansion of dissent which we have been tracing. The later
years of Davies' ministry in Virginia coincided with the period
of the French and Indian War. Following the defeat of Braddock in the summer of 1755, the frontier counties were constantly exposed to the ravages of savage warfare. Many families
were forced to take flight and some congregations, including
Craighead's, were scattered.[122] The war, however, brought its
advantages to the dissenters. It was upon the Presbyterian
population in the Valley that the brunt of Indian attacks fell,
and in Hanover and elsewhere the members of that denomination took a vigorous part in winning the conflict. Churchmen
and dissenters were brought together by the common fear of a
French victory which would check expansion to the west and
possibly result in the loss of their rights as Englishmen. More
than this, there was great apprehension lest a French victory
should be followed by a Roman Catholic occupation.

The part which Davies took in the war was by no means
small. More than once his vigorous sermons gave his people
new courage and shook them from their lethargy, for he made
patriotism a part of the Christian's religion, and defending his
country a part of his duty.[123] In the spring of 1758 when the

[120] MS. Records of Hanover Presbytery; Colonel Gordon's *Journal*, May
25, 1760, October 12, 19, November 7, 21, 25, 27, 1760, and *passim*.

[121] Colonel Gordon's *Journal, loc. cit.*, pp. 228 ff.; *Watchman of the South,*
September 19, 26, 1844; *Watchman and Observer,* November 20, 1845; Foote,
Sketches, First Series, p. 354.

[122] Davies to Mr. C., February 7, 1757, in *Letters;* Foote, p. 283; Webster,
op. cit., p. 437.

[123] Davies, *Religion and Patriotism the Constituents of a good Soldier.*
A sermon preached in Hanover, August 17, 1755; *Virginia's Danger and
Remedy,* Williamsburg, 1756.

work of raising recruits by voluntary enlistments was languish-
ing, it was a stirring appeal by Davies that once more aroused
the citizens of Hanover to action and resulted in the formation
of a new company of soldiers.[124] In these patriotic addresses
Davies' oratory is seen at its best as when he urges: "For our
Country must be defended: and if nothing but Force can con-
strain you to take up Arms in its defence, then Force must be
used: . . . Something must be done! must be done by you!
Therefore instead of assuming the State of Patriots and Heroes
at home, to Arms, and away to the Field, and prove your Pretensions sincere. Let the Thunder of this Imprecation rouse you
out of your Ease, and Security. 'Cursed be he that doth the
work of the Lord deceitfully; and cursed be he that keepeth back
his Sword from Blood.' " No matter what the subject was or
the occasion, Davies never lost the opportunity to invite enlist-
ment in the army of God, to urge men to "proclaim eternal War
against all Sin," to quit themselves well and be strong.

Under circumstances like these it would have been folly for
the government to stir up religious antagonisms and it is not
surprising that the obstacles put in the way of the dissenters
became fewer.[125] To say the least, it would have been embar-
rassing for the authorities to oppose Davies, whose services in
recruiting regiments and firing the patriotism of the colonists
were so valuable, and upon whose coreligionists the defence of
the frontier mainly fell. Hence Davies found himself quite
at liberty in carrying on his ministry after his return from England in 1755.[126] Others, like Todd and Wright, were not molested when they used unlicensed houses and made excursions
to distant parts.[127] The latter says that by reason of the inflic-

[124] *The Curse of Cowardice.* A sermon preached to the militia of Hanover County in Virginia. See especially pp. 10-11 for his portrayal of the
horrors of Indian warfare, and pp. 22, 25 for his strong appeal for soldiers
to take the field.
[125] *Cf.* Jernegan, in *Source Problems,* p. 189. In 1758 Governor Fauquier
assured the Presbytery that he would always exert himself "to support the
Act of Toleration, and secure the peaceable enjoyment of its immunities to
all his majesty's subjects who conform thereto." MS. Records of Hanover
Presbytery, 1758.   [126] *Cf.* Foote, p. 296; Hughes, *loc. cit.,* p. 77.
[127] Reverend Patrick Henry complained that these men violated their
licenses by preaching in private houses in his parish and that Todd often

tions visited upon the colony, men were beginning to believe that the New Light clergy were right after all. He added, "I now preached anywhere being so distant from the metropolis and the time being so dangerous and shocking."[128] Thus the French and Indian War aided the cause of the dissenters and contributed in no slight degree to the winning of religious toleration.

In other respects, too, conditions favored the Presbyterians. The passage of the Twopenny Acts in 1755 and 1758 marked the beginning of a crisis in the relations between the Established Church and the colonial government which was to culminate in the famous Parsons' Cause and leave the prestige of the Establishment much damaged.[129] The attitude taken by the clergy in this controversy made them unpopular and led to further defection from the Anglican Church. These disputes over salaries, happening just at the time when the Presbyterians were rendering patriotic services to the colony, and when the people, because of the burdens of the war, were least in the mood to contribute to the support of a clergy whose usefulness was questioned by many, contributed doubly to the cause of the dissenters. Perhaps it was the added fortune of the Presbyterians that the climax to the struggle occurred in Hanover County, their stronghold in eastern Virginia, and that the popular party had Patrick Henry for their spokesman. By this time (1763) Davies had passed from his earthly labours and left their continuation to the hands of others.

In 1758 Davies received a call to the presidency of the College of New Jersey. Being uncertain as to the wisdom of ac-

went outside his legal bounds. He also says that Wright preached five months and then left the colony without qualifying according to law. Dawson MSS., date mutilated. See also Foote, pp. 297-308.

[128] Foote, p. 308. Officially the Presbytery observed the terms of the Toleration Act and requested nothing more than enjoyment of the liberties it conferred. See address to Governor Loudoun in 1756 and to Fauquier in 1758, in MS. Records of Hanover Presbytery.

[129] On this see any standard biographies of Patrick Henry, as those by Tyler and Morgan. Ann Maury's *Memoirs of a Huguenot Family*, is a source, and also there are many documents in Perry. Eckenrode, *Separation of Church and State in Virginia*, Chap. II, sets forth the main facts. A. P. Scott has a study on the constitutional aspects of the case in *Pol. Sci. Quar.*, Vol. XXXI, pp. 558-577.

cepting the offer, he left it to the judgment of the Presbytery. The latter decided that his loss to the colony would be "very dangerous to the important interests of religion among us," and persuaded him at first to remain.[130] In declining the presidency, Davies stated that he believed his work in Virginia was more important; that his friend Samuel Finley was better qualified for the office than he was; that he did not wish to lay himself open to the charge of being ambitious for preferment.[131] The trustees of the College were not to be denied in their efforts and laid the matter before the Synod of New York and Philadelphia, which dissolved Davies' pastoral connections in Virginia in order to secure his removal to Princeton. In July 1759, he preached his farewell sermon and Hanover Presbytery granted him his dismission.[132]

When he left Virginia Davies was probably the most celebrated representative of American Presbyterianism. The move proved to be an unfortunate one and in the change from the vigorous outdoor life to a confining position, he soon lost the health he had regained in Virginia. He succumbed on February 4, 1761. Though he had already accomplished a great work, death caught him in his thirty-eighth year.

Before Davies left Virginia, the Presbyterian Church entered into a new period of its history marked by the healing of the schism and the union of the Old Side and New Side wings into the Synod of New York and Philadelphia. This occurred in 1758, by which time the passions of the revivals had subsided. Thus it might be said that the close of Davies' ministry marked also the close of the first phase of the Great Awakening. The Old Side members, Craig, Black, and Miller, who in earlier years had opposed the New Lights, were now joined with the Hanover Presbytery.[133] Naturally conservative, the Presbyteri-

[130] MS. Records of Hanover Presbytery, September 13, 1758.

[131] Letter of Davies, October 18, 1758, in *The Presbyterian* for July 10, 1833.

[132] The sermon gives Davies' reasons for finally deciding to leave Virginia. It can be found in any complete edition of his sermons and in abbreviated form in the *Memoirs*, pp. 85-92.

[133] MS. Records of Hanover Presbytery, 1758. The first session of the enlarged body was held in Cumberland County, July 12, 1758. Craig and

7763

ans in Virginia now settled down to a period of quiet existence and no other extensive revival occurred among them until the one which emanated from Hampden-Sydney College broke out in 1787.

Following the departure of Davies, Hanover County rapidly lost prestige as the center of Virginia Presbyterianism. The congregations met with discouragements in their attempts to obtain a successor to Davies and became enfeebled by the emigration of many of the leading members to the western counties.[134] It was served by supplies until 1763, when the young David Rice accepted a call to its pastorate.[135] His relations with his congregation do not seem to have been happy and the remuneration was insufficient, so that in a few years he removed to Bedford County to take charge of three congregations, including that of the Peaks of Otter.[136]

After the Hanover revival there seems to have been a tendency for Presbyterianism to shift more and more to the westward, and to confine its efforts mainly to the Scotch-Irish. This was particularly true after the rise of the Baptists in the late 'sixties, which movement became very general in eastern Virginia and displaced the Presbyterians in many localities. The weakening of Presbyterianism in the eastern counties was further emphasized by the rapid spread of the Methodists from the southeastern counties, Brunswick and Sussex being as their center. The second great Presbyterian revival, as we shall see, was

Miller at first had doubts about taking their seats as their Presbytery of Donegal did not heartily concur in the union of the Synods. They were consequently admitted as "correspondents" to this first session. See also "Old Hanover Records," in *Watchman and Observer,* November 20, 1845.

[134] William Hill, "Reverend Cary Allen," *Pres. Quar. Rev.,* IV, p. 55; Foote, *Sketches,* Second Series, p. 79. Hill's step-father, Daniel Allen, was one of those who removed from Hanover after the departure of Davies, and his half-brother, Cary Allen, became prominent, along with himself, in the revival of 1787.

[135] MS. Records of Hanover Presbytery, October 7, 1763; Foote, Second Series, p. 79. Rice was born in Hanover County in 1733, studied under Todd and Waddell and took his A.B. at Princeton when Davies was President. He was licensed as probationer in November, 1762. See his *Memoirs,* pp. 55-56, in Bishop, *History of the Church in Kentucky.*

[136] Rice's *Memoirs,* pp. 58 ff.; Foote, Second Series, p. 79. In 1738 David Rice moved to Kentucky, largely for economic reasons.

confined wholly to the western Scotch-Irish counties.[137] This tendency was due in part to the westward emigration of many Presbyterian families but principally, perhaps, to the scarcity of ministers. The Hanover Presbytery was for some years the only one in all the South, and it took care of all the missionary work that was done.[138] Supplies were sent regularly to the Presbyterian congregations in North Carolina, and in 1770 Orange Presbytery was formed to include in it the Carolina ministers.[139] The records show that there were always many vacancies which could not be cared for, a condition which did not improve as the mission field expanded westward into Kentucky and Tennessee.[140] From its formation in 1755 to its reorganization in 1786 Hanover Presbytery included just forty-four ministers, not a large number considering the great extent of the field.[141] This was largely due to the very high educational standard required of their ministers, which also greatly handicapped the Presbyterians in the race with the Baptists and Methodists.

While we are to bear in mind the above mentioned tendencies and conditions clearly observable after Davies' time, we must not be left with the impression that the Presbyterians were completely swept off the stage in eastern Virginia. Todd remained for many years to continue the work of his former colleague, while in the Northern Neck Waddell served from 1762 until 1776, when the breakdown of his health caused him to remove to Augusta County.[142] Waddell's eloquence delighted

[137] See below, Chapter VII.

[138] G. P. Hays, *Presbyterians*, p. 113.

[139] MS. Records of Hanover Presbytery, *passim*. At this time, 1770, there were fifteen members in Hanover Presbytery which number was reduced to nine by the separation of the North Carolina members, MS. Records, April 25, 1770 and April 10, 1771.

[140] During the decades 1760 to 1780 the number of ministers fluctuated around a dozen, the number of accessions being about balanced by losses through death or removal. By 1785 there were twenty-five ministers, but Abingdon Presbytery was cut off from it and in 1786 Lexington and Transylvania Presbyteries were formed, so that the number was reduced to eight. The fact that these Presbyteries were in other states shows how large the mission field had been. See Hays, *op. cit.*, p. 113; *Watchman and Observer*, December 18, 1845. MS. Records for number of ministers.

[141] Foote, Second Series, Chaps. IV, VI, and VIII for the members.

[142] In his later years he settled in Louisa County. Foote, First Series, pp. 375 ff.

his father-in-law, Colonel Gordon,[143] and many other admirers among the élite. Philip Fithian tells us that "the People of Fashion in general countenance and commend him. . . . Mr. and Mrs. Carter speak well of him, Mr. and Mrs. Fauntleroy also, and all who I have ever heard mention his name."[144]

In 1763 Whitefield came to the Northern Neck on his sixth visit to America and kept up the spark of the revival there and in a few other places.[145] Passing through Virginia on his way south, a year or two later, he notices a great contrast between conditions then and a quarter of a century previous when he visited the colony.[146] The embers of evangelicalism were everywhere smouldering but it was the Separate Baptists, not the Presbyterians, who were to stir them afresh.

After Waddell's removal in 1776, the Presbyterians lost their grip on the Northern Neck.[147] Supplies were sent by the Presbytery but the denomination dwindled in the face of the onslaughts of the Baptists and the dispersements caused by the Revolutionary campaigns.[148]

In conclusion, we note that the success of Davies and the Presbyterians in Virginia had a wider significance than the mere establishment of another group of religionists in the colony. It was a portent of a social and political as well as a religious revolution in the life of the colony—the beginning of a movement from below which was to constantly push upward the

[143] Gordon expresses his admiration time and again in his *Journal*, along with his disgust for the parsons of the Established Church. *W. and M. Quar.*, XII, pp. 4, 5, 6, etc.

[144] *Journal and Letters*, p. 118 (1774).

[145] Gordon's *Journal*, August 28, 1763, *W. and M. Quar.*, XII, p. 8. Whitefield was in poor health and Gordon fitted him out with " a chair & horse for £47.10." See also Tyerman, *Whitefield*, II, 468.

[146] Tyerman, II, 479. Philip Slaughter in his *History of Bristol Parish* prints a most entertaining letter dated at Petersburg, April 1765. It contains someone's impression of Whitefield and is full of sarcasm and disgust, probably fanned by the fact that Whitefield was an Englishman. Pp. 23 ff.

[147] In 1768 Waddell had become involved in a controversy with Parson Gibberne who made a most scurrilous attack upon him for preaching in his pulpit upon invitation of his parishioners. The letters which were exchanged are found in Rind's *Virginia Gazette*, July 21, 1768 and August 18, 1768 Supplement. One of Gibberne's letters is addressed to "the Irreverend Mr. James Waddell."

[148] *Watchman of the South*, September 26, 1844.

common folks to a respectable plane in society and politics. This upheaval began in the church and gained in momentum by reason of the zeal of the leaders, the number of adherents, the popularity and reasonableness of its program.[149] It was, in short, a mass movement and directed aright, as it was, it could not fail.

The Presbyterians represent the first phase of this internal revolution. Opposed sharply at first as fanatics and schismatics, they gradually lost this stigma attached to the name of "New Lights,"[150] made deep inroads upon the solidarity of the Anglicans, and gained numerous accessions from the upper class.[151] It was a social portent of no little significance that the Presbyterian ministers met with much success in the conversion of gentlemen and at the other extreme, of slaves. The fact that Davies, single-handed, had won the battle for complete toleration for non-conformists was in itself an achievement sufficient to gain respect for the denomination he represented. We have seen that even the rich and the great began to realize that the political influnce wielded by the dissenters was not to be ignored. Under the leadership of Patrick Henry and their ally, Thomas Jefferson, they were to actually wrest the leadership in the Assembly from the planter régime.

Until the Great Awakening, the Established Church and the government were closely allied and both were controlled by the planter politicians. The dissenters fought the battle for religious liberty, well knowing that the overthrow of privilege in the Church must precede the establishment of political equality. By 1760 the first victories had been won. A rival sect with a government responsive to popular wishes had established itself

---

[149] Cf. J. W. Smith, "Devereux Jarratt and the beginnings of Methodism in Virginia," J. P. Branch Hist. Papers of Randolph-Macon College, I, 3.

[150] Writing in 1761 to Peter Munford (Montford), Wright says that as the revival spread "a great number were then ambitious to become New Lights, who before hated and scorned the name. Some of the bitterest enemies were conquered and made willing to deny themselves and take the cross." Letter in Webster, op. cit., pp. 624 ff.

[151] In 1755 a correspondent in Richmond wrote: "When I go among Mr. Davies' people religion seems to flourish: . . . it is very agreeable to see the gentlemen at their morning and evening prayers, with their slaves devoutly joining with them." Quoted in Webster, p. 557.

and obtained recognition in the very stronghold of Anglicanism. The democratic ideas which it represented disturbed for the first time the complacency of the ruling group.[152]

With the winning of toleration the Presbyterians settled down to a quiet existence and the early animosities between them and the Anglicans, for the most part, disappeared. Other dissenters, however, were not content to stop short of complete religious liberty and the disestablishment of the Anglican Church. For these Davies and his colleagues paved the way. "The crust of privilege was broken and democratic ideas in religion and politics spread and strengthened. At the same time the moral and spiritual life of the colony was deeply influenced, and the foundation was laid for the conquest of Virginia to evangelical Christianity."[153]

[152] Eckenrode, *Separation of Church and State in Virginia*, p. 34.
[153] *Ibid.*

CHAPTER V

The Baptist Revival

When Davies closed his mission in Virginia in 1759, the Baptists in the colony were so few in number and unimportant that they were practically unnoticed.[1] Within a few years they became the revivers of the revival and by the time of the Revolution it is estimated that they counted ten thousand members, which number had doubled by 1790.[2] In the latter year Asplund, the compiler of the Baptist *Annual Register*, recorded over two hundred churches and one hundred and fifty ordained ministers for the denomination in Virginia.[3]

With the Baptist movement the Great Awakening entered an even more popular and extravagant phase than when the Presbyterians were its sole representatives. Their religious zeal and enthusiasm, the rapid increase in their numbers, coupled with their despised social standing, aroused an opposition to the Baptists which developed into persecution. The term "New Light" now became attached to the Baptist ministers and people with a fresh opprobrium, for they were the plainest of the everyday people, often unlettered and ignorant.[4] Presbyterianism, "with its intellectual demands of an elaborate creed" and its high standards of education for its ministry, was at best restricted in its appeal. It was never able to reach and to stir the common folk as the Baptists did. "The people needed a distinctive symbol and a comparatively formless faith; they found the one in adult baptism by immersion, and the other in the wide compass of Bible teaching wherein the devout and emotional

[1] John Leland, "The Virginia Chronicle," in *Works*, p. 105. Leland was a contemporary of the revival as was Fristoe, cited below.

[2] Various estimates have been gathered by W. T. Thom in his *Struggle for Religious Freedom in Virginia: the Baptists*, pp. 39-42, note 68. See also Leland, pp. 116-117.

[3] The *Annual Register of the Baptist Denomination in North America*, p. 24; *cf.* John Rippon's *Baptist Annual Register* for 1790, p. 100. The membership was more than one-third of the total number in North America at the time.

[4] William Fristoe, *History of the Ketocton Baptist Association*, p. 63.

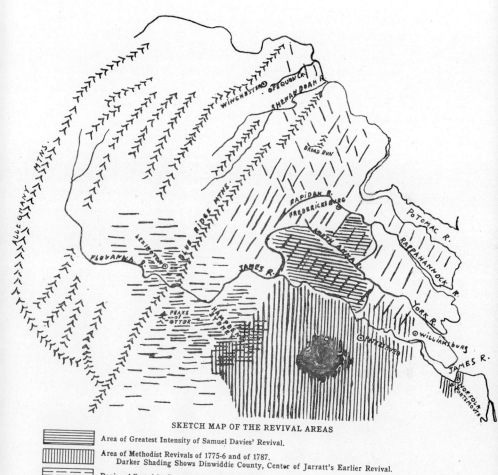

SKETCH MAP OF THE REVIVAL AREAS

 Area of Greatest Intensity of Samuel Davies' Revival.

Area of Methodist Revivals of 1775-6 and of 1787.
Darker Shading Shows Dinwiddie County, Center of Jarratt's Earlier Revival.

Region Affected by Presbyterian Revival of 1787.

Region Where the Baptists Became Predominant as a Result of the Great Awakening. Note How
They Displaced the Presbyterians in the Area of Davies' Earlier Revival.

The Regular Baptists Established Themselves in This Region.
They United With the Separate Baptists in 1787.

soul finds what it seeks."[5] "They wanted an organization, a ministry, a preaching, responsive to their emotions. The Baptist organization supplied the demands of their thoughts and their emotion, and on a plane congenial to their habit of speech and life."[6]

As was the case in other churches, the Great Awakening caused a division among the Baptists into conservative and revivalist wings. Those who belonged to the former group were called Regulars, while the latter were known as Separates.[7] The Regular Baptists first settled in Berkeley County in 1743 and began to spread over the northern part of the colony.[8] An important settlement was made on Ketocton Creek, in Loudoun County, east of the Blue Ridge, about 1755 as a result of Indian depredations. Ten years later the churches in Virginia obtained dismissal from the Philadelphia Association and formed themselves into the Ketocton Regular Baptist Association.[9] Largely through the activities of David Thomas, the Regulars made good progress in northern Virginia, and in 1767 in Orange County they met the rising tide of Separates who were advancing in wave after wave of revivals upward from the south. Here an effort to unite the two groups failed and more than twenty years were to elapse before such a union was consummated.[10] By 1770 the Regulars had a total membership of six hundred and twenty-four, had ten churches scattered in seven counties,

[5] Thom, p. 32. See also Howison, *History of Virginia,* II, 165.
[6] Thom, p. 32.
[7] See R. B. Semple, *History of the Rise and Progress of the Baptists in Virginia.* There was a third group called the General Baptists who settled in Surry and Isle of Wight counties about 1714. They originally came from England and held to Arminian doctrines. They did not become identified with the revival and in 1765 they joined the Regular Baptists. Semple, pp. 444 ff.; Campbell, *History of Virginia,* p. 553; David Benedict, *History of the Baptist Denomination,* II, 24-25. Beale's edition of Semple is used unless otherwise indicated.
[8] Semple, pp. 375 ff.; Thom, p. 11.
[9] Fristoe, *op. cit.,* p. 7; Semple, p. 388; Leland, p. 105. The churches at this time were four in number, namely, Ketocton in Loudoun County, Smith's Creek in Shenandoah County, Mill Creek in Berkeley, and Broad Run in Fauquier.
[10] Semple, pp. 23, 383-4; Leland, p. 105.

and were well established in the region north of Fredericksburg and Orange County.[11] Their only church south of the James was far away in Halifax County, but it may be that Regular Baptists were among those who about this time began to arouse the fears of Devereux Jarratt by their appearance in Amelia and adjacent counties.[12] Whoever they were, they were too aggressive to be checked, even with the later coöperation of the Methodists.

It was in the hands of the Separate Baptists, however, that evangelicalism was to become again a dynamic force in Virginia. They, and not the Regulars, became the continuators of the revival. The Separates were Presbyterian in origin, having their rise in New England about 1744 at the time of the great revival of Edwards and Whitefield.[13] Withdrawing themselves from the established churches, they organized themselves on the plan of Independents, placing all authority in the hands of the local churches. Their leading preacher, Shubal Stearns, became a Baptist in 1751.[14] In obedience to what they considered a divine call, Stearns and a few followers left New England in 1754 and, after a brief stay in Berkeley and Hampshire Counties in Virginia, the company passed on into Guilford County, North Carolina, where they established themselves permanently on Sandy Creek in 1755.[15] Their first church consisted of sixteen members. In a remarkably short time the number swelled to over six hundred and Sandy Creek Church became the center

[11] Thom, p. 11; Fristoe, pp. 8-13.

[12] Jarratt, *Autobiography*, pp. 105, 107.

[13] Fristoe, pp. 22-23; L. Burkitt and Jesse Read, *History of the Kehukee Baptist Association*, pp. 37-38, where the reasons for the withdrawal are given as follows: "1. Because they (the Presbyterians) were too extravagant in their apparel. 2. Because they (the Separates) did not believe their form of church government to be right. But chiefly because they (the Presbyterians) would admit none to the ministry only men of classical education, and many of their ministers apparently seemed to be unconverted. They were then called Separate Newlights."

[14] J. B. Taylor, *Virginia Baptist Ministers*, I, pp. 13-18, for sketch of Stearns; J. D. Hufham, *North Carolina Baptist Historical Papers*, 3rd Paper, Part I, pp. 5 ff. for Stearns and the Sandy Creek revival.

[15] Hufham, 3rd Paper, pp. 6-7; Semple, pp. 13-14.

of a phenomenal revival which spread north and south. In Virginia the Separates became the most active of the evangelicals and were the greatest factor in destroying the Establishment and securing religious liberty.

Springing as it did from the Great Awakening, the Separate Baptist movement everywhere had in it the fire and fervour of the Whitefield revival. It was this that distinguished it most from the Regular wing of the church. Unlike the latter, too, the Separates did not adhere to the London Confession of Faith (1689) which had been adopted in 1742 by the Philadelphia Association, but adopted the Bible as the broad platform of their beliefs.[16] Fristoe says: "The regular Baptists were jealous of the separate Baptists, because, as yet, they never formed nor adopted any system of doctrine, or made any confession of their faith more than verbally; and it was thought unreasonable, that if they differed from all other denominations why they should not in a fair, open and candid manner make known their principles to the world, and in so doing, act as children of the light; and on the other hand the separate Baptists supposed the adopting a confession of faith would only shackle them and that it would lead to formality and deadness, and divert them from the Bible. . . ."[17] The Regular Baptists were orthodox Calvinists, while the Separates tended strongly towards Arminianism, or the doctrine of free grace.[18] We are told also that the latter "thought the Regulars were not sufficiently particular in small matters such as dress etc."[19]

[16] Leland, "Virginia Chronicle," in *Works*, p. 105.

[17] *History of the Ketocton Baptist Association,* pp. 21-22; *cf.* Semple, p. 67.

[18] C. C. Bitting, *Notes on the History of the Strawberry Baptist Association of Virginia, 1776-1876,* pp. 10-11; J. S. Bassett, "Development of the Popular Churches after the Revolution," *Proc. Mass. Hist. Soc.,* Vol. XLVIII, p. 261; J. T. Smith, "Life and Times of the Reverend John Leland," in *Baptist Quarterly,* V, 237.

[19] Semple, p. 67. Leland tells us that the early Virginia Baptists were very particular in dress. The men cut off their hair "like Cromwell's round-headed chaplains, and the women cast away all their superfluities so that they were distinguished from others. . . ." "Virginia Chronicle," in *Works,* p. 117. The churches often had to exercise discipline in matters of dress.

The Separates appear to have been more evangelical than their conservative brethren who, they believed, were not sufficiently strict in receiving church members.[20] When the Regular Baptists of the Kehukee Association wished to form closer affiliations with the Separates, the latter objected that their principles were at a variance because the former retained many members who had been baptized in a state of unbelief.[21] The Separates emphasized faith as essential to baptism.

In other ways the two groups within the Baptist Church were distinguished. Leland tells us that among the Regulars the work "was solemn and rational; but the Separates were the most zealous and the work among them was very noisy. The people would cry out, fall down, and for a time lose the use of their limbs, which exercise made the bystanders marvel; some thought they were deceitful, others that they were bewitched, and many being convinced of all would report that God was with them of a truth."[22]

In the Separate Baptist revival we note the presence of various phenomena, both motor and sensory, such as the muscular contortions known as the "jerks," excessive trembling, falling, rolling on the ground, crying and "barking" like dogs.[23] These

[20] Burkitt and Read, *op. cit.,* p. 39; Semple, pp. 449 ff.

[21] This was in 1772. The points of disagreement are given in Burkitt and Read and were: 1. The Regulars did not sufficiently emphasize experience in receiving members for baptism. 2. They contained members who acknowledged that they were baptized before they believed. 3. The Regulars indulged in too much superfluity of dress. The second was the most weighty objection. Pp. 38-39. Also Semple, pp. 449 ff.

[22] Leland, p. 105; given also in Thom, p. 17.

[23] See Thom, p. 17. We have many evidences of these exercises. Daniel Fristoe tells of a meeting attended by 2,000 where he saw "multitudes, some roaring on the ground, some wringing their hands, some in extacies, some praying, some weeping; and others so outragious cursing and swearing that it was thought that they were really possessed of the devil. I saw strange things today. . . ." Quoted in Morgan Edwards MS. Materials Towards a History of the Baptists in Virginia. John Williams in his MS. Diary frequently mentions shouting, trembling, convulsions, and once, "The Devil a Rageing & Blaspheming which kindled the Flame of the Christians, and the Lord." When William Hickman first attended a Baptist meeting "numbers fell, some were convulsed and others were crying out for mercy." Quoted in Spencer, *Kentucky Baptists,* I, 153. Edwards, *op. cit.,* gives other examples. See also Semple, pp. 15, 24 and *passim.* Williams MS. Diary and a

forms of reflexes, due largely to sympathetic like-mindedness and suggestibility, are characteristics of the primitive mind in which the power of inhibition is easily overcome by a highly developed imagination and the emotions.[24] Such manifestations as we have noted, invariably start with the lower and uneducated classes, especially under conditions of a large crowd, when meetings are protracted or are held at frequent intervals and when the skillful exhorter directs attention to some single idea, as salvation or hell. By constant repetition of the central theme, the crowd is brought to a high pitch of excitement and the emotions of fear and joy in particular are translated into muscular and sensory reflexes. The effect is increased by the singing of a variety of short, violently contrasted verses which are commonly known and which make a vivid impression on the mind, especially when meetings are held at night.

The existence of the above manifestations is certainly indicative of the social sphere of the Baptist revival. While the Presbyterian "New Lights" were often accused of such extravagances as we note among the Separates, we have no such evidence of their existence as we have for the latter.[25] The superior education, the more careful mental training, and the calmer leadership of the Presbyterian ministers would be sufficient to account for their holding in restraint and in fact discounting such revival excesses as we have noted.

copy of Edwards MS. History are in the Virginia Baptist Historical Society, Richmond. The original of Edwards is in possession of the Crozer Theological Seminary.

[24] The psychology of the revival is best treated in F. M. Davenport, *Primitive Traits in Religious Revivals*. An excellent article on the same subject is in *The Christian Review*, Vol. IX, entitled "The Great Awakening," and inspired by the appearance of Tracy's book of this same title. See also *Evan. and Lit. Mag.*, V, 306 ff.

[25] This is certainly true of Davies' revival. Wright wrote in 1761 that "amidst the whole of the work, there has been scarcely any tincture of enthusiasm." He says that the converts "were rather tempted to unreasonable diffidence, than like the Separates to go and preach to others," and also that there were remarkably few apostates considering the extent of the work and that "among uncultivated souls." Letter in Webster, *op. cit.*, pp. 626-627.

Since the peculiar physical and mental manifestations were often mistaken for true conversion and yet might arise wholly from a highly developed imagination coupled with nervous instability, revivals of religion have inevitably resulted in a large number of apostacies.[26] On the basis of the foregoing explanation it is very apparent that one might experience all of the so-called revival phenomena and yet have not the least sense of spiritual conviction.[27] It is also easy to see how persons who actually were opposed to the revival and how even exceedingly self controlled individuals might, without the slightest religious sentiments, be drawn into the vortex of contagion and imitation under conditions of proper intensity. We have many such examples in both the Separate Baptist and Methodist revivals. Such cases illustrate the "law of spread" which is referred to by Davenport.

It was the tendency in the eighteenth century, as it has been in all ages, to attribute the abnormal and irrational to the mysterious and supernatural power of God or the Devil. As we see them now, the most logical explanation of such phenomena is to be found in the operations of the laws of individual and social psychology.[28] This can be said without denial of the fact that revivals have had a large place in the development of the Church and that with all their objectionable features they are in harmony with the natural laws of action and reaction, ebb and flow.[29] This type of religious propaganda was particularly adapted to the South, because of the isolation of rural life and the small amount of education which was accessible to the small farmers and plain folks.[30]

[26] Davenport, *op. cit.*, pp. 247 ff. See also below, p. 176.

[27] The revival visions, trances, and hallucinations can be explained on the grounds of self-hypnotization through suggestibility and prolonged concentration on a single subject or idea. See Davenport, pp. 227-8.

[28] The pathological explanation can hardly suffice for any more than sporadic cases, certainly not for whole communities. Davenport, p. 220.

[29] See J. E. McCulloch, "The Place of Revivals in American History," *Meth. Rev.* (So.), Vol. LI, p. 681.

[30] Bassett, "Development of the Popular Churches after the Revolution," *loc. cit.*, p. 266. *Cf.* P. G. Mode, "Revivalism as a Phase of Frontier Life," in *Journal of Religion*, July, 1921.

The training and preaching of the Separate Baptists were of the type to encourage the extravagant aspects of the revival. There was among the denomination a decided tendency to underrate education. This was no doubt due to the intense antipathy towards the Established Church in whose ministry education was emphasized at the expense of personal piety, and also to the fact that the results they attained convinced the Separate Baptists that gifts of heart were more important than theological training. To them the call of God was the only essential for the ministry, and God could minister through the weakest of the human race "unassisted by human learning, and abundantly enrich their minds with spiritual ideas, which is impossible for any person to acquire, though acquainted with all the different languages in use in the world, and though they understood all the arts and sciences taught by man."[31] In a certain sense their lack of education was a decided advantage to these zealous preachers, for it placed them on the same plane with those to whom they ministered, and a strong bond of sympathy developed between the two.[32] Then, again, we must remember that the exigencies of the revival were great. With no established ministry upon which to draw, it was not a case whether the Separate Baptists should have an educated or an uneducated ministry, but whether they should have the latter or none at all.[33]

If these men lacked an education, they certainly were endowed with native ability, good common sense, profound religious convictions, and a sacrificial zeal that did not flinch even before persecution. Feeling themselves called of God, they did not hesitate to invade the parishes of the established clergy. They were, most of them, unwilling to seek a license for preaching from the state and rode far and wide to proclaim the truth.[34]

[31] Fristoe, op. cit., pp. 31-38, for qualifications which a minister ought to possess.

[32] J. A. Broadus, "The American Baptist Ministry 100 Years Ago," in Baptist Quarterly, IX (1875), pp. 1-20 at p. 17.

[33] Ibid., p. 14.

[34] David Thomas, The Virginian Baptist, Part I, contains a discussion of the Baptist doctrines. See also Fristoe, op. cit., pp. 17-21. The one great common doctrine for all Baptists was adult baptism. Beyond that they

Coupled with their evangelical preaching they made sharp attacks on the Established Church with its infant baptism, its ecclesiastical arrangements, and its pleasure-loving parsons, who often led the opposition to the Baptists. In their bitterness towards the Anglicans, the Separates left no stone unturned to bring about the ultimate downfall of the state-supported church.[35] In this respect they far surpassed all other denominations in the colony.

Certain peculiarities of address distinguished the preaching of the Separate Baptists. Probably the most striking of these was a mannerism known as the "holy whine," which had its origin in open air preaching and consisted of a rising and falling of the tone to relieve the strain.[36] It became a habit and was long continued as an appropriate form for the pulpit discourse. In addition they indulged in vehement gesticulations, odd whoops, and an impassioned manner which moved their congregation to tears, tremblings, screams and fallings.[37] Their reputation is well illustrated by the instance given by Morgan Edwards, who mentions a man as saying "he had rather go to hell than be obliged to hear a baptist in order to go to heaven." Soon after he listened to Dutton Lane preach and fell to the ground roaring out, "Lord have mercy upon me for I'm a gone man." After continuing in this state for about an hour, he experienced conversion.[38] Semple tells us: "The people were greatly astonished having never seen things on this wise before. Many mocked, but, the power of God attending them, many also trembled."[39]

were by no means agreed. As we have seen, the Separates were the most evangelical.

[35] Hawks, Ecclesiastical Contributions, Virginia, pp. 121-22, 127.

[36] Broadus, loc. cit.

[37] Semple, pp. 15-16; Campbell, History of Virginia, pp. 553-4.

[38] MS. Materials Towards a History of the Baptists in Virginia.

[39] Pp. 15-16. Morgan Edwards makes an interesting comment on Richard Major who was bred a Presbyterian and embraced the Baptist tenets. He became minister of Little River Church in Loudoun County in 1766. Says Edwards: "Very successful—Began with reading sermons—sometimes read what was not in."

Judging from the statement of David Thomas, we are led to believe that the Regular Baptists disapproved of the "enthusiasm" and demonstrations of the Separates. In answer to an objection against the Baptists that the Holy Scriptures did not countenance their excesses, Thomas wrote in 1774: "As these horrid vociferations and obstreperous commotions, mentioned in the objections, never were the effect of my preaching, nor are approved of by our churches as any part of religion, I am no ways obliged to vindicate any or all of them."[40]

The fact that the Regular Baptists were willing to apply for licenses under the Toleration Act and that they were not so demonstrative as the Separates, caused them to escape serious persecutions.[41] Thomas and others itinerated much without molestation, most of their enemies supposing that their licenses did not limit them to particular houses. The fact that they had Thomas, a learned man, in their midst also gained for them a respect not enjoyed by the Separates.[42]

The Separate Baptists occupied in the popular mind a very definite social status. They had the reputation of being the meanest of the mean—a poor, illiterate, ignorant and awkward set of enthusiasts.[43] Fristoe tells us that they were generally "of the mediocrity, or poorer sort among the people—instances have been very few, of persons being called who were rich in this world—and we have been encouraged to believe that it gave

[40] *The Virginian Baptist,* p. 63.

[41] Thom, p. 11; MS. Sketch of Jeremiah Moore (Va. Bap. Hist. Soc.), p. 4. The Regulars did not escape persecution altogether. In his early years David Thomas was more than once assaulted. Once he was pulled down from his pulpit and dragged out of the house in a barbarous manner. At another time an attempt was made to shoot him and once a snake was thrown in the midst of the congregation "but no hurt done." Taylor, I, 44, Semple, pp. 382-383, Edwards MS. History. Richard Major, a Regular, met with much opposition in Loudoun County. The instances of persecution of Regulars are comparatively few, however.

[42] Thom, p. 11; Semple, p. 383. Thomas held the degree of M.A. from Brown University.

[43] R. B. C. Howell, *Early Baptists of Virginia,* after speaking of the despicable reputation of the Baptists, says that as a matter of fact they were as a whole "in all respects, equal at least to the same number of men and women taken promiscuously from society in this or any other country." Pp. 131 ff. Nevertheless the *belief* concerning them was a fact.

clearer proof of the genuine quality of religion among us. . . ."[44]
Again, he says of these early Baptists: "The cant word was
that they are an ignorant, illiterate set—and of the poor and contemptible class of people."[45] David Thomas cites as an objection
to his denomination that none of the rich or learned ever joined
them and that they were considered "the meanest people in the
world which could not be the case, were you so worthy of notice
as you pretend to be. Were you in the right, can it be thought
that men of the brightest parts, cultivated with a liberal education, would not be able to discern it."[46]

This attitude of contempt became so widespread as to per-
vade all classes, even the poorer.[47] Benedict, the Baptist historian, records how in the early part of his ministry "a very
honest and candid old lady who had never been far from her
retired home said to me in a sober tone, 'Your society are much
more like other folks now than they were when I was young.
Then there was a company of them in the back part of our
town, and an outlandish set of people they certainly were. You
yourself would say so if you had seen them. As it was told to
me, you could hardly find one among them but was deformed
in some way or other. Some of them were hare-lipped, others
were blear eyed, or hump-backed, or bow legged, or clump
footed; hardly any of them looked like other people. But they
were all strong for plunging and let their poor ignorant children run wild, and never had the seal of the covenant put on
them.' "[48]

By 1790 a social revolution had occurred in Virginia. The
Baptists counted many influential and wealthy members among
them and were as respectable as other denominations.[49] They

[44] *History of the Ketocton Baptist Association*, p. 148.
[45] *Ibid.*, p. 64.
[46] *The Virginian Baptist*, pp. 54-55. In reply Thomas defends the Baptists.
[47] Howell, *op. cit.*, pp. 131 ff. An example is seen in the case of William
Hickman, who thought of the Baptists as false prophets and babblers until
he went to hear them and then his wife was disgusted at his change in
attitude. Quoted in Spencer, *Kentucky Baptists*, I, 153. See below, p. 121.
[48] *Fifty Years Among the Baptists*, pp. 93-94, and given in Thom, p. 19.
The *Virginia Gazette*, August 15, 1771, informs us of common accusation
against the Baptists in that they were "a pack of ignorant enthusiasts."
[49] See Semple, p. 59 and below Chapter IX.

had won the battle for religious liberty, prejudices had subsided, they were ready to take up plans for establishing an institution of learning and, most significant of all, to give to the world a history of their achievements. To fully appreciate the significance of this upheaval it will first be necessary for us to take account of the spread of the Separate Baptists, the nature of the opposition to them, and the causes of their success.

From Sandy Creek as a center Stearns' revival was carried north and south by his preachers. Daniel Marshall was delegated to spread the gospel in the adjacent parts of Virginia. As a result, in 1760 a church was constituted in Pittsylvania County and Dutton Lane, a convert, became its first pastor.[50] For a decade it seems that the Regular Baptists led in the work in Virginia. The popular opposition to the Separates during this period was very strong, with the result that the number of churches increased but slowly.[51] Until 1765 the work was confined to the region south of the James. Even at the beginning of 1770, there were not more than four churches south of this river and only three on the north side.[52] At this time, we have seen, the Regular Baptists had ten churches, chiefly in the northern part of the colony. After 1770, however, the growth of the Separate Baptist movement was phenomenal. When the Virginia Association held its first session in May 1771, delegates from fourteen churches representing 1,335 members were present.[53] In 1773 the Association was divided into Southern and Northern Districts, the James river being the dividing line.[54] In May 1774 the Northern District included at least twenty-four churches with an aggregate membership of 1,921, while in October the Southern District received letters from thirty churches which reported 2,083 members.[55] This was truly a remarkable growth considering the opposition to the Baptists and shows that the year 1770 marks roughly the popular reaction in favor of the denomination.

The Separate Baptist ministers were indefatigable both in zeal and energy. Men like Daniel Marshall and Samuel Harriss

[50] Thom, p. 13; Semple, p. 17. [51] Cf. Thom, pp. 16 ff.
[52] Ibid., p. 28, and Semple, pp. 24, 42.
[53] Semple, p. 70. [54] Ibid., p. 77. [55] Ibid., pp. 79-80.

travelled far and wide wherever an occasion to preach was within reach, and they became founders of many churches.[56] Harriss was one among the early Separates who was of respectable standing. He is referred to by Semple as "a man of great distinction," and could boast of respectable parentage and an education which was good for his day. In Pittsylvania County he held various offices including those of church warden, sheriff, justice of the peace, colonel of the militia and even burgess.[57] He joined the Separate Baptists early in the movement, being ordained ruling elder in 1759. Harriss was particularly identified with the revival in the counties north of the James, especially in Culpeper and Orange Counties.[58] People sometimes came from a distance of a hundred miles to his meetings, while to travel forty or fifty was not at all uncommon. Hundreds of men at times camped on the grounds in order to stay through the meetings and we are told that sometimes the floor would be covered with persons who had been "struck down under conviction of sin."[59]

Many others equalled Harriss in their efforts. Jeremiah Moore thought he travelled far enough to have reached twice around the world, had he been directed to that end.[60] He preached principally in Virginia and Maryland, but also visited the Carolinas, Tennessee, Kentucky, Pennsylvania and other northern colonies. Lewis Lunsford travelled day and night, even in the most inclement weather. He visited the Valley and on three occasions, it is said, his journeys extended to Kentucky.[61] James Ireland's preaching embraced a regular circuit which included places in Shenandoah, Frederic, Culpeper and Fauquier Counties. He says: "There were not many places upon the waters among the back mountains that were then inhabited, but what I visited."[62] He often preached three times a day and once at

[56] Semple, pp. 13 ff.; Taylor, *Virginia Baptist Ministers,* I, 18-24 on Marshall, and 31-39 on Harriss. Edwards says that Harriss was bred a Churchman and embraced the Baptist faith in 1759.

[57] Semple, p. 18 note; Edwards MS. History.

[58] See Semple, pp. 19 ff.

[59] *Ibid.,* but see above, pp. 110-112, on the psychology of the revival.

[60] Taylor, I, 219.   [61] *Ibid.,* p. 141.

[62] James Ireland, *Life,* pp. 189-190. The Virginia Baptist Historical Society, Richmond, has a copy of this valuable biography.

night without regard to weather or fatigue. In the fourteen years of his ministry in Virginia prior to 1791, John Leland baptized seven hundred persons and preached about three thousand sermons.[63] Similarly, John Waller baptized more than two thousand persons and assisted in the constitution of eighteen churches. For many years he had the ministerial care of five churches for which he preached steadily.[64] These are only a few, and are fairly typical, of the men who represented the Separate Baptists. They help us to understand the spirit and character of the movement. As the revival spread in wave after wave each one sent forth new prophets to carry the tidings. Often illiterate, still they met with remarkable success, preaching and winning converts in defiance of magistrates, mobs and prisons.

No other sect in Virginia suffered the amount and variety of persecution which the Separate Baptists bore. This first took the form of popular violence to which, beginning in 1768, legal prosecution was added. For about a decade after their first settlement at Sandy Creek, the sect was contemptuously ignored by the governmental authorities who evidently did not regard the movement as dangerous.[65] Popular opposition, however, began early and the instances of it are so numerous that we can only indicate its general character. When Samuel Harriss first went north of the James into Culpeper County, in 1765, after preaching a sermon he was driven out by a mob armed with sticks, whips and clubs.[66] On one occasion in Orange County, he was pulled down by a ruffian, dragged about now by the hair, now by the leg, but his friends rescued him. At another

[63] Letter of Valediction (1791), in *Works,* pp. 171, 173.
[64] Taylor, I, 83, 85.
[65] Semple, p. 29. However, this was not true of individual observers. As early as September, 1759, James Craig, minister in Cumberland Parish, Lunenberg County, wrote a letter in which he reports that wherever the Baptists appeared people flocked over to them. "In Halifax one Samuel Harris, formerly Burgess for that County, and one William Murphy, so ignorant that he cannot read plain, or write his name, have raised and propagated a most shocking Delusion, which threatens the entire subversion of *true Religion* in these parts. These *ignorant Enthusiasts* profess themselves to be Antipaedobaptists." Dawson MSS. September 8, 1759 (Library of Congress).
[66] Semple, p. 20, and Thom, p. 13.

time "he was knocked down by a rude fellow, while he was preaching."[67] We do not hear, however, that Harriss was ever molested in his own county where he was known and respected. Here, as Thom notes, "the social element was in his favor."[68]

Harriss was only one of many to suffer violence of this sort. On more than one occasion John Waller was severely beaten, as in 1771, in Caroline County, when the parson, his clerk and the sheriff led an attack upon him. The parson even ran his whip down Waller's throat to silence him and he was then pulled down and lashed severely. Sore as he was, Waller went on preaching after the departure of his persecutors.[69] John Taylor often faced the rage of the mobs and once in the midst of worship was approached by twenty young men "armed with instruments of death" who broke up the meeting.[70] Similarly, John Koontz, Lewis Lunsford, William Webber, James Ireland, David Barrow, John Pickett, Elijah Baker and others too numerous to mention were threatened and suffered various forms of violence.[71]

Besides kicks and cuffs and dragging by the hair, we hear of preachers being plunged into mud until they were nearly drowned, out of ridicule for the Baptist rite of dipping.[72] Preachers were insulted by drunken ruffians and once, at least, a live snake and a hornet's nest were used to break up meetings.[73] In addition many attacks were made upon preachers during service in the form of abusive language, while attempts to interrupt baptism and cast ridicule upon the ordinance seem to have been somewhat common.[74] Often their enemies tried to do away with the Baptist preachers while they were in prison. Thus an attempt was made to blow up James Ireland when in

[67] Semple (1810 ed.), p. 382.

[68] *Op. cit.*, p. 16.

[69] This instance is given in Williams' MS. Diary who recorded it shortly after it happened. Edwards' MS. History also tells of it.

[70] Taylor, I, 233.

[71] Taylor, *passim*, and Semple (1810 ed.).

[72] This was the experience of David Barrow and a colleague. Taylor, I, 164.

[73] *Cf.* Thom, p. 17, who gives references.

[74] Fristoe, pp. 78-79; J. D. McGill (compiler), *Sketches of the History of the Baptist Churches of the Rappahannock Association,* pp. 13-14.

Culpeper jail in 1770, and at another time poisonous fumes were burned at the door and window of his prison in an effort to suffocate him.[75] Instances of persecution while the preachers were in prison are frequent.

Considering the fact that the Baptists represented a distinctly popular cause, it is interesting to note the reasons for the opposition of even the lower classes to them. Probably this was due to the strange mannerisms of the preachers, the novelty of their doctrines, the prevalence of the revival phenomena which many dreaded would seize them, and the general reports that the Baptist preachers were "wolves in sheep's clothing."[76] The accusations lodged against the sect caused many to revile their very name. Ireland's early attitude is probably quite typical. He "entertained the most violent prejudices against them" and vowed in the name of the Trinity that he would never become a Baptist.[77] So, too, William Hickman "was sure they were the false prophets" and hoped he would never see one of them.[78] Often men would prevent members of their families from going to hear the Baptists or from being baptized in order to avoid the stigma attached to such an action.[79] The sect was regarded as sacrilegiously cruel in neglecting the baptism of children, while Fristoe tells us that it was even broadly circulated that as soon as the Baptists were numerous enough, they intended to "fall on their fellow subjects, massacre the inhabitants and take possession of the country."[80] It was some years before the masses were disillusioned and realized that these sectaries were really reformers who were fighting their battles, and not mere incendiaries.

[75] Ireland, *Life,* p. 166. He was taken to jail amidst the cursings and abuses of persecutors while missles of various sorts were hurled at him during the whole night.

[76] See Fristoe, p. 68. It is frequently mentioned that the Baptist doctrines were new and strange and that their preaching made "a great noise" in the neighborhood.

[77] *Life,* pp. 71-72.

[78] Quoted in Spencer, *Kentucky Baptists,* I, 153.

[79] Fristoe, p. 68. William Hickman kept his wife from being baptized for some months.

[80] Fristoe, *History of the Ketocton Baptist Association,* p. 65; Thom, p. 19; Benedict, *Fifty Years Among the Baptists,* pp. 93-94.

Beginning in 1768 the Baptists had to face legal prosecution in addition to the violence and defamation of mobs. This continued until the outbreak of the Revolution, during which period it appears that about thirty-four ministers were imprisoned, some on several occasions.[81] The first instance of actual imprisonment occurred on June 4, 1768, in Spottsylvania County, when John Waller, Lewis Craig, James Childs, James Reed and William Mash were arrested as disturbers of the peace.[82] One of the charges brought against them was that "they cannot meet a man on the road but they must ram a text of Scripture down his throat." The court offered to release them if they would cease preaching for a year and a day and give security to the amount of two hundred pounds. This they refused to do and they were imprisoned. Craig was released after four weeks, but the others were held for forty-three days. "While in prison they constantly preached through the grates. The mobs without used every exertion to prevent the people from hearing, but to little purpose."[83] Morgan Edwards says that they were set free in order to get rid of them. At any rate, they were discharged without condition.

This first case is a typical one.[84] It is to be noticed that these preachers were arrested on peace warrants and also that disturbing the peace consisted mainly in preaching and in "ramming" texts of Scripture down the throats of the people. In this connection Fristoe informs us: "As the law was silent about dissenters and no mode prescribed for their preaching, nor prohibition of it, nor for punishing them on the account of it, justices of the peace and courts of justice, took a different plan, pretended they were not persecuting religion when the

---

[81] C. F. James, *Documentary History of the Struggle of the Baptists for Religious Freedom,* contains the names which are also given in Thom, note 38. See also Leland, *Works,* p. 107. Philip Gatch, the Methodist, tells us that Waller was confined in jail for a total of a hundred and thirteen days in different counties. *Memoirs,* p. 51. A summary of the persecutions is in the *Religious Herald,* April 6, 1871.

[82] Semple, pp. 29-32; Edwards' MS. History gives all the names.

[83] Semple, p. 32. Edwards makes a similar statement.

[84] I have examined a number of orders for the arrest of Baptist preachers, letters of warning to them, etc., in the Virginia Baptist Historical Society. Some of these are in the original and some are copies.

Baptist preachers were taken and imprisoned, but that it was the peace and good order of the community they were aiming at; and so shifted the ground—they were not brought to the bar for religion, nor for their religious opinions, nor any of their rites, modes or religious ceremonies, but as disturbers of the peace, the perverters of good order, and the calling unlawful assemblies together, taking the people from their necessary employment on their different farms and plantations, bringing the people into habits of idleness and neglect of their necessary business and interesting pursuits and thereby reducing the inhabitants to want and distress."[85]

An examination of other evidence sustains Fristoe. Thus on January 12, 1771, in Chesterfield County, Joseph Antony and William Webber were committed to jail "on a warrant issued against them for misbehaviour by Itinerant preaching . . . being of that sect of dissenters from the Church of England commonly called Ana Baptist."[86] The warrant for the arrest of John Waller, Robert Ware, James Greenwood, William Webber, Richard Faulkner and Thomas Wafer, issued in Middlesex County on August 10, 1771, charges them with having been present

at the house of James McKan in this County at a Conventicle or unlawful assembly of many Persons exceeding the number of Ten besides the household . . . there met together under the pretence of the exercise of Religion in other manner than according to the Litturgy and Practice of the Church of England And they . . . have at other times and Places taken upon themselves to Preach or Teach to the Persons so unlawfully Assembled not having Episcopal Ordination to Teach or Preach the Gospel according to the Canons of the Church of England neither have They professing Themselves to be Protestant Teachers or Preachers dissenting from the said Church of England, Qualified themselves . . . according to . . . an Act of Parliament . . . for exempting Their Majesty's Protestant Subjects dissenting from the Church of England from the Penalties of certain Laws nor is the house of the said James McKan a Place for the meeting or Congregation of Protestant Dissenters for Religious Worship according to the directions of the said Act of Parliament: and they . . . do labour and persuade

[85] *History of the Ketocton Baptist Association*, p. 71. Note the economic argument.

[86] MS. copy in Va. Bap. Hist. Soc. See also *Va. Mag. of Hist. and Biog.*, XI, 416.

many Persons in Communion with the Church of England to dissent from the same and utter doctrines Destructive of the Peace of Society to the subversion of all Religious Establishments, the exciting & raising Factions in the minds of his Majesty's Subjects contrary to the Laws of the Colony and against the Peace of our Lord the King his Crown and Dignity.[87]

In the orders for their commitment we are informed that upon their examination these men asserted that they had "no power or authority for which they stand charged but from above." The foregoing is typical of both the attitude of the authorities and the Baptist preachers. The latter, in truth, believed that their commissions came from on high and no earthly authority could prevent them from their duties.

We find that these orders for arrest and commitment read much the same.[88] The Baptist preachers convened people without qualifying according to law and were therefore guilty of breach of the peace and misbehavior. To this common charge was sometimes added the accusation of "raising Sedition and Stirring up Strife amongst his Majesties Liege People."[89] The vagrancy law was always at the disposal of the officials.[90] Eleazer Clay was one of the few men of some wealth and influence who joined the Baptists when they were still a despised sect.[91] He at once became a preacher and, although he laboured in a county noted for its persecutions (Chesterfield), he was

[87] Original MS. in Va. Bap. Hist. Soc.

[88] Others in the Va. Bap. Hist. Soc. either in the original or copy are for John Pickett, February 26, 1770, Fauquier Co.; Joseph Antony and William Webber, January 12, 1771, Chesterfield; Augustine Eastin, June, 1772, Chesterfield; John Tanner and John Weatherford, June 4, 1773, Chesterfield; Jeremiah Walker, August 6, 1773, Chesterfield (on the Chesterfield cases see *Va. Mag. of Hist. and Biog.*, XI); Nathaniel Saunders and William McClanahan, August 21, 1773, Culpeper; John Waller, Robert Ware, and John Shackleford, March 21, 1774, Essex; Lewis Lunsford, October 2, 1775, Richmond Co.; David Tinsley, February, 1774, Chesterfield; Elijah Baker, May 27, July 1, July 28, 1778, Accomac, in case of Church Wardens vs. Elijah Baker. Case dismissed August 25. Other cases in Semple and Taylor.

[89] Original MS. order for the arrest of Saunders, McClanahan, "and their abettors," Culpeper, August 21, 1773. Also in others.

[90] Church Wardens vs. Elijah Baker, was a vagrancy case. Accomac, 1778. Copy in Va. Bap. Hist. Soc.

[91] See Semple, p. 270.

never apprehended. When asked why he did not arrest Mr. Clay, Colonel Cary, the magistrate replied: "Mr. Clay had a livelihood, but these others are taken up under the vagrant law."[92] Cary's attitude certainly has a social significance.

The records of these cases are often incomplete.[93] The Baptist preachers were offered the alternatives of giving surety for good behavior or serving a term in prison. A few of them bound themselves to cease preaching in the county,[94] but most of them preferred imprisonment.[95] Lewis Craig's spirit was probably that of the great majority when he told the jury: "I take joyfully the despoiling of my goods for Christ's sake. While I lived in sin the jury took no notice of me."[96] This, we are told, caused John Waller, who was one of the grandjurymen, to become a Baptist. At another time Craig was released from Caroline prison on promising good behaviour but he stipulated that preaching should not be construed a forfeiture of his recognizance.[97] Morgan Edwards says: "No reply was made to this for I believe they were tired of him."

It is a fact that it was hard to know just what to do with these persistent and ubiquitous Baptists. Imprisonment did not

[92] *Religious Herald,* August 29, 1872.

[93] W. G. Stannard's exhaustive examination of the Chesterfield court records yielded but meagre results. He found the records imperfectly kept. *Va. Mag. of Hist. and Biog.,* XI, pp. 415 ff.

[94] A copy of Lunsford's bond which he gave in Richmond County in 1775 is in the Va. Bap. Hist. Soc. as is one from Shackleford in 1774, Essex County. Some others gave bond but it was not usual. Leland says it was sometimes done when there was reason to believe that the court would not bring suit upon them. He says that he never heard of but one instance of such a suit and that one was dismissed. Ministers would give bonds and immediately begin to preach, not considering it as a breach of peace. See Leland, p. 107. In 1771 Lewis Craig gave security in Caroline County but regretted it and began preaching again and was imprisoned for three months. McGill, *Hist. of Churches of Rappahannock Association,* p. 26. Semple says that occasionally security was given in hopes of obtaining licenses. This was Lunsford's idea in Richmond County, but not obtaining the license he later regretted that he had not gone to jail (1810 ed.), p. 418.

[95] Thus Waller wrote from Urbanna prison (Middlesex) that he and Webber were afraid to sign any bond not to preach "for fear of sinning against God." MS. Va. Bap. Hist. Soc., September 20, 1772, to James Mills, a magistrate, whom he asked to release Webber on account of his poor health. See another letter of Waller's from the same prison a year earlier, in Semple, pp. 481-483, and *Religious Herald,* January 18, 1828.

[96] Edwards, MS. History.   [97] *Ibid.*

stop their preaching and only caused their numbers to increase.[98] Parson James Craig wrote to Commissary Dawson: "They pray for persecution, and therefore if you fall upon any severe method of suppressing them, it will tend to strengthen their cause."[99] Obviously, then, when persecution came it was in answer to prayer and the Lord was with the Baptists. Neither mobs, nor prison walls, nor threats, nor hunger, nor insults could silence the imprisoned preachers, or check the popularity of the Baptist doctrines.[100] Indeed, the persecution only caused the popular reaction in their favor. It is not surprising that more than once Baptist preachers were released to be rid of them.

It is necessary to emphasize the fact that the Separates generally did not recognize the right of civil authorities to regulate preaching or places of worship. In religious matters they claimed that their authority was from God alone. Therefore, they were not at all inclined to comply with the Act of Toleration, either by licensing their places of worship or taking the oaths. Their conception that as ministers it was their duty to go into all the world and preach wherever they could, made them unwilling to confine themselves to particular places.[101] Likewise, it was inconsistent with their views of truth to subscribe to the required articles of the Church of England, as the law demanded. In short, the Toleration Act conflicted with the Separatist idea of religious liberty. They were unwilling to accept anything less than complete freedom of conscience and worship.

The position of the Separates was, of course, not one which could be recognized in a court of law. On the other hand, in the few instances in which they were willing to comply with the law, there was a disposition to treat them unfairly. When

[98] Semple, p. 271, gives Chesterfield County as an example and remarks "that, generally the Baptist cause has flourished most extensively where it has met the severest opposition in the outset." See also p. 33 and Campbell, p. 555.

[99] Dawson MSS., September 8, 1759.

[100] James Ireland, *Life,* is very typical. See pp. 164 ff. and 177 ff. *Cf.* Weatherford's experience in Taylor, I, 52.

[101] McGill, *Hist. of the Churches of the Rappahannock Association,* p. 14. See also *Religious Herald,* May 7, 1874.

William Webber and Joseph Antony were arrested in Chesterfield County, in January 1771, they offered to take the oaths and subscribe to the test, but the court decided "that their doing so in this Court will not authorize them to preach as the said act directs."[102] The County Courts claimed to be without authority to grant licenses for preaching places and the Colonial Court placed the narrowest interpretation possible on the Toleration Act.[103] The latter took the ground that only one place might be licensed in a county, and that a license was for the house and not the man.[104] It did not grant unrestricted right to preach. Fristoe says that the Colonial Court once refused a license for a Baptist meeting-house in Richmond County on the grounds that the Presbyterians already had one there.[105]

Another practical difficulty in the way of obtaining licenses was in securing certification from two magistrates that the signers of the petition were inhabitants of the place. Owing to prejudice this was not easy to do. Before the Court would grant the license, the dissenting minister must pass an examination before an Anglican clergyman and it was no easy matter to find a friendly parson who would grant the certificate of qualifications.[106] Even if the petition was put through, it was by no means certain that a license would be obtained. There was a decided prejudice against the Baptists and in 1772 two petitions were sent to the Burgesses saying that although the Baptists were willing to conform to the spirit of the Toleration Act and are loyal and quiet subjects, the indulgence which is granted to Presbyterians and Quakers and other dissenters is denied to them.[107] We do not wonder that there developed in the denomination that strong spirit of independence which demanded the complete abolition of privilege for the Anglican Church. We can also discover the social discontent lurking in

[102] *Va. Mag. of Hist. and Biog.*, XI, 416; MS. copy in Va. Bap. Hist. Soc.
[103] MS. copy of petition of Ware and eleven others (Middlesex County).
[104] Fristoe, *History of Ketocton Baptist Association*, p. 72.
[105] *Ibid.*, p. 73.
[106] *Ibid.*, pp. 74-75. *Cf.* Ireland's experience in obtaining a license, *Life*, pp. 177-178.
[107] *Journal of House of Burgesses*, February 12 and March 14, 1772, from Lunenberg and Caroline counties.

the statement that it "was intolerable for one set of men to make application to another set of men (cap in hand) and in the most humble posture, ask their consent and allowance, to worship the God that made them. . . ."[108]

One other method of checking the Baptists was to fine them for non-attendance at church. Fristoe tells us that little notice was taken of non-attendance when Anglicans absented themselves from worship, "but so soon as the new-lights were absent they were presented by the grand jury and fined according to law; whether such a fine was ever collected or not we cannot certainly say—however the attempt to make them pay appeared very unreasonable."[109] He adds that it was burdensome enough for the Baptists to be compelled to support a church from which they derived no benefits, without being confined for non-attendance. A complete examination of the county records would probably reveal a considerable number of presentments for this cause. In Middlesex County, at the May term in 1771, there were fifteen, while there were seven in May 1772 and eleven in May 1773.[110] The names of some prominent Baptists appear and some of them were fined repeatedly. We are told there were quite as many presentments at the other quarterly terms and that "most of those presented were fined each time five shillings and the cost—very few were excused."[111]

Turning to the various causes of the opposition to the Baptists, we find that they were regarded by many, and with good reasons, as lawbreakers who ought to be punished. Even those who considered that the Toleration Act did extend to them saw that most of the Baptists did not care to avail themselves of its terms.[112] That the Baptists insisted that they were called

---

[108] Fristoe, pp. 73-74.

[109] *History of the Ketocton Baptist Association*, p. 69.

[110] MS. copy of the court records certified by P. T. Woodward, clerk of court in 1873. Va. Bap. Hist. Soc.

[111] Letter of P. T. Woodward, April 28, 1873.

[112] "An Address to the Anabaptists Imprisoned in Caroline County, August 8, 1771," in Purdie and Dixon's *Virginia Gazette,* February 20, 1772. Very hostile to the Baptists and written by a lawyer. An article in defense of the Baptists appeared in the same weekly for August 15, 1771. It was an answer to those who claimed that the Act of Toleration did not extend to the Colony and held that if this were the case, neither did the penalties

of God was of little weight. Indeed, some ridiculed this claim and challenged the preachers to produce credentials beyond their bare words. In support of the legal activities of the authorities was cited the scriptural advice, "Beloved, believe not every Spirit but try them whether they be of God, since many false Prophets are gone out into the World."[113] The Baptists were also reminded that the Scriptures enjoined obedience to the magistrates who do not bear the sword of justice in vain.[114]

Secondly, there was a fear that the success of the Baptists would involve the ruin of the Established Church.[115] We have many evidences of the activity of the Anglican clergy against the sect and Leland tells us that they raised the cry of their craft being in danger.[116] James Craig saw only fatal consequences to the church from the Baptist movement "unless the principal persons concerned in that delusion are apprehended, or otherwise restrained from proceeding further."[117] Another friend of the Establishment asked: "What do you mean here by Conversion? Not from Idolatry, or Paganism to Christianity. Those you apply to are already, or pretend to be, christians. I own I can fix no Meaning to this Term, as you use it, but their forsaking the Established Church and becoming of your Opinion."[118]

A third cause was the general impression that the Baptists were a menace to society. Their doctrines were considered as

which the act repealed, for these laws "can reach no farther than the annulling Power of the repealing act." He asks on what grounds were the Baptists punished if the Toleration Act did not apply to Virginia? The writer of the "Address" holds that their imprisonment could be justified on grounds of common law, if necessary, since the Baptists were a menace to society.

[113] "Address to the Anabaptists," loc. cit. Also see article by Philoepiscopus in Dixon and Hunter's Virginia Gazette, December 13, 1776.

[114] Letter of William Bradley, a magistrate, to Nathaniel Saunders, dated Culpeper, October 6, 1770, and warning him not to preach. Va. Bap. Hist. Soc., which has a number of other Saunders papers.

[115] Fristoe, op. cit., pp. 67, 80; Leland, "Virginia Chronicle," in Works, p. 106.

[116] "Virginia Chronicle," loc. cit., p. 106; see Semple, Taylor, Ireland, Fristoe and others. Cf. Fithian, Journal and Letters, p. 118 (1774).

[117] To Dawson, September 8, 1759, Dawson MSS.

[118] "Address to the Anabaptists," loc. cit.

subversive of religion and morality. One in particular, which was alluded to with its consequences, was " 'that after Conversion a Man cannot sin unto Death'; by which you take off all religious Restraints from Men of abandoned Principles, who, having been once dipped in your happy Waters, are let loose to commit upon us Murders, and every Species of Injury, when they can do it secretly so as to avoid temporal Punishment."[119] It was also pointed out that often the effects of the Baptist preaching was to destroy homes: "Wives are drawn from their Husbands, Children from their Parents, and Slaves from the Obedience of their Masters. Thus the very Heartstrings of these little Societies which form the greater are torn in sunder, and all their Peace destroyed."[120] It was even felt that the Baptists were planning the destruction of the state. When Waller and several others were arrested in Middlesex in 1771, they were one by one taken into a room and searched for firearms, being charged "with carrying on a mutiny (meeting ?) against the authority of the land."[121]

Fourthly, the Baptist preachers were considered as false prophets and strollers, who by art and strategem intoxicated the brains of poor people until they were horribly deluded.[122] Their piety was considered a sham and hyprocricy and their loud praying as ostentatious.[123] Their gospel was looked upon as a "religious madness," a "terrible Distemper" which raged "with the greatest Fury," an "Enthusiastic and Superstitious Delusion."[124] Many of their practices were disgusting to conserv-

[119] *Ibid.* Craig says that those who are received as truly converted and are immersed "are then ascertained of eternal happiness, they can sin no more and cannot relapse being under the irresistible influence of the Holy Ghost." Dawson MSS. as above.

[120] "Address to the Anabaptists," *loc. cit.*

[121] Letter written by Waller while in Middlesex jail, August 12, 1771, given in Semple, pp. 481-3 and in *Religious Herald,* January 18, 1828. The former prints "meeting" where the latter has "mutiny."

[122] Bradley's letter to Saunders, October 6, 1770, mentioned above, contained much along this line. It is quite lengthy.

[123] *Ibid.* Bradley wrote that he could not see that loud praying was any more a true sign of godliness than loud laughing was of true pleasure. He refers to the Baptists "Bauling" so as to be heard for a half mile.

[124] Craig to Dawson, November 5, 1759, Dawson MSS. Craig also described some of these characteristics, namely, that some of them profess to

ative people. In Pittsylvania County, John Wright, the Presbyterian, "mightily opposed and slandered them to their faces" and once wrote to Samuel Harriss, "the more I consider that kind of religion among the baptists and the religion of my bible, the more fully I am convinced that it is an awful delusion."[125] Similarly, the Methodists regarded adult baptism as without scriptural foundation and Jarratt was very outspoken against the Baptists. He regarded them as deceivers and even published a pamphlet in order to cast ridicule upon them.[126] He apologizes that some of the things he says may appear to be "grovelling" to his readers "but then they will consider that I could not well rake in the dirt without stooping low."

The Baptists were represented as being sprung from the Anabaptists of Münster, whose excesses had made their name odious in Christendom.[127] Later on, when the Baptists had become socially established they wished to write their history so as to prove that they were always plain and honest folks, and "to convince the impartial inquirer that we with propriety disown any affinity with the Madmen of Münster, which has been so often attempted to be Fixed upon us by abusive pen and rancurous tongues."[128]

In addition, the assuming of the holy calling of the ministry by any layman or mechanic, simply upon his own assurance

have received the gift of the Holy Ghost by which they can tell whether or not a person has actually been converted, and their emphasis on the definiteness of the experience of conversion as a sign of true Christians. These, we have seen, were considered features of those who espoused the Great Awakening in the North.

[125] Morgan Edwards, MS. History of the Baptists of Virginia. The Regular Baptists in Loudoun County "met with much opposition from the presbyterians and mocking." *Ibid.* This is where Richard Major, former Presbyterian, was located.

[126] *An argument between an Anabaptist and a Methodist on the subject and mode of baptism.* . . . This originally appeared in manuscript form in 1781 but must have had a wide circulation as a minister in Delaware received one of the first copies. It was reprinted in 1814 and in this form is available in the Library of Congress. My information is taken from the introductory preface.

[127] *Cf.* Howison, *History of Virginia,* II, 166.

[128] MS. Circular Letter of the Roanoke Association, May, 1789 (Va. Bap. Hist. Soc.).

from God without any special training or other commission,
was regarded by many as an outrage to the sacred function and
a disgrace to religion.[129] The apostles, it was pointed out, had
gifts to perform miracles but no such evidence could be offered
by these Baptist "invaders of the function." That such as these
should claim to truly interpret and expound the Scriptures was
considered preposterous.

A fifth cause of bitterness against the sect is seen in their
violent attacks upon the Established Church. Whether true or
not, the Baptists believed that the Anglican clergy were their
arch-persecutors.[130] Consequently, it is easy to see how they
may have been rash and even indecent in their condemnation of
the Establishment. At any rate, there was a firm belief that the
Baptists were exceedingly free in abusive and scandalous in-
vective against the Church.[131] In a calm and dispassionate
manner an Anglican clergyman, who had taken pains to examine into the dispute and who laboured to secure a better
understanding between his people and the Baptists, advised the
latter: "I doubt not but you might enjoy your Religion in
Peace and Quietness, if you would forbear to concern yourselves with those who are of the Church; who are Christians
as well as yourselves."[132] He further wrote that if the reports
that had come to him were true, "worse could not be said of the
Pagans and Idolators, who sacrificed their Children to Moloch,

[129] Dixon and Hunter's *Virginia Gazette,* December 13, 1776, article by
Philoepiscopus.
[130] *Ibid.* Thom, p. 27, thinks it doubtful if as a class the clergy took an
active part in the persecutions of the Baptists. There are many individual
instances in which the parsons were the leaders but it must be remembered
that there were about ninety clergymen in the Establishment in 1776.
[131] This was the burden of a very sane and dispassionate letter from William Green, a rector, to Nathaniel Saunders, dated February 7, 1767.
It is a plea for a charitable and Christian spirit between Anglicans and
Baptists and quotes much Scripture on love, charity and judging others.
The writer addresses Saunders because he has learned that the latter is
much more moderate in his behaviour than most of his brethren and therefore hopes that he will admonish his brethren to have more of the spirit
of Christ. He was a believer in freedom of opinions among Christians of
all denominations. I learned that the writer was a parson from the *Religious
Herald,* June 5, 1873, which mentions the letter. I do not know of its existence in print. MS. Va. Bap. Hist. Soc.
[132] *Ibid.*

than has been said by some of your Society concerning the Church and its Members; The Ministers not excepted. For my part, I think Men who will behave in such a Manner, cannot reasonably expect to be treated with common decency or respect; nor can they have the least pretensions to Candour, Modesty, or good Manners: And whether they can have any Portion of the meek Spirit of Jesus is only known to God." He did not believe that the Baptists looked upon other Christians as brethren "in the Scripture sense of the word," and pleaded for a more charitable and Christian spirit between the denominations. Letters like this help us to see that there was much misunderstanding and that not all of it came from the Anglicans.

A sixth cause for the opposition to the Baptists is seen in the economic argument which took the form that the Baptist meetings called too many from their labour. Fristoe says that at times the number of males at meetings was actually counted by enemies and their lost wages totalled and this loss would be blamed on the "wretched new-lights."[133] The latter were accused of bringing people into habits of idleness and reducing them to want and distress. The poverty of most Baptist preachers, along with the lowly status of the members, no doubt added weight to this argument.[134]

Finally, we have already discussed the social identity of the Baptists, which must not be overlooked as a cause for much persecution of the denomination.[135] Surely such a movement could contain nothing that was worth respect, and its votaries must be wildly deranged.

Despite all this opposition, the Baptists flourished. Indeed, many of the charges against them were turned to good effect and only confirmed them in their convictions.[136]

---

[133] *History of the Ketocton Baptist Association*, p. 72.

[134] See Fristoe, p. 64; Thomas, *Virginian Baptist,* pp. 54-55. A MS. petition from the Church people of King William County, November 21, 1778, advances against the Baptists that their meetings are disorderly, their leaders immoral and dissipated, "whereby the poor are seduced from their labour, and our negroes from their duty." Va. State Library.

[135] See above, pp. 115-116.

[136] Thus it was pointed that the poor and lowly were the first followers of the Nazarene himself. Fristoe, p. 64.

Looking into the causes of this great popular religious movement we note, first of all, "the fact that the Baptists presented the great evangelical movement in the way which appealed most strongly to the masses."[137] No doubt the fact that their wandering preachers were without learning or patronage, poor in station, unrefined in manners and awkward in their address, made them all the more effective. They stood in sharp contrast to the clergy of the Establishment and their sermons were the burning appeals of enthusiasts. Their gospel, based on the principle of direct personal communion with God, stirred to the core masses who had hitherto been unreached by the Establishment or even by the Presbyterians with their educated ministry and somewhat elaborate creed.

The social factor, as Thom has pointed out, was strongly at work in the Baptist movement.[138] It explains much of the vindictiveness towards the Establishment which was identified with the ruling class. In it for the first time the people found an organization, a ministry, and a preaching congenial to their thinking, their emotions, their habit of speech and station in life. Their leaders were their own spokesmen and there was not a taint of exclusiveness in their organization. For the first time unlettered men were given full opportunity to think for themselves and to lead others. In an age when social classes were sharply defined, their assertiveness was at first ridiculed and then resented. The cavalier at whom Leland stamped his foot was insulted by his independence.[139] We see here a social upheaval in progress. As the masses continued to assert themselves they gained recognition, became more and more like other people, and won respect in the eyes of the world. Along

---

[137] Eckenrode, *Separation of Church and State in Virginia,* p. 38.

[138] *Op. cit.,* pp. 32-35.

[139] The incident is told in Smith, "Life and Times of the Reverend John Leland," *Baptist Quarterly,* V, 235, as follows: Leland was once interrupted in his preaching by a cavalier under the pretence of civil authority. Leland writes: "I gave a heavy stamp on the floor, and said, 'In the name of God forbear!'" After a colloquy the Colonel and his party left. When he returned home his mother asked him what the Baptist preacher had said to him. "Why he stamped at me," was the reply, "and made no more of me than if I had been a dog! I'll have no more to do with them."

with this process they threw off odd and disgusting manner-isms, paid attention to education, became more rational and conservative, and gained recruits from the well-to-do classes.[140] This process was completed with the second great Baptist re-vival in the years following 1785,[141] when they became probably the most numerous denomination in Virginia.

Politically, the times favored the Baptists. Liberty was in the air and republican principles were rapidly gaining ground. Their liberal religious views were in accord with the growing liberalism in politics. For the same reason that many of the colonists regarded British laws regulating commerce as unjusti-fiable and therefore refused to observe them, the Baptists con-sidered the laws dealing with religion as incompatible with natural rights and disregarded them.[142] Their defiance of the statutes was symbolical of the growing spirit of independence. The legal prosecution which followed placed them in the light of sufferers for the cause of religious freedom. More and more a strong element in the colonies, represented by Madison, Jef-ferson, and Henry, viewed the Established Church and its clergy as incompatible with the principles of the Revolution and became champions of the Baptists. To such as these the democratic or-ganization of the Baptist churches made a strong appeal.[143] The fact that the Baptists strongly espoused the Revolution also greatly aided their cause, although legal prosecution did not wholly cease for some years after its outbreak.[144] Likewise it

[140] The social revolution is considered in Chap. IX, where further evi-dence is presented.

[141] See Chapter VII.

[142] Eckenrode, *Separation of Church and State in Virginia*, pp. 37-38.

[143] See E. F. Humphrey, *Nationalism and Religion in America*, 1774-1789, p. 367 and Chap. XIII; Gaillard Hunt, "James Madison and Religious Lib-erty," *Am. Hist. Ass'n. Report*, 1901, Vol. I, pp. 165-171, espec. p. 167. *Writings of James Madison* (Hunt ed.), I, 19-21, for a classic statement of the influence of the Baptist persecutions upon Madison. For other relations of the Baptists with Madison and Madison's part in securing religious free-dom in Virginia, see below, Chap. VIII, espec. pp. 203-4. The whole sub-ject of the political philosophy of the religious leaders and its practical application is also considered in Chap. VIII, below.

[144] Mention has been made of the prosecution of Elijah Baker for vag-rancy in 1778. It was in the same year that the House of Delegates refused to refund to Jeremiah Walker his prison fees for the time he was in Ches-terfield jail in 1773-4. It endorsed the view that Walker's preaching was a

required another great evangelical revival before the denomination outlived the social stigma which was attached to it.[145]

Finally, the economic cause was at work. More and more the payment of taxes to the Established Church was becoming intolerable, as the Parsons' Cause revealed. The irritation was intensified by the new religious antagonism. The economic issue was closely identified with the political argument, for double taxation in the church, to which dissenters were subjected, was just as inconsistent with the revolutionary philosophy as double taxation in the state.[146]

By the time of the Revolution the Baptists formed a considerable body of ardent religionists in the colony. With the outbreak of the war they began a vigorous struggle for religious liberty, which did not end until Church and State were completely divorced. This was one of the results of the Great Awakening which will be considered elsewhere, and it was closely identified with the development of democracy in politics. In that it gave them a chance to strike for religious freedom, the war came opportunely for the Baptists, but with it came also the first decided halt in the progress of the revival. In the Association of 1776 the letters from the churches brought "mournful tidings of coldness and declension."[147] For the next few years the Associations were but thinly attended and but little was done beyond taking measures for removing the grievances in the laws. The usual number of sixty or more corresponding churches dropped to about thirty or forty. Semple says: "This declension is accounted for, by some of the let-

breach of the peace. *Jour. of the House of Delegates,* November 14 and 20, 1778.

[145] As evidence of this we have the many contemptuous references to the Baptists in the legislative petitions of the Revolutionary period, of which the one from King William County, already mentioned, is a fair sample. Jarratt's pamphlet against the Baptists, written in 1781, might also be cited as evidence.

[146] This complaint that paying for the support of a church which they could not attend was an obligation inconsistent with natural rights appears again and again in the petitions to the legislature for relief. *E.g.,* Memorial of Hanover Presbytery, October 24, 1776; Petition of the Baptists of Prince William County, June 20, 1776. See also *Journal of the House of Delegates,* October 16, 22, November 1, 9, 1776, etc. *Cf.* Humphrey, p. 377.

[147] Semple, p. 86.

ters, as arising from too much concern in political matters, being about the commencement of the revolution. Others ascribe it to their dissensions about principles, etc. Both, doubtless, had their weight."[148]

From the religious standpoint, the principal reason for the check in the Baptist movement was due to the fact that another strongly evangelical group became heir to the revival. Socially, too, it was free from exclusiveness, but being identified with the established order, at least in name, it escaped the persecutions suffered by the Baptists. We refer to the counter-awakening in the Anglican Church under the leadership of Devereux Jarratt and his Methodist allies. The year 1776 marked the first great Methodist revival in Virginia and it definitely placed that group to the fore as the continuators of the Great Awakening.

[148] *Ibid.*, p. 86. It was in 1776 that Waller and his followers, having embraced Arminian principles, withdrew from the Baptists. This shows the strength of the Methodist influence.

CHAPTER VI

DEVEREUX JARRATT AND THE METHODIST MOVEMENT

When Devereux Jarratt began his ministry in the Anglican Church in 1763, he was a thorough evangelical. Converted under the influence of the New Light Presbyterians,[1] he was a product of the Great Awakening. A firm faith in the doctrines of the Established Church, a love for its beautiful and dignified service, and a belief in the apostolic origin of its form of organization, determined him to take orders in it rather than in the Presbyterian Church.[2] The general prejudice against dissenters also caused Jarratt to believe that he would find a greater field of usefulness in the Anglican communion.

Except for his boon friend and co-labourer in the revival, Archibald McRoberts, it seems that Jarratt stood practically alone among the Anglican clergy in his evangelical views. "No one," he says, "was ever more cordially abhorred by the clergy in general" than was he.[3] Again he tells us, "I was opposed and reproached by the clergy—called an enthusiast, fanatic, visionary, dissenter, Presbyterian madman and what not. . . ."[4] This attitude towards Jarratt did not change for many years, nor did his colleagues in the ministry lend their support to his revival.[5]

Jarratt's significance lies in the fact that, like the larger Methodist movement, he represents a counter-awakening in the Established Church. From the Presbyterians he carried the influences of the Great Awakening to the Anglicans. Had that

[1] See above, p. 34. He began his ministry as rector in the parish of Bath, Dinwiddie County, in his thirty-first year.

[2] Jarratt, *Autobiography*, pp. 59, 152-153. To the end of his days Jarratt never lost confidence that the Episcopal Church would arise "and be in some measure respected according to her real worth." Also he saw in the state supported Anglican church a more permanent support than in the Presbyterian system of annual subscriptions which also "subjects the minister to the caprice of so many people. . . ." *Ibid.*, p. 59.

[3] *Autobiography*, pp. 99-100.   [4] *Ibid.*, p. 86.

[5] Jarratt to John Wesley, June 29, 1773, in *Arminian Mag.*, IX, pp. 397-398.

JOSEPH PILMOOR

Church, through its clergy, proven responsive to the evangelical tendencies which Jarratt represented, there is no reason to believe that it would not have been saved. However, it refused to accept the revival and in this attitude it showed that it had become an anomaly. Single-handed it was unable to resist successfully the rising tide of evangelicalism that was sweeping the colony, and when the Methodists drew apart into an independent organization the Anglican Church was hopelessly weakened.

Jarratt's preaching at once began to attract attention, for his parishioners had never listened to the like before. He tells us: "I endeavored to expose, in the most alarming colors, the guilt of sin, the entire depravity of human nature—the awful danger mankind are in, by nature and practice—the tremendous curse to which they are obnoxious—and their utter inability to evade the sentence of the law and the strokes of divine justice, by their own power, merit or good works."[6] To the end of his days Jarratt continued to be a believer in personal and experimental religion, and this marked him as a true son of the Great Awakening. He emphasized the fallen state of man and the necessity of spiritual regeneration through faith in God, as the first essential in the Christian experience. Hell, heaven, the judgment, the tortures and pangs of the damned, and the joys of the saved, were all real to him.[7] He preached extempore and, in common with the evangelical school, he used the direct appeal in the second person.[8] In his address he displayed the warmth and zeal that marked the revivalists everywhere,[9] and many of his appeals might well have fitted into the sermons of a New Light Presbyterian, a Separate Baptist, or a Methodist. He preached

---

[6] *Autobiography,* p. 89.

[7] *Cf.* Jarratt's *Sermons, passim,* especially the following: "The Miserable State of Man by Nature; and the Way of Recovery by Faith in Jesus Christ"; "The Sum of the Gospel"; "On the Mediation of Christ Jesus"; "The Dominion of Christ"; "Christ, the Redeemer"; "On Happiness; or the truly happy man described"; "The Christian's Conflict and Triumphant Exit."

[8] *Sermons,* I, Preface, p. viii, and *passim.*

[9] John Williams, a leading Separate Baptist, records hearing Jarratt preach in 1771 and describes his manner as warm and zealous. MS. Diary of John Williams (Va. Bap. Hist. Soc.).

against all the vices and for all sinners. None escaped his warnings and petitions to mend their ways. Upon all he called to repent and be saved.

Under Jarratt's vigorous preaching people were soon awakened and a real religious concern developed among his parishioners. As the interest in religious things deepened, Jarratt began to hold week-day prayer meetings in private houses, which, he remarks, "was a great novelty in a minister of the church."[10] These meetings not only were of spiritual benefit, but also of social significance. It was here, Jarratt tells us, the "poorer sort, who at first may be shy in speaking, soon wore off their shyness, and spoke as freely as others."[11] In these prayer services we see in actual operation the pushing upward of the lower classes to a plane of equality with their former superiors. It was the Great Awakening with its evangelical doctrines which first brought them this opportunity to assert themselves, thus contributing to the social revolution.[12]

The religious concern created among the people of Bath could not be restricted by the bounds of a single parish. The news of the strange work attracted people to come from many miles to see and hear for themselves. Says Jarratt: "My churches were now crowded, from time to time with a concourse of strangers, both far and near." Some of these were awakened by the vigorous sermons they heard and in turn excited others to come so that "convictions and conversions increased and spread into counties still more remote."[13] One of Jarratt's churches (Butterwood) soon became too small to accommodate half the congregation and it had to be enlarged from time to time.

Associated with Jarratt in this work of reviving the Church was Archibald McRoberts, a neighboring rector. Concerning the latter, William Watters, one of the earliest Methodist itinerants, wrote: "He was the first minister of the Church of Eng-

---

[10] *Autobiography,* p. 91.   [11] *Ibid.,* p. 92.
[12] For further discussion see below, Chap. XI.
[13] *Autobiography,* p. 94.

land that ever I heard preach christian experience."[14] Jarratt would have been only too glad to avail himself of the services of others like McRoberts, had they been at hand, and we do not wonder that he encouraged the Methodists when their separation from the Establishment seemed remote.

Jarratt and McRoberts worked together in spreading the gospel—by travelling, by exchanging pulpits, and by assisting one another in many ways. By 1772 the revival had "extended itself in some places for fifty or sixty miles around."[15] Jarratt was frequently called upon to travel many miles in order to meet his preaching engagements. It often became necessary to hold open-air meetings either because the congregations were too large for the churches or because it was convenient sometimes to appoint a meeting at a place where there was no church. As the work spread Jarratt formed societies out of the new converts and gradually the bounds of his circuit widened until it "extended to a circle of five or six hundred miles—east, west, north and south."[16]

In the counties of Sussex and Brunswick, the Methodist revival was just beginning and, from the year 1773 on, Jarratt's revival was merged into this wider movement. Wesley's itinerants made Jarratt's work their own and carried the flame that he had kindled far and wide.[17] It was in 1773 that the first meeting between Jarratt and the Methodist pioneer, Robert Williams, took place in Petersburg, and the following year the first Methodist circuit in Virginia was organized. Jarratt saw

[14] William Watters, *A Short Account of the Christian Experience and Ministerial Labours of William Watters*, p. 58. Hereafter we shall refer to this title as Watters' *Life*.

[15] Jarratt, *Brief Narrative of the Revival of Religion in Virginia. In a letter to a friend*, September 10, 1776. The letter is to Thomas Rankin and contains other communications to and from various persons describing the work. This is our most valuable source on the revival of 1776. It is incorporated in Asbury's *Journal*, Vol. I (Philadelphia, 1792), pp. 157-170, and is published separately in several editions. Our references are to the Asbury *Journal* unless otherwise indicated. See also Jesse Lee, *A Short History of the Methodists*, p. 43. Lee was also a participant in the revival and we are told that his parents were awakened under the preaching of Jarratt.

[16] *Autobiography*, p. 96.   [17] Jesse Lee, *History*, p. 43.

in the Methodists an instrument for reviving religion in the Church of his faith, as well as for combating the rising tide of Baptists, who were gaining numerous adherents in places where he had been accustomed to preach, and whom he regarded as a menace to the cause of the true religion. "I did what I could to prevent this evil," he writes, "but it was too much for any one man to do."[18] In another connection we have seen that later he even wrote a pamphlet in answer to their tenets in the form of a dialogue, but the Baptists had come to stay.[19]

For many years Jarratt worked hand in hand with the Methodist itinerants and we shall be meeting him time and again. Before launching into that larger movement, however, it seems well to call attention in a special way to the increased demands upon Jarratt's services which arose from the spread of that revival. The field of his labours became greatly enlarged and carried him into more than a score of counties in North Carolina and Virginia. He mentions having visited Halifax, Warren, Franklin and Granville counties in North Carolina; while in Virginia his itineracy embraced Brunswick, Greensville, and Southampton, on the south; Lunenberg, Mecklenburg, Charlotte, Prince Edward, Nottoway and Amelia, on the west; Cumberland, Powhatan, Chesterfield, Henrico, Hanover, Caroline, King and Queen, and King William, on the north; New Kent, James City, Charles City, Surry and Sussex, on the east.[20] In all, he visited twenty-nine counties in the two states.

In 1779 Jarratt's labours were increased by the loss of McRoberts, who left the Establishment to set up an Independent Church and later to join the Presbyterians.[21] McRoberts and Jarratt remained on good terms, but the former had no use for the Methodists whom he branded "a designing people, void of

---

[18] *Autobiography*, p. 107.

[19] See above, p. 131 and note. Also Asbury, *Journal*, May 28, 1780.

[20] *Autobiography*, p. 97. Professor Wm. E. Dodd commented to me that these were the counties where the Revolution was all but unanimously supported.

[21] *Ibid.*, p. 101; William Meade, *Old Churches, Ministers and Families of Virginia*, I, 448-9.

the generous and catholic spirit of the gospel," and "entirely under the influence of the Pope John."[22] He thought that but little good could come from their illiterate preachers who were labouring under a misguided zeal.

During these years Jarratt preached an average of five sermons a week and administered the sacrament to many hundreds of communicants.[23] Although involved in many duties outside of his parish, he never neglected his own people and faithfully attended the three churches in Bath. That he seldom failed to keep his appointment is revealed in the fact that of two hundred and seventy sermons in one year of which we have record, one hundred and fifty were delivered in his own parish.[24]

The phenomenal spread of Jarratt's revival after 1773 was due to the fact that it really became a part of the great Methodist awakening. In fact, it lost its identity and Jarratt merely became a colleague, although an invaluable one, of the Wesleyan itinerants. Methodism did not become a vital religious force in Virginia until the arrival of the pioneer Robert Williams, early in 1772. The latter seems to have been the first preacher of that denomination to visit the colony.[25] Jarratt calls him "a plain, simple hearted, pious man,"[26] and "an artless, indefatigable preacher of the gospel."[27] Arriving at Norfolk, he began his ministry in typical Methodist fashion by taking his stand on the Court House steps, and, after singing a hymn and kneeling in prayer, he preached to an astonished and, we are told, somewhat disorderly crowd who had never before seen nor heard the like.[28] So unaccustomed were the people to evangelical preaching that the use of such words as "hell," "devil," and

---

[22] McRoberts to Jarratt, July 13, 1780, in Jarratt, *Autobiography*, p. 149.
[23] *Autobiography*, pp. 97-98; "Testimony of Devereux Jarratt in favor of Evangelical Doctrines," *Evangelical and Literary Magazine*, IV, 178.
[24] *Autobiography*, pp. 97-98.
[25] Jesse Lee, *Life of John Lee*, p. 12; Jarratt, *Autobiography*, p. 107. Sketch of Williams in M. H. Moore, *Pioneers of Methodism in North Carolina and Virginia*, pp. 47-51. See also W. W. Bennett, *Memorials of Methodism in Virginia*, pp. 47 ff.
[26] *Autobiography*, p. 107.   [27] *Narrative*, p. 159.
[28] Jesse Lee, *History*, p. 40; Bennett, *op. cit.*, p. 51; Moore, *op. cit.*, p. 48.

"damned," in a sermon was misconstrued as swearing. Such was the commencement of a revival that was to reap astonishing fruits within a few years.

During the first year of his ministry Williams laboured chiefly in the vicinity of Norfolk and Portsmouth, where, as a result, Methodism was permanently planted.[29] Two other itinerants soon came to help in the work. In the summer of 1772 Joseph Pilmoor travelled through the southeastern counties, preaching at Norfolk, Portsmouth and other places,[30] while in the fall the young William Watters accompanied Williams on a journey from Baltimore through the eastern counties to Norfolk.[31]

Early in 1773 Williams was invited to Petersburg, where some had caught the spirit of the awakening.[32] After preaching in the town for some weeks, he itinerated in the surrounding country where an extensive revival soon broke out. According to Jesse Lee, Williams was the first Methodist preacher to come into that part of the colony.[33] It was here that the meeting with Jarratt took place in 1773, and he and McRoberts gave the Methodists a hearty welcome to their parishes.[34]

No doubt Williams caught a new inspiration from his meeting with Jarratt and he departed from him to spend the rest of the year in preaching and gathering members in the counties south of Petersburg. He carried the gospel into the northern part of North Carolina.[35] In 1774 he formed the first circuit in Virginia. This was the Brunswick circuit, which extended from Petersburg to beyond the Roanoke in North Carolina, embracing the area in which Jarratt's revival was most pronounced.[36] We may well call this region the cradle of Methodism in the South.

[29] Bennett, pp. 51-52.
[30] *Ibid.*, p. 53; Watters, *Life*, p. 2.   [31] Watters, pp. 26-28.
[32] Bennett, pp. 56-58, letter of Gressett Davis to John Wesley, July 11, 1780.   [33] *History*, pp. 42-43.
[34] Jarratt, *Narrative, loc. cit.*, p. 159; Watters, *Life*, p. 34.
[35] Jesse Lee, *History*, p. 43; W. L. Grissom, *History of Methodism in North Carolina*, I, p. 42.
[36] Jesse Lee, *History*, p. 51.

The result of Williams' labour is recorded in the Minutes of the first Methodist Conference in America, which met at Philadelphia July 14, 1773, in which Virginia is reported as having 100 members out of a total of 1160 for the colonies.[37] Of the ten preachers assigned by the first Conference, two went to Virginia—Richard Wright, to Norfolk, and Robert Williams, to Petersburg. The next year 218 members were reported to the Conference from the Brunswick circuit, while through the faithful efforts of Wright seventy-three were reported from Norfolk.[38]

Williams, the pioneer, lived just long enough to witness the fruition of his labours in the outbreak of the great revival of 1775-6 and he carried the news of it to Asbury in April, 1775, The latter records in his *Journal:* "I met with Brother Williams from Virginia, who gave me a great account of the work of God in those parts—five or six hundred souls justified by faith, and five or six circuits formed."[39] He soon was stationed at Norfolk himself, but he found this a barren field as compared with the reports that reached him from Brunswick.[40]

Williams died on September 26, 1775. The first of the Methodist itinerants to preach a sermon in Virginia, he was also the first to be called from the field. In his brief ministry he had planted Methodism permanently in Virginia. His simple and sincere devotion and earnest evangelical preaching had stirred many.[41] To Williams also belongs the credit of starting the

[37] Minutes, 1773, in *Minutes of the Methodist Conferences annually held in America from 1773 to 1794 inclusive.* Philadelphia, 1795; Lee, *History,* p. 9.

[38] Minutes, 1774. However, in 1775, Asbury found "about thirty persons in society" at Norfolk "after their manner but they had no regular class meetings." *Journal,* May 29, 1775. But he preached to many more. Norfolk was not included in Brunswick circuit.

[39] Asbury, *Journal,* April 28, 1775. Asbury is wrong as to the number of circuits, however. See below, p. 156.

[40] See Asbury, *Journal,* May 29, 1775 ff., especially June 14, and November 6, 1775.

[41] See Lee, *History,* p. 37. We are told that it was Williams' effective preaching that won the prominent Baptist, John Waller, over to the Arminian views. See above, Chap. V, note 148, and Taylor, *Virginia Baptist Ministers,* I, 82.

practice of printing and circulating books and tracts,[42] thus making the Methodist press a factor in the expansion of the revival. The distribution of Wesley's pamphlets no doubt opened the way in many places for the Methodist preachers. The Conference, however, soon took over this work as a denominational enterprise and before the end of the century it had grown into the Methodist Book Concern.[43] Williams also organized the first circuit in Virginia, although the first *society* seems to have been formed by Pilmoor in the summer of 1772.[44] There is no account of a society organized by Williams before 1774.[45]

With the beginning of Williams' revival, Jarratt's connection with the Methodists became more intimate. It must be remembered that Methodism began as a revival within the Anglican Church in America, as well as in England. Its adherents frankly professed an attachment to the Established Church, which Wesley himself asserted, and, as simple laymen, its ministers refrained from administering the sacraments, leaving this function to the parish ministers.[46] Because of this, Jarratt became an indispensable ally. He was assured that the Methodists had come "to build up and not to divide the church," and that their preachers insisted that "all who left the Church left the Methodists."[47] Nevertheless, the Methodists were evangelical and represented a spirit quite contrary to that which prevailed in the Establishment, while in their constituency they were practically a popular church.[48] For these reasons they made impor-

[42] Lee, *History,* pp. 48-49; Bennett, p. 70. See below, pp. 165-166.

[43] See Minutes, 1773, Rules 4 and 5; Lee, *History,* p. 129; F. A. Archibald, *Methodism and Literature,* pp. 20-21.

[44] Pilmoor's "Journal" in J. P. Lockwood, *The Western Pioneers or Memorials of the Lives and Labours of the Reverend Richard Boardman and the Reverend Joseph Pilmoor,* pp. 151-2, and in Grissom, *op. cit.,* pp. 33-34.

[45] Lee, *History,* p. 51.

[46] Hawks, *Ecclesiastical Contributions, Virginia,* p. 133; J. S. Anderson, *History of the Church of England in the Colonies,* III, p. 261; Jarratt, *Autobiography,* p. 108.

[47] Jarratt, *op. cit.,* p. 108.

[48] See Bassett, "Development of the Popular Churches after the Revolution," *Proc. Mass. Hist. Soc.,* Vol. XLVIII, pp. 254-268.

tant contributions to the social upheaval in Virginia and in bringing about that change in religious conceptions which, under the impetus of repeated revivals, was transforming the colony.[49]

That a strong bond of sympathy between Jarratt and Wesley's itinerants should develop, was inevitable. Were not these men instruments of God, come to preserve the unity of the Church and to call sinners to repentance? Not only did Jarratt encourage folks to join the Methodists, but he even aided the latter in forming societies.[50] His home was always open to the itinerants as they came round the circuit and meetings were regularly held in the rector's barn, which Watters tells us was "well fitted up with seats and a pulpit. . . ."[51] These ties of friendship and coöperation were not broken until the Methodists severed their connection with the Establishment and formed themselves into an independent Church.[52]

Four preachers were assigned to Virginia by the Conference of 1774, one to Norfolk and three to the Brunswick circuit. The circuit was ridden on the six weeks plan, the itinerants traveling at intervals of two weeks. In the latter part of 1774, reports of more than ordinary outbursts of religion in most parts of the circuit began to spread.[53] These continued current through the winter and spring of 1774-5 and, in April of the latter year,

---

[49] Cf. Eckenrode, Separation of Church and State in Virginia, p. 34. As we shall see (Chap. VIII), the Methodists did not play the part in politics which the Baptists and Presbyterians did.

[50] Jarratt, Autobiography, p. 110; J. W. Smith, "Devereux Jarratt and the beginnings of Methodism in Virginia," J. P. Branch Hist. Papers, I, pp. 16-17.

[51] Watters, Life, p. 58; Jarratt, Autobiography, pp. 108-109; also Philip Gatch, Memoirs (compiled by John McLean), p. 53, who says, "He fitted up his barn for our accommodation, and it became a regular preaching place, where quarterly meetings were occasionally held. The hospitalities of his home were generously conferred upon us, while he was truly a nursing father to Methodist preachers."

[52] Jesse Lee says that the letters published in the form of Jarratt's Autobiography "shew that he was more severe in his spirit against the Methodists than they who knew him ever thought him to be." Lee does not think that Jarratt would have consented to the publication by Coleman of the letters from Jarratt. History, pp. 81-82, note.

[53] Jesse Lee, History, p. 51.

Asbury received the news from Williams that five or six hundred had already been awakened.[54]

In the summer of 1775, Thomas Rankin, accompanied by Jarratt, made a tour through the southern part of Virginia and into North Carolina.[55] In both colonies the chapels overflowed with the large congregations and outdoor meetings had to be arranged. The following entry in Rankin's *Journal* when he was in North Carolina in July 1775, is typical of the revival scenes: "On Tuesday, 30, was our Quarterly Meeting. I scarce ever remember such a season. No chapel or preaching place in Virginia would have contained one third of the congregation."[56] Everywhere on the circuit both blacks and whites were eager for the gospel and Rankin tells us that he was "preached" almost to the point of exhaustion. The same must have been true of Jarratt, also.

The outstanding leader of the revival in 1775, however, was neither Rankin nor Jarratt, but George Shadford, who was assigned to the Brunswick circuit by the Conference of 1775 and entered upon his work the same summer. Shadford is said to have been the foremost revivalist of his day and, therefore, was a most effective preacher.[57] When he came to Virginia he says he was depressed in spirit, but before long he became the chief instrument in this great awakening of Methodism. When he began to preach he was amazed at the results, for seldom was a meeting held which did not produce its converts. Among the first of the latter was a dancing master who had a large and profitable school which he now gave up. Joining the Methodists, he became a school teacher.[58]

Under Shadford's preaching the societies were kindled with a new ardor. The revival gained fresh momentum until the whole circuit felt its influence.[59] Shadford's services were, how-

---

[54] See above, p. 145, and note 39.

[55] Rankin's *Journal* in Grissom, *op. cit.*, p. 43. Rankin's *Autobiography* is found in Thomas Jackson, *Lives of Early Methodist Preachers,* Vol. III.

[56] *Loc. cit.,* p. 44.

[57] Moore, *Pioneers of Methodism in North Carolina and Virginia,* p. 56. Sketch of Shadford covers pp. 56-70. Shadford's *Autobiography* is in Jackson, *op. cit.,* III, 173-219.

[58] Shadford's *Autobiography, op. cit.,* pp. 207-208.

[59] Moore, *op. cit.,* p. 65.

ever, cut short by the approach of the Revolution, for he was one of those conscientious Englishmen who could not honestly renounce allegiance to his king. There was no alternative but to return to England, where he continued in the pulpit until 1791.[60] Unquestionably American Methodism suffered a great loss by Shadford's decision. We wish he had told us more about his work in Virginia in 1775, but upon this part of his career his autobiography is most meagre. Nevertheless, we catch a passing glimpse of the figure of this great revivalist as he moved rapidly from one society to another, arousing the indifferent and firing the zeal of the Christians until he himself "could scarcely believe them when they told him."[61] The results of his work and of Rankin's and Jarratt's are evident in the fact that about six hundred members were added to the societies in the Brunswick circuit during 1775. In no place, says Jesse Lee, was the revival equal to the one in Brunswick where Shadford was travelling.[62]

The revival reached its culmination in the winter and spring of 1776.[63] It started almost simultaneously at three different points on the circuit, two, significantly enough, in Mr. Jarratt's parish of Bath, in Dinwiddie County, and the other in Amelia, a region, according to Jarratt, that had hitherto been noted for indifference to matters of religion.[64] Eye-witnesses, as Jarratt and Jesse Lee, testify as to the extent and intensity of the revival of 1776. The former remarks that it was "as great as perhaps ever was known, in country places in so short a time," while Lee, who was present at many of the meetings calls it "the greatest revival of religion I have ever seen."[65]

[60] *Ibid.*, p. 68.

[61] Shadford's *Autobiography, op. cit.*, pp. 207-208.

[62] Jesse Lee, *History*, p. 53. See also Rankin to Wesley (1778) in Jarratt's *Narrative*. This letter dated later than Jarratt's *Narrative* is appended to it both in Asbury and the 1779 edition of the *Narrative*. Asbury I, 171 ff.

[63] Jarratt's *Narrative* deals especially with the revival in 1776. See also Lee, *History*, pp. 54 ff. and his *Memoirs* by Minton Thrift. Also L. M. Lee, *Life and Times of Jesse Lee.*

[64] *Narrative* in Asbury, I, 159-160.

[65] *Ibid.* Thrift, *Memoirs of Jesse Lee*, p. 16. See also A. M. Courtenay, "The Reverend Devereux Jarratt" in *Meth. Rev.* (So.), Vol. XLVII, pp. 336-349, at p. 344.

Many details have come to us of various meetings from the hands of those who were participants. A record of them would involve us in useless repetition, as everywhere the revival scenes were similar. Meetings were held for hours during the day and sometimes lasted through most of the night.[66] All accounts, of course, dwell on the number of converts—ten, fifteen, or even twenty sometimes in a single day.[67] People who had been indifferent for years were now awakened. They were of all ages, from all classes, including many blacks. Everywhere there seemed to be an eagerness to hear the word preached, and people were sometimes converted in their class meetings, even though no preacher was present. One of Jarratt's neighbors wrote that he had been exhorting for seven years "but very few would hear. Now . . . there are few that will not hear."[68] There were, undoubtedly, many who, like Jesse Lee, were "glad to go to meeting by night or by day," and who were willing to travel many miles on foot to hear the gospel preached.[69] Wherever there was exhorting or preaching, it seems that people were seized with the revival spirit and there were not enough ministers to take care of the work.

The final phase of the revival began with a fresh outburst which took place at a quarterly meeting, held on May 2, 1776, at Boisseau's Chapel, in Dinwiddie County, where Jarratt preached. The accounts of both Jarratt and Lee agree as to the extensive influence which emanated from this meeting.[70] Its spirit was carried far and wide by those who went home. Dinwiddie, Amelia, Brunswick, Sussex, Prince George, Lunenburg, and Mecklenburg counties all shared in this epoch of the awakening, which continued unabated throughout the summer under

[66] Thus Jarratt tells of a meeting held among his neighbors which continued "all night and till two hours after sunrise." To McRoberts, May 3, 1776, in *Narrative*.

[67] Jarratt mentions thirty converts in two days among his parishioners "besides others, of other parishes" and again of forty within eight days to his knowledge. A neighboring preacher, Saunders, says it was common on Sundays for ten, fifteen or twenty to find the Lord. See Jarratt's *Narrative*.

[68] Thomas Saunders' account, July 29, 1776, in Jarratt's *Narrative*.

[69] Thrift, *Memoirs of Jesse Lee*, p. 16.

[70] Jarratt's *Narrative*, p. 161, and Lee, *History*, pp. 55-56.

the preaching of Thomas Rankin, who delivered his first sermon at Boisseau's Chapel on the last day of June.[71] Here, and at other places, he preached to hundreds at a time with great effect. Doors and windows were left open so that the crowds without could hear, while often the emotions of the audience drowned the voices of the preachers and compelled them to stop.[72]

Again Rankin carried the revival into North Carolina, and, returning to Virginia, held another quarterly meeting at Mabury's (often written Mabry's) dwelling house in Brunswick, July 30-31, 1776, where the same scenes were repeated.[73] Even the critical situation developed by the war did not interrupt the work for some months. Indeed, if we may believe Jarratt, the interest in the revival was so intense that the disputes between England and the colonies for a while "seemed now in most companies to be forgot."[74] Before the work had spent itself, it was found that 1,800 had been added to the Methodist societies in the course of a single year,[75] while the number of circuits had increased to six.[76]

No account of the revival of 1775-6 could be complete without special mention of the rôle of Devereux Jarratt. Shadford, to be sure, was the outstanding leader in 1775 and Rankin in 1776, but Jarratt was one of those who worked quietly but zealously and effectively all the time. Not dependent upon any Conference to send him into the field as the Methodists were, his services were continuous. In order that his people might have a share in the work of the Methodists and join their societies, if they chose, Jarratt requested that his parish be included in the Brunswick circuit. Many societies were formed among his parishioners and in a few months he "saw more fruit of his labours than he had done for many years."[77] On May 11, 1776,

[71] T. Rankin to Wesley (1778), in Asbury's *Journal*, I, 173.
[72] *Ibid.*, and Lee, *History*, p. 57.
[73] Letter to Wesley, *loc. cit.*, p. 175.
[74] Jarratt's *Narrative*, p. 162.
[75] Rankin to Wesley, *loc. cit.*, p. 172; Lee, *History*, p. 59. Rankin says that when Shadford came to Virginia there were 2,664 in society to which 1,800 were added in a single year.
[76] Brunswick, Fairfax, Hanover, Pittsylvania, Amelia and Sussex. See below, p. 156.
[77] Rankin to Wesley, *loc. cit.*, p. 171.

Jarratt himself wrote, "Sometimes fifteen find the Lord at one meeting." As many as three score in and near his parish had been awakened since the recent quarterly meeting at Boisseau's Chapel, where he had preached on May 2.[78] His part in the work was thus an active one, and he stands with Williams, Shadford and Rankin as a promoter of the revival. He frequently preached, met the classes, held love-feasts and administered the sacraments.[79] Jesse Lee says that he was most useful in the revival, and his heart was closely united to the Methodists in doctrine and discipline.[80]

There was one feature of the revival that Jarratt did not exactly like and that was its emotional element. All of the conditions conducive to the various revival phenomena were present in the movement we have just been studying. There were the large, closely packed crowds of men and women, mostly from the uncultured and illiterate classes and including many Negroes, who were particularly susceptible to the emotional appeal.[81] There were the protracted meetings, sometimes extending in intervals over several days, as the quarterly meetings. There were frequent night meetings which added color to the environment and heightened the effects of the emotional element. There were also the skilful exhorters who placed sustained emphasis on the physical torments of hell and the joys of heaven. Lastly, there were the familiar hymns and spiritual songs born in the revival, written by the Wesleys to express all that Methodism stood for, which were adapted to every emotion of the soul, and which set the converted on fire with enthusiasm and shot pungent darts of fear through the hearts of the unsaved.

Under such conditions it was natural that the physical and sensory reflexes should appear in a very high degree and the

---

[78] Rankin to Wesley, p. 172. See also Jarratt to McRoberts, May 2, May 3, and May 7, 1776, in Jarratt's *Narrative*.

[79] Lee, *History*, p. 54. As the Methodists did not yet administer the sacraments and since so few of the Anglican clergy were in accord with them the burden of this work naturally fell upon Jarratt.

[80] *Ibid.;* also Rankin to Wesley, *loc. cit.*, p. 171.

[81] Davenport, *Primitive Traits in Religious Revivals,* Chaps. II, V, and *passim;* "The Great Awakening," *Christian Review,* IX, pp. 389 ff. Rankin tells us that sometimes hundreds of Negroes were among his congregations.

various accounts are unanimous as to the presence of these manifestations. Lee tells us: "I have been at meetings where the whole congregation would be bathed in tears; and sometimes their cries would be so loud that the preacher's voice could not be heard. Some would be seized with a trembling, and in a few moments drop on the floor as if they were dead; while others were embracing each other with streaming eyes, and all were lost in wonder, love and praise."[82] A local preacher in Sussex wrote to Jarratt under date of July 29, 1776: "It is common with us for men and women to fall down as dead under an exhortation; but many more under prayer: perhaps twenty at a time. And some of them have fallen to the earth, have shown the same distress, wringing their hands, smiting their breasts, and begging all to pray for them."[83]

The above descriptions are typical of the revival scenes everywhere. They frequently occurred, even under Jarratt's preaching, much to his distress. He was very reluctant to approve of these physical and sensory manifestations, for to him they seemed to be only useless confusion more in keeping with a "drunken rabble" than a congregation of worshippers. He writes: "In some meetings there has not been that decency and order observed which I could have wished. Some of our assemblies resembled the congregation of Jews at laying the foundation of the second temple in the days of Ezra—some wept for grief; others shouted for joy, so that it was hard to distinguish one from the other. So it was here: the mourning and distress was so blended with the voice of joy and gladness that it was hard to distinguish the one from the other, till the voice of joy prevailed: the people shouting with a great shout, so that it might be heard afar off."[84]

Jarratt did not doubt the genuineness of the work of grace, but he wished it might go on without the loud outcries, the tremblings, the fallings and convulsions, the babel of confusion. He was somewhat reconciled to these phenomena, however, by reading a defence of them by President Edwards, who observed

---

[82] Thrift, *Memoirs of Jesse Lee*, p. 16.
[83] In Jarratt's *Narrative, loc. cit.*, p. 165.
[84] *Narrative*, especially his letters to McRoberts, May 2 and 7, 1776.

that the work was always deepest and greatest whenever they were most present.[85] Jarratt himself was compelled to admit that as the emotional element abated "the work of conviction and conversion abated too."[86] In his perplexity he hardly knew what course to pursue, seeing that it took much wisdom "to allay the wild, and not damp the sacred fire." Not wishing to check the revival by openly inveighing against the irregularities, he contented himself with advising the preachers in private, and he, himself, took all the pains he could to keep them within the bounds of propriety "that our good might not be evil spoken of."[87] In his attitude towards Methodist "enthusiasm," Jarratt displayed the Anglican's sense of decorum.

We have already offered a brief explanation of the psychological causes of the revival phenomena, and need only repeat here that, in counting converts, too often physical emotions arising not from conviction and remorse for sins, but wholly from the fear of the certainty of punishment, despair of escape from divine wrath, or even joy and exultation at the prospect of final deliverance, were mistaken for an essential change of heart.[88] We know, too, that in revivals of religion, people, and even the preachers, often crave for the appearance of the "exercises," mistaking them for indisputable marks of true conversion. In many cases the result has been that after the excitement has passed away, a state of apathy succeeds and the supposed convert relapses into his sinful ways, even doubting the efficacy of salvation.[89] We are also reminded that through contagion

---

[85] *Narrative*, p. 164.

[86] *Ibid.*, p. 165; *cf.* p. 168. Jesse Lee makes a similar statement. *History*, p. 53.

[87] *Narrative*, p. 168.

[88] *Cf.* "The Great Awakening," *Christian Review*, IX, 387 and Davenport, Chap. XI.

[89] See *Evangelical and Literary Magazine*, V, 306 ff.; Davenport, pp. 247 ff.; *Christian Review*, IX, 390 ff. On September 10, 1776, Jarratt wrote that "many, since their first joy abated have given way to doubts and fears, have had their confidence in God much shaken and have got into much heaviness. Several have passed through this and are now confirmed in the ways of God. Others are in it still; and chiefly those over whom Satan had gained an advantage, by hurrying them into irregular warmth, or into expressions not well guarded. I have seen some of these in great distress, and just ready to cast away hope." *Narrative*, p. 169.

and the "law of spread" people who are utterly indifferent to religious sensibilities are sometimes swept into the vortex of emotion. Thus Jarratt tells us that careless people of the "politer sort" who went to the meetings out of curiosity, "fell down on their knees, and cried for mercy among the rest."[90] Such examples are plentiful in the history of religious awakenings.

Whatever objections one may have to revivals of religion, their importance in the development of the Christian church must be admitted.[91] If there are always apostates, there are always those whose lives are permanently changed for the better. So it was in the Methodist revival of 1776. It is difficult to estimate results in any definite way, but the increase in membership and in the number of circuits during this period, as shown in the Conference Minutes, proves to us that many were brought into the societies and that religion began to flourish in new regions. Brunswick circuit, the only one in Virginia at the beginning of the revival, reported 218 members to the Conference held in May, 1774. A year later the number had increased to 800 and before the next Conference met, in May, 1776, 811 more had been gathered in by the revival, bringing the total for that circuit to 1,611.[92]

The total number of Methodists claimed for Virginia in 1775 was 955 as against 291 for the preceding year.[93] In 1776 the number had increased to 2,456, not including 683 members for Carolina, which was reported separately in this year. This was half the total membership in America, and considerably more if North Carolina be included. Since the revival had not spent its force when the Conference met in May, 1776, we note that the membership a year later was reported at 3,449, not

[90] Jarratt to McRoberts, May 2, 1776, in *Narrative*.

[91] See J. E. McCulloch, "The Place of Revivals in American History," *Meth. Rev.* (So.), Vol. LI, pp. 681 ff.; Peter G. Mode, "Revivalism as a Phase of Frontier Life," *Jour. of Religion*, July, 1921, pp. 337-354. Lee, *History*, pp. 53, 56, says that some things were done in the revival which might be called imprudent and that in some meetings there was not the order which could have been wished.

[92] Conference Minutes, 1774, 1775, 1776.

[93] Some of these were included in Carolina.

including North Carolina.[94] This increase took place despite the shadow of suspicion which the war had cast over the denomination. In all other parts of America the societies remained stationary.[95]

The increase in the number of circuits in Virginia also shows the expansion of Methodism through the revival. In 1775 the Brunswick circuit embraced fourteen counties in Virginia, and what were known as Halifax and Bute counties in North Carolina.[96] A new circuit, Fairfax, appears in the Minutes of 1775 with thirty members. This embraced the country along the Potomac from Dumfries in Prince William county to Leesburg and possibly as far west as the Blue Ridge.[97] A hundred members were added to this circuit before the next Conference.[98]

Hanover and Pittsylvania, with 270 and 100 members respectively, appear on the Minutes of 1776, bringing the total number of circuits to four. Hanover covered a large territory, stretching originally over parts of six counties on both sides of the James River. It was soon found necessary to alter it so as to include only the territory north of the river.[99] It will be remembered that this was a field in which the Separate Baptists had done fruitful work and had "rolled back the wave of persecution."[100] In addition, Jarratt and McRoberts had preached in those parts with good effect, and when Philip Gatch was sent there in 1776, he found no accommodations for the large crowds and had to preach to them out of doors.[101] It was "like a new world of grace" to him.

During the last year of the revival, 1776, two more circuits, Amelia and Sussex, were formed, being cut off from Bruns-

[94] Minutes, 1777. North Carolina reports 930. Brunswick circuit reports 1,360 but had been divided by this time. The members were distributed: Brunswick 1,360; Fairfax 330; Hanover 262; Pittsylvania 150; Amelia 620; Sussex 727. The Methodists were pretty careful not to carry any delinquent members. See below, pp. 163-4, on their local organization.

[95] The total for America at this time was 6,968.

[96] Moore, *Pioneers of Methodism in North Carolina and Virginia,* p. 78.

[97] Bennett, *op. cit.,* p. 74.   [98] Minutes, 1776.

[99] Gatch, *Memoirs,* pp. 50, 55, 56. Lee, *History,* p. 51. Gatch was assigned to the Hanover circuit in 1776. In 1778 the circuit was again divided into two four-weeks circuits, the northern section taking the name Fluvanna. *Cf.* Bennett, pp. 95, 98.

[100] Gatch, p. 51.   [101] *Ibid.*

wick. They appear on the Minutes of May, 1777, with 620 and 727 members respectively. During the revival, therefore, the number of circuits in Virginia grew from one to six. In the same period the number of ministers assigned to Virginia steadily increased from two in 1773 to four in 1774, and six, or nearly one-third of the total number in America, in 1775. In 1776 nine preachers were sent into the colony.[102]

The revival of 1775-1776 has been designated as the greatest awakening in the history of American Methodism. To the men of the time who have left us accounts of it, as Jesse Lee, Jarratt, Thomas Rankin, and Francis Asbury, it appeared most phenomenal in its results. Lee, who wrote his history of the Methodists in 1810, says that his pen "cannot describe the one half of what I saw, heard and felt. I might write a volume on this subject and then leave the greater part untold."[103] According to the same writer, the awakening affected an area of from four to five hundred square miles, including Dinwiddie, Amelia, Sussex, Brunswick, Prince George, Lunenburg and Mecklenburg counties. Jarratt says that seven or eight of the sixty-two counties were vitally touched and that it was confined in them to the circuits regularly visited by the preachers.[104] Nevertheless, he was convinced of the permanency of the work and, in September, 1776, when it had abated, wrote that up to that time he had not heard of one apostate.[105] Although the zeal of many had flagged and others were in a state of doubt, still many profligates had been "effectually and lastingly changed into pious, uniform christians." People of all ranks had been reached and in many regions a change had been wrought which was to leave a permanent impress upon the religious life of the Old Dominion.

Sporadic revivals continued to occur in Brunswick, Sussex and Amelia circuits during 1777, but as the war progressed and

[102] Minutes for the years in question.

[103] *History*, p. 59.

[104] *Narrative*, pp. 169-170 (probably the counties mentioned by Lee). Rankin says that the revival spread through fourteen counties in Virginia besides Bute and Halifax counties in North Carolina. Letter to Wesley, *loc. cit.*, p. 172. This corresponded with Brunswick circuit.

[105] *Narrative*, p. 170.

was finally carried to the South, the Methodists laboured under increasing disadvantages.[106] This was due to several reasons. In the first place, the denomination was still a part of the Anglican Church and, therefore, identified with the Tory cause. Then, again, Wesley himself firmly espoused the cause of England and was outspoken in supporting the power of Parliament to tax the colonists and in denying to the latter any rights under the laws of nature, while at the same time they claimed those of British born subjects.[107] All British subjects, he held, cede to the King and Parliament "the power of disposing without their consent, of both their lives, liberties and properties." If the colonists did not forfeit any *rights* by emigrating they at least "by natural effects," lost certain privileges as the right to vote and be represented in Parliament. The colonists inherit all the privileges of their ancestors who emigrated to America, but no more. It was a part of the original constitution of England that Parliament had the right to tax all subjects whether they voted or not. Wesley believed that the Revolution was a pre-determined scheme of a group of uncompromising Republicans headed by Samuel Adams and supported by the Congregationalists and Presbyterians.[108] His attitude did not help the cause of his followers in America. In addition, the actions of some of the loyalist American preachers were obnoxious and many of the Methodists, both preachers and laymen, were conscientious objectors and refused to fight when drafted.[109]

Under these conditions it was easy to stir up opposition to the sect and, as Garrettson said, they "began to labour under heavy political trials."[110] Jesse Lee says that it was only necessary to call a Methodist a Tory and people could go ahead and

[106] Lee, *History*, p. 62; Jarratt's *Narrative*, 162.

[107] *A Calm Address to Our American Colonies*, Bristol, 1775, pp. 4-7. This pamphlet brought forth scores of replies in defence of the colonies. See the bibliographies on anti-Methodist publications by R. Green and C. H. Cavender.

[108] *Reflections on the Rise and Progress of the American Rebellion*. This was published anonymously in London, 1780. *Calm Address*, pp. 13-15.

[109] See Freeborn Garrettson, *Life* (ed. Nathan Bangs), pp. 65, 121-22; Lee, *History*, p. 60; and Lee's experience as related in his *Memoirs*, by Thrift, pp. 28 ff.

[110] *Life*, p. 58; see also Watters, *Life*, pp. 49-50.

treat him as they pleased.[111] Moreover, the war caused the loss
of some of the best preachers, as Shadford and Rankin, who
returned to England. When, in the later years of the conflict,
the fighting was actually carried to the South the Methodist
societies were, no doubt, much demoralized. In 1780, for the
first time, the membership for the South began to fall off
slightly and only one new circuit was added to Virginia in 1781,
and none in 1782. With the close of the war, the Minutes show
a rapid recovery. In 1785, twelve of the fifty-two circuits,
twenty-five of the one hundred and four preachers, and probably one-third of the 18,000 members which the denomination
claimed in America, were in Virginia.[112]

The severance of the American Colonies from England and
the disappearance therewith of the authority of the Anglican
Church made necessary the organization in America of an independent Methodist Episcopal Church. This was achieved by the
historic Conference which gathered at Baltimore on Christmas
Eve of 1784.[113] The action was approved by Wesley, who saw
that it was necessary in order to preserve the existence of
the denomination in America, and who, therefore, ordained
Thomas Coke as Superintendent and Richard Whatcoat and
Thomas Vasey as Elders with powers to administer the sacraments.[114] The Christmas Conference elected Coke and Asbury
as Superintendents or Bishops, the latter being previously or-

[111] *History*, pp. 74-75.

[112] Bennett, *op. cit.*, p. 226. The Minutes do not give the details for 1785
and Bennett bases his statement on the Minutes of 1784.

[113] The story of this gathering can be read in any of the standard histories of American Methodism, as those by Atkinson, Bangs, Buckley,
Stevens, Tigert. The lives of Watters, Garrettson, and of Thomas Ware
contain the impressions of participants and the latter has an article entitled
"The Christmas Conference of 1784" in the *Meth. Mag. and Quar. Rev.*,
January, 1832, pp. 96-104. See also Gatch for the account of a contemporary. Coke's *Journal* and Asbury's *Journal* are to be counted among the
sources. L. M. Lee, *Life and Times of Jesse Lee* is based on contemporary
evidence. J. J. Tigert, *Constitutional History of American Episcopal Methodism*, is best for the constitutional questions involved.

[114] See Wesley's letter dated Bristol, September 10, 1784, and published
with the Minutes of 1785. Also Tigert, *op. cit.*, p. 197, who calls it the
Magna Charta of American Methodism. Lee, *History*, p. 91; J. M. Buckley,
Const. and Parl. Hist. of the M. E. Church, pp. 40 ff.

dained by Coke.[115] In addition twelve elders were set apart whose duties consisted in travelling over the circuits and administering the sacraments and otherwise superintending the work in the absence of the Bishops.[116] The elections of three deacons completed the hierarchical organization of the Church, though the adoption of a form of Discipline constituted no small part of the work of the Conference.[117]

For the Methodists of Virginia, the important result of the organization of a Methodist Episcopal Church in America was that the societies could now receive the sacraments from the hands of their own preachers. The question of administering the ordinances had been perpetually before the Conferences, and at one time, 1779-80, almost caused a secession of the southern ministers. Until the authority of England was definitely overthrown in the colonies, Wesley insisted that the right to administer sacraments was a prerogative of duly ordained clergymen and did not belong to the Methodists. This made the latter dependent upon the Anglican clergy and it was revolting to the Methodists to have to receive the sacraments from men who were generally of loose morals and spiritual indifference.[118] On the other hand, to omit the ordinances that were so clearly a duty could not be thought of. To be sure, Jarratt rendered timely services in this respect but he could not take care of the work alone. As the war progressed and the Established Clergy deserted their parishes, the situation became more acute. The people could not understand why their ministers could not administer the sacraments when their work had met with such divine approval. It was surely an anomalous situation and one which did not prevail in any other denomination.

[115] The latter title was not officially used until in the Discipline of 1787. Wesley had named Asbury as joint superintendent with Coke but Asbury insisted on election by the Conference also. See Buckley, p. 48.

[116] David Sherman, *History of the Revisions of the Discipline of the M. E. Church.*

[117] This first Discipline is given in Tigert, *op. cit.*, Appendix VII.

[118] Lee, *History*, p. 48. The Baptists and Presbyterians practiced closed communion. The former baptized only on confession of faith and by immersion while the latter would not baptize children unless one of the parents was a Presbyterian. See Buckley, p. 37.

Some of the preachers felt the same way, but the Conferences were loath to take action. Nevertheless, the matter could not be postponed forever and, in 1779, at the regular Conference which met in Virginia, it was decided to assume the authority of administering sacraments.[119] Asbury and the northern preachers had held a separate Conference in Delaware and were not present.[120] The reason assigned for the action taken by the southern ministers was: "Because the Episcopal Establishment is now dissolved, and therefore, in almost all our circuits the members are without the ordinances—we believe it to be our duty."[121]

The action of the Conference for a time threatened to disrupt the Church, since the northern preachers were almost unanimously opposed to it. In 1780, however, the matter was compromised, it being agreed to suspend the ordinances for one year, pending a reference of the matter to Wesley. At the end of this time a general Conference would meet in Baltimore to effect a settlement.[122] Largely through the efforts of Asbury, who made an extended tour through Virginia and North Carolina, the Conference which met in 1781 agreed to return to the old plan and give up the administration of ordinances.[123] A year later it was decided "to put the people out of Society when they received, and the preachers when they administer the ordinances if they have been previously warned."[124]

The want of duly ordained ministers with authority to administer the sacraments hastened the break with the Anglicans. Thomas Ware tells us that the anomalous position of the preachers tended to paralyze the efforts of the Church and that many who were awakened by the zeal of the Methodists "were kept from uniting with us because we could not administer to

[119] Gatch, *Memoirs*, p. 68; Garrettson, p. 111; Watters, p. 73; Lee, *History*, pp. 69-70 and *Memoirs* by Thrift, pp. 23-24.

[120] See Asbury, *Journal*, April 28, 1779; Watters, pp. 71 ff. This Conference had no official standing. Garrettson, p. 111; Gatch, p. 70.

[121] These proceedings are given in Gatch and are quoted in L. M. Lee, *op. cit.*, pp. 78-80.

[122] Watters, *Life*, p. 80; Garrettson, p. 111; Lee, *History*, p. 73, and *Memoirs*, p. 24.

[123] Asbury, *Journal*, April 24, 1781.

[124] *Ibid.*, I, 337-8.

them all of the ordinances."[125] The arrival in 1784 of Coke, Whatcoat, and Vasey, properly ordained, was the first definite step away from the Establishment. The separation was completed by the Christmas Conference, as we have already seen. With it came the breach with Jarratt, who had laboured hard to remedy the complaint of the want of ordinances and to prevent the inevitable separation.[126] But the times were against him.

The newly organized Church had hardly entered upon its career in Virginia when a second great revival began which inaugurated a period of remarkable expansion. This revival was part of a general movement which affected also the Baptists and Presbyterians.[127] When it was over, the Methodists had penetrated every part of the Commonwealth and, says Leland, the Baptist, "they exceed all societies in the state in spreading their books and tenets among the people.[128] Before passing to the general revival movement which completed the victory of evangelical Christianity, it would seem well to point out briefly some features of Methodism which gave it a decided advantage over its Baptist and Presbyterian rivals.[129]

1. The highly centralized organization under the Bishops, combined with the adoption of the itinerant system of spreading the gospel made for both strength and flexibility in the Methodist system.[130] It was a great factor in the success of the evangelical movements that the Bishop could send his preachers wherever he chose.[131] The itinerancy enabled Methodism to

[125] Ware, *Life and Travels,* pp. 104-5.
[126] Jarratt, *Autobiography,* p. 114. In later years Jarratt became reconciled with the Methodists. He preached for them at a conference held in Petersburg in 1790. "Friends at first are friends again at last," is Asbury's comment upon the reconciliation; while Jarratt wrote, "The Methodists and I are on pretty friendly terms." *Cf.* A. M. Courtenay, "The Reverend Devereux Jarratt," *Meth. Rev.* (So.), Vol. XLVII, 349.
[127] See Chapter VII.
[128] "Virginia Chronicle," in *Works,* p. 101.
[129] The writer has developed this subject more fully for a later period in a paper entitled, "Some Factors in the Expansion of Frontier Methodism, 1800-1811," *Journal of Religion,* January, 1928, pp. 98-120.
[130] See John Atkinson, *Centennial History of American Methodism,* Chap. VII.
[131] See Sherman, *History of the Discipline* (3rd ed, 1890), p. 182, on the duties of Bishops.

keep pace with the expanding religious needs of the country to a remarkable degree,—in fact, it made Methodism a vast missionary system. Moreover, the circuit system kept the churches constantly supplied with ministers, and frequent changes of the latter gave the people the benefit of a varied and, as it were, a collective ministry.[132] Jesse Lee says that the preachers "saw that it would be best for themselves and for all the people to have frequent changes of gifts, and of congregations."[133]

2. The lay ministry or system of local preachers, made up of those who followed regular lay vocations during the week but who devoted some of their time, particularly the Sabbaths, to preaching and organizing classes in their own neighborhoods, secured to the denomination the services of many gifted men whose talents would have been lost had the Church relied wholly upon the itinerancy.[134] Without bearing the responsibilities of the regular ministry, and receiving no remuneration, the local preachers served the Church with diligence and supplemented the work of the itinerants in a most able manner. They were frequently the pioneers of the Church in new regions, organizing classes even before the arrival of the circuit rider.[135]

3. The local organization of the Methodists was well designed for keeping the Church vigorous and militant. The societies were divided into classes and bands in which the members could be held to strict accountability. The class leaders were appointed and removed by the itinerants.[136] The classes were governed by strict rules which the leaders were required to enforce.[137] Members were admitted to the classes by tickets which were issued quarterly by the preacher so that delinquent

---

[132] L. S. Burkhead (ed.), *Centennial of Methodism in North Carolina*, contains suggestive articles by E. M. Marvin and W. S. Black on the early itinerancy. See also Atkinson, *op. cit.*, for excellent discussion. The Conference of 1775 planned for some of the preachers to change in three months and others in six months. In 1780 it was agreed that all should change in six months. *Cf.* Lee, *History*, pp. 52, 71.

[133] Lee, *History of the Methodists*, p. 52.

[134] Sherman, *History of the Discipline*, pp. 202 ff., for duties of local preachers.

[135] *Cf.* Gewehr, *loc. cit.*, pp. 106-109.   [136] Sherman, p. 193.

[137] Given in Lee, *History*, pp. 30-33, and in Sherman or any M. E. Discipline for the period in question.

members could be easily dropped. Thus the purity and vigor of the Church was maintained. The bands were smaller groups, all men or all women, all married or all single, for more intensive spiritual cultivation.[138] It will be readily seen that the classes and bands supplied the Methodists with a system of personal oversight over the members which the nature of the itinerancy prevented. The organization in small units emphasized the importance of every believer and made Methodism social as well as active. It was a unifying agency and developed in the denomination, an *esprit de corps* which could not easily be broken.[139]

4. The Methodists were peculiarly fortunate in having a hymnody that was born in their own revival and designed to express the religious beliefs and experiences of that denomination.[140] This statement gains more weight in view of the fact that early Methodism had no fixed creed or set of doctrines, but rather regarded Christian experience and conduct as the main tests of membership. The hymns of the Wesleys supplied the denomination with something like a platform and were a great factor in indoctrinating the masses in the evangelical principles for which it stood. The hymnal has, in fact, been called "a poetic confession of faith."[141] That the Methodists realized the value of singing their own hymns, and singing them well, is seen in the fact that in the Discipline was a section on "The Spirit and Truth of Singing."[142] The variety of meter in the hymnal greatly enhanced its value as a medium for extending the revival.

5. In their theology the Methodists made a broader appeal than did either the Baptists or Presbyterians. In contrast to the

---

[138] Sherman, pp. 139-140 for the band rules.

[139] See the suggestive article on "Theory of Methodist Class Meetings," by W. J. Sasnett, in *Meth. Quar. Rev.* (So.), V, 265 ff. and also one by J. P. in *ibid.*, III, 575 ff.

[140] On this subject see David Creamer, *Methodist Hymnology*, N. Y. 1848; W. F. Tillett, "Methodist Hymnology," in *Meth. Quar. Rev.* (So.), Vol. LII, pp. 333-48; E. R. Hendrix, "Evolution of the Methodist Hymnal," in *ibid.*, Vol. LV, pp. 3-18.

[141] Tillett, *loc. cit.*, p. 345.

[142] Sherman, pp. 136-7, or any Discipline of the period. In this the ministers were told, "In every large society let them learn to sing, and let them always learn our tunes first." They were urged to "exhort every person in the congregation to sing, not one in ten only."

doctrines of predestination and the final perseverance of all
saints, as held by the Presbyterians and many of the Baptists,
the Methodists believed in Arminianism, or the universal re-
demption of all true believers. This doctrine was much more
easily comprehended than was Calvinism and had the advantage
of placing everyone on an exactly equal plane in the sight of
God. In addition, the catholicity of the denomination was well
adapted to reach the great unchurched masses.[143] No doctrinal
or dogmatic requirements were exacted for admission into the
Methodist societies. The only condition was that a person be a
true seeker after the Christian experience and possess a true
desire to be saved from his sins. As evidence of this desire,
members must observe certain rules of conduct and avoid
certain practices regarded as unchristian. The one thing emphasized by the Methodists was a right heart and on this basis the
societies were open to all alike. On the contrary, Presbyterians
and Baptists held to closed communion, excluding from their
sacraments all who did not adhere to certain doctrinal demands.
Whereas doctrinal matters become a divisive factor among both
these sects, such was never the case with the Methodists.

6. We have seen that the pioneer Williams made use of the
press, and that Leland noted the diligence of the Methodists in
spreading their books among the people. The press became a
factor of ever increasing importance in the spread of the revival.[144] From its very beginning the Methodist Church has
been a printing Church and Wesley placed his denomination
in the lead in the printing and distribution of cheap religious
literature. Five years after the organization of the Church in
the New World the Book Concern was instituted.[145] The

[143] The classic statement of the Methodist position is given in Wesley's
sermon "On a Catholic Spirit," *Works* (Emory ed.), I, 346-55, espec. at
349-50. See also W. J. Conoly, "The Catholicity of Methodism," *Meth.
Rev. Quar.* (So.), October, 1916, pp. 718-28; Charles Adams, "Wesley the
Catholic," *Meth. Quar. Rev.* (N. Y.), Vol. XXXII, pp. 177-198; J. A. Faulkner, "Certain Aspects of Early Methodism," *So. Meth. Rev.*, N. S. III, 1887,
pp. 179-192; W. P. Lovejoy, "Influence of Methodism," *Meth. Rev.* (So.),
Vol. LI, pp. 371 ff.

[144] See, especially, F. A. Archibald, *Methodism and Literature.*

[145] *Ibid.*, p. 20; Lee, *History*, p. 129. John Dickens was made Book Steward in 1789 with headquarters at Philadelphia.

Methodists were not only their own publishers but also their own book agents. It was a duty incumbent upon every circuit-rider to distribute books, tracts and sermons. In this way Methodism became a permanent influence in thousands of homes. The social and religious value of a common literature in countless scattered societies is easily seen, for it served to bind the members in harmony of spirit, aided in their educational uplift and in the fixation of the Methodist principles.[146]

It remains to note only the fact that the Methodists in Virginia were spared from the persecution and official opposition to which the Baptists and Presbyterians had been subjected before them. If for no other reason, the fact that the denomination was Anglican in its connections and therefore could not be considered as subversive of the Established Church should be sufficient to account for this. Then, too, the days of persecution were practically over when their great revival started and the colony was mainly concerned with the crisis with England. In name, the Methodists were identified with the established order. In fact, they represented a strong popular movement as can be seen in the character and training of their ministry, the nature of their appeal, and in the constituency of their societies. Although the Methodists of Virginia never inherited the social stigma attached to the early New Lights and later to the Baptists, they nevertheless contributed greatly to the social and religious revolution in the colony.

[146] Archibald, Chaps. XXII, XXIV.

CHAPTER VII

Post-Revolutionary Evangelism

A study of the Great Awakening in Virginia could scarcely be complete without at least a survey of the post-revolutionary revivals. The Revolution had sharply arrested the progress of the evangelical principles, while at the same time it had practically swept the Establishment from the stage.[1] It required yet another Awakening to complete the victory of evangelical Christianity, to gather into the Church those who were left unprovided by the dissolution of the Establishment, and to bring to full fruition the transforming processes which had sprung from this revival of personal religion.

Prior to the Revolution the Great Awakening in Virginia was represented in each of its phases by some one denomination—first, the New Light Presbyterians, then the Separate Baptists, and finally, the Methodists—each seeming to take up the work where the other left it, thus making the movement a continuous one down to the war. In its final stage, which we are about to enter, all three of the above denominations fell common heir to the revival, and simultaneously experienced a new Awakening which covered the entire state. This Awakening commenced in different regions in 1785, reached its crest everywhere about 1787-8, and, before it had subsided, had added new thousands of members to the Baptist, Presbyterian, and Methodist churches.[2]

A feature of this revival, at least in certain regions, was the coöperation between the different denominations to secure the best results. Philip Gatch tells how Methodists, Baptists, and Presbyterians united in the work in Buckingham County where

[1] In 1776 there were ninety-one Anglican clergymen in Virginia. In 1783 there were only twenty-eight and of these only fifteen had parishes. Bassett, "Development of the Popular Churches after the Revolution," *Proc. Mass. Hist. Soc.*, Vol. XLVIII, pp. 255-257. He uses the phrase "suspended animation" to describe the condition of the Anglican Church in Virginia from 1784 to 1811.

[2] See Semple, *History of the Baptists in Virginia*, p. 58; Leland, *Works*, pp. 24 ff.; Bennett, *Memorials of Methodism in Virginia*, pp. 231, 242 ff.; Foote, *Sketches of Virginia*, First Series, pp. 406 ff.

all three denominations were flourishing, and he refers to James Sanders, of the Baptists, and to Drury Lacy, of the Presbyterians, as ministers of high standing. "We dwelt together in unity. We preached with and for each other and the Lord again favored the neighborhood with his presence."[3] On the other hand, the Presbyterian ministers, with their superior intellectual attainments, were apt to look somewhat askance upon the uneducated Methodists and Baptists who appealed to the emotional and whose meetings were attended with exaggerated physical demonstrations. This was the case when the popular Methodist orator, James O'Kelly from North Carolina, came to Prince Edward County and held a few meetings near Hampden-Sydney College.[4]

1. THE REVIVAL AMONG THE METHODISTS

As in 1776, the Methodist revival which began about 1785 was most pronounced in the southern counties of Virginia, particularly in Brunswick, Sussex, and Amelia circuits, though it was by no means confined to these.[5] So extensive was the movement that Jesse Lee says it far exceeded the earlier revival, and attracted such attention that an account of the work was published in the newspapers and spread all over the United States.[6] He himself was so impressed that he wrote: "Such a time for the awakening and conversion of sinners was never seen before among the Methodists in America."[7] "Many of the old Christians, at that time, believed that the knowledge of God, would, in that revival, cover the face of the earth; and, that there would not be left in that part of the world, one soul who

---

[3] Gatch, *Memoirs,* pp. 88, 92, 94.

[4] Foote, *Sketches,* pp. 412-413.

[5] Jesse Lee, *History,* pp. 129, 133; also his *Life of John Lee,* p. 15; Philip Bruce to Bishop Coke, March 25, 1788, in *Arminian Mag.* (American), II (1790), p. 564.

[6] Lee, *History,* p. 134.

[7] *Ibid.,* p. 129. Lee appears to have been just as enthusiastic about the revivals of 1775-6 and probably the earlier movement was just as intense but it was more restricted. The Methodists were now well established and had many more ministers and a more perfect organization so that it is easy to account for Lee's attitude on both occasions. It was probably the extent of the later revival which impressed him so much.

should remain unconverted. The people generally expected, when they were going to meeting, that they should see souls converted to God before they returned home; and according to their faith, so it was in a general way."[8]

The revival seems to have reached its crest in the mid-summer of 1787 and it was attended by the usual physical and emotional outbreaks which characterized the earlier awakening. The most famous meetings were the quarterly meetings held at Mabry's Chapel on Brunswick circuit, July 25 and 26, and at Jones's Chapel in Sussex circuit, July 27 and 28.[9] The quarterly meetings were always big occasions for the Methodist societies,[10] and under the impetus of the revival additional hundreds attended the above mentioned gatherings. R. Garrettson, a witness of the events we are describing, estimates that there were perhaps four thousand present at the meeting at Mabry's Chapel and, so far as he could learn, one hundred and fifty were converted.[11] Jesse Lee says that thousands attended and above one hundred souls were awakened in two days, while Philip Cox wrote to Bishop Coke at the very time of the meeting that "hundreds were in loud cries for mercy. The second day was much greater: it is thought above a hundred whites found peace with God, besides as many negroes on that day."[12]

The meeting at Jones's Chapel on Sussex circuit was on the same scale. Under the influence of converts of the Mabry's meeting the work had commenced even before the preachers arrived and the shouts of the people, we are told, were heard a

---

[8] Jesse Lee, *Life of John Lee,* p. 16.

[9] Philip Cox to Bishop Coke, July, 1787, in *Arminian Mag.* (American), II, pp. 91 ff. Lee, *History,* p. 130.

[10] These were occasions for the administration of the sacrament of the Lord's Supper. They lasted for two days and were attended by the members from miles around—twenty, thirty, and even forty. The travelling preachers for the circuit were present, as well as some of the local preachers, and would deliver one sermon after another and also hold the love-feast, that is, the breaking of bread between members. See Coke, *Journal,* April 8, 1785, on quarterly meetings.

[11] R. Garrettson, February, 1788; in *Arminian Mag.* (English), XIII (1790), p. 303.

[12] Lee, *History,* p. 130. Cox, *Arminian Mag.* (American), II, pp. 91-92.

half mile from the chapel.[13] When the preachers came upon the scene some three score were down upon the floor "groaning in loud cries to God for mercy." Preaching was out of the question, for the ministers could not make themselves heard above the cries of the distressed. "Such a sight," writes Garrettson, "I never had before; numbers of saints in ecstacies, others crying for mercy, scores lying with their eyes set in their heads, the use of their powers suspended, and the whole congregation in agitation."[14]

The estimate by participants places the number who attended the meeting on the first day at no fewer than five thousand, with many more on the second. The preachers had difficulties in reaching all. Cox tells us: "We preached to them in the open air and in the chapel, and in the barn by brother Jones's house at the same time. Such a sight my eyes never saw before and never read of either in Mr. Wesley's journals or any other writings . . . except the account in the scripture of the day of Pentecost."[15]

The same scenes were enacted on the second day. The crowd continued to grow and Garrettson estimates that he preached to fifteen hundred in the woods. Many scores, both blacks and whites, were prostrated for hours. In particular the Negroes "lay struggling till they beat the earth with their hands, head and feet, while others kicked holes in the ground."[16] The power of suggestion and self-hypnosis in this revival is shown by the fact that even the more restrained were swept from their feet. "Here were many of the first quality in the country, wallowing in the dust with their silks and broadcloths, powdered heads, rings and ruffles and some of them so convulsed that they could neither speak nor stir."[17] For such a great gathering the statement that about two hundred whites and half as many blacks professed conversion seems conservative enough.[18]

[13] R. Garrettson, loc. cit., pp. 303-4; Philip Cox to Coke, loc. cit., pp. 92-93; Lee, History, p. 130.   [14] Loc. cit., pp. 303-4.   [15] Loc. cit., pp. 92-93.
[16] Garrettson, loc. cit.; Lee, History, p. 131; Davenport, Primitive Traits in Revivals of Religion, Chap. V on the "Religion of the American Negro."
[17] Cox, loc. cit.; Lee, History, p. 131. Cf. Davenport, op. cit., Chap. XII on "Conversion by Suggestion."
[18] Cox, loc. cit.

The scenes that we have been describing were repeated, though on a lesser scale, in all the societies that felt the grip of the revival. John Lee wrote to his brother, Jesse, from Prince George County under date of October 4, 1787: "All the white persons in my father's family have joined in class with the Methodists, and profess to be happy. Our class has increased to forty members; and our circuit has been enlarged to six weeks; and I suppose near a thousand souls have been converted in this circuit within a few months past. Such a work of God we have never seen before. The great work began in July, and I was the third person that found peace with God. . . . Within four weeks from the time that I was converted, I believe one hundred of our neighbors were brought to God."[19]

Philip Cox speaks of many meetings in Sussex and Brunswick circuits that were attended by awakenings and revival scenes. It was nothing for meetings to continue for six or seven hours at a time and last until midnight. Societies everywhere were alive to the work, and, if we may believe the reports, some that formerly could count upon only twenty or thirty in a weekday meeting now attracted as many as a thousand.[20] Many who came to oppose the work, swearing bitter things against the Methodists, were unexpectedly stricken and went home shouting praises for what God had wrought.[21] It was not uncommon for people to cease work in the fields in order to hold prayer meetings, and conversions usually followed.[22] "There was so much time spent by the people in running to meeting, by day and by night, in the neighborhood, and so little work done, that many of the religious people thought that they should hardly make bread to eat, but the crops were tolerably good; others were looking for all the people to be converted in a short time; but their expectations failed them. . . ."[23] Nevertheless people everywhere were reached in prayer-meetings, in class-meetings, in houses and fields until hundreds were added to the church

[19] Jesse Lee, *Life of John Lee*, p. 28.
[20] R. Garrettson, *loc. cit.*, p. 302.
[21] *Ibid.* and Lee, *History*, p. 132. *Cf.* Davenport, Chap. XI, espec. pp. 225 ff.
[22] Lee, *Life of John Lee*, p. 25; *History*, p. 134.
[23] Lee, *Life of John Lee*, p. 27.

in the course of the year. The presence of a preacher, we have seen, was by no means necessary for the continuation of the work; once under way, it gathered force of its own momentum. Young converts, as John Lee, commonly began to exhort and hold meetings immediately, and, no doubt, their zeal was a great factor in the spread of the revival.[24]

In the spring of 1788, Philip Bruce wrote to Coke from Portsmouth, Virginia, of the extraordinary work in that vicinity, "vast numbers flocking into the fold of Christ from every quarter. In many places in this circuit, as soon as the preacher begins to speak, the power of God appears to be present; which is attended with trembling among the people, and falling down; some lie void of motion or breath, others are in strong convulsions: and thus they continue, till the Lord raises them up, which is attended with emotions of joy and rapture. When one gets happy it spreads like a flame: so that one after another they arise to join in the praises. . . ."[25] Great as the work was at Portsmouth, Bruce adds that "it loses all report" with the happenings in Sussex and Brunswick where Philip Cox and John Easter laboured.[26]

Although the revival progressed in many places in the spring of 1788, it had passed its crest.[27] Returning at this time from a circuit in Maryland, Jesse Lee notes a remarkable change that has taken place among the people of Virginia. "I have never seen anything more like taking the kingdom by violence than this," he writes, and he was firmly convinced of the efficacy of the work.[28] According to Bennett, the entire area south of the James River from the Blue Ridge to the sea was affected

[24] *Life of John Lee,* pp. 18 ff., espec. 25-26. John Lee's conversion is a good example of how the revival gripped the individual.

[25] Bruce to Coke, March 25, 1788, in *Arminian Mag.* (American), II, p. 563.

[26] *Ibid.* Bishop McKendree was converted in the revival on the Brunswick circuit under the powerful preaching of John Easter. Robert Paine, *Life and Times of William McKendree,* I, 38.

[27] The summer of 1785, however, marked the beginning of extensive revivals among the Methodists of Kentucky. See letter of James Haw to Asbury in *Arminian Mag.* (American), II, pp. 202-4. Miss Catharine Cleveland's study, *The Great Revival in the West,* covers the great southwestern revivals of which the above was only the preliminary.

[28] Minton Thrift, *Memoirs of Jesse Lee,* p. 97.

by the Awakening.[29] As to the number of converts, it is estimated that 1,600 were gathered in on the Sussex circuit, about 1,800 on the Brunswick and 800 on the Amelia, during the year when the revival was at its height.[30] These circuits, however, lay within the strongholds of Methodism in Virginia where the revival was most pronounced. Considering the way in which all classes from the well-to-do to the Negroes were reached, these statements do not seem to be exaggerated. No doubt there were many instances where whole families, like that of the Lees, "joined in class with the Methodists."

Under the impetus of two brief but intense revivals the expansion of Methodism in Virginia had been phenomenal and was attracting the attention of other denominations. Leland, the Baptist, wrote in 1790 that the Methodists, who had never spread much in Virginia until 1775, were now scattered all over the state and in some places were very numerous. They were "the most fortunate in increasing their number of preachers of any society in Virginia. . . . Their ministers are very constant preachers, and they exceed all societies in the state in spreading their books and tenets among the people."[31]

2. The Revival Among the Baptists

The revival among the Baptists began about 1785 in the region of the James River and affected both the Regulars and Separates. Although it continued to spread until 1791 or 1792, it reached its culmination in the years 1787-9. It was most marked in the Dover, Goshen, Culpeper and Ketocton Associations.[32] These Associations included all of the counties above the James River in eastern midland and northern Virginia. Particularly marked was the revival in some of the churches in the Northern Neck, in King and Queen, Caroline, Culpeper,

---

[29] Bennett, *op. cit.*, p. 242.

[30] Lee, *History*, p. 133; R. Garrettson, *loc. cit.*, p. 307. In the spring of 1788 Philip Bruce wrote that he had been informed by Cox that between 1,200 and 1,500 whites besides a great number of blacks had been converted in Sussex circuit. Bruce to Coke, *loc. cit.*, p. 564. From John Easter in Brunswick he learned "that by the best account he can make, there have been 2,000 whites converted in his circuit this past year." *Ibid.*

[31] Leland, "Virginia Chronicle," in *Works*, p. 101.

[32] Semple, p. 61 note.

Orange, Madison, Spottsylvania, Louisa, Fairfax and Stafford counties.[33] Between the Baptists and the Methodists, therefore, all of eastern Virginia was swept by this phase of the Great Awakening, with the James River as the dividing line between the areas of their respective activities.

The existing evidence of the revival among the Baptists is rather fragmentary but such as it is, it is convincing. The time of greatest intensity seemed to be, as stated by Leland, from the fall of 1787 until the spring of 1789. His field of labours was an area of about twenty square miles including the corners of Orange, Culpeper, Spottsylvania and Louisa counties. From October 1787 until March 1789, he baptized about four hundred people; three hundred of these in 1788, or more than he had baptized in any preceding year.[34] When the work seemed to slacken in one neighborhood, it broke out in another.

The reports from the Associations that were affected by the revivals show large numbers of converts. Thus to the Dover Association, which included churches in the counties between the James and the Potomac in eastern Virginia, reports of a great revival, almost throughout the district, were read in the letters from twenty-one churches in May 1789.[35] The revival still continued in the fall and it is stated that hundreds were baptized in the course of the year. By the spring of 1790, however, the work had subsided in a very considerable degree.[36]

In one of the churches in this Association, namely, Upper King and Queen, the original church record-book has been preserved.[37] In it we can see the effects of the revival in the large number of baptisms that occurred. Under the date of August 24, 1788, we are informed that their pastor baptized fifty mem-

[33] See Semple, p. 61, note, cf. tables of the churches in the Associations mentioned.
[34] Leland, *Works,* p. 27.   [35] Semple, p. 121.   [36] *Ibid.,* p. 122.
[37] MS. Church Record-book of Upper King and Queen Church (in Va. Bap. Hist. Soc.,) September 21, 1788, October 20, November 25, December 5, February 14, 1789, March 22, April 16, June 21, 24, July 1, 28. There are several of these books for other churches which go back to the colonial period but most of them have been destroyed. In them were kept the minutes of the regular monthly meetings and other matters as the number of baptisms. They deal mostly with the disciplining of members, pastoral relations and support, etc.

John Leland

bers who had been received at different meetings in the course of about fifteen days. The following month over sixty were baptized, and thereafter until the midsummer of 1789 regular additions of ten, twenty, and even thirty members to the church occurred monthly. In respect to this church Semple says: "A greater work of grace has probably never been known in Virginia within the limits of one church."[38] He adds that many respectable people were included in those who were baptized during this revival. Theoderick Noel was pastor at the time, concerning whom we are informed his "talents for a preacher seemed to be calculated for a revival."[39]

Other churches of the Dover Association in which large harvests were reaped during the post-Revolutionary revival were Morattico and Nomini churches in the Northern Neck, where Lewis Lunsford and Henry Toler respectively laboured, and Tuckahoe church in Caroline.[40] Nomini church was constituted in April, 1786, with seventeen members; at the end of the year there were seventy-three. Under the impetus of the revival this number increased to 222 in 1788 and to 300 in 1789.[41] At Tuckahoe church, in the northeastern part of Caroline County, about 300 were baptized by John Shakleford during this period of the Awakening.

We have similar accounts from churches in the Goshen, Orange, Culpeper and Ketocton Associations, but the details need not concern us here.[42] In fact, there are few details to record other than the general statement of extensive revivals in 1788-9, with considerable increases in membership. The effects of the Awakening on the Regular Baptists are seen in

[38] Semple, p. 160.
[39] Ibid., p. 164.
[40] Ibid., pp. 61 note, 181-2; 175, 156.
[41] Ibid., p. 175.
[42] For Goshen Association see accounts in Semple of the following churches: County Line (Caroline and Spottsylvania counties); Waller's or Lower Spottsylvania; Pamunkey (Orange); Wilderness (Spottsylvania); Goldmine (Louisa). Semple, pp. 208-9, 198-9, 220, 203, 216.
For Culpeper Association: Crooked Run (Culpeper); F. T. (Culpeper); Rapid Ann (Madison); Blue Run (Orange). Ibid., pp. 233, 237, 238, 241.
For Ketocton Association: Bull Run (Fairfax); Chappawamsic (Stafford). Semple, pp. 402, 404.
See also pp. 184, 427 for Orange and Greenbrier Associations.
The mention of the revival is usually most brief but it is there and gives us an idea of the revival area.

the fact that whereas only twenty-three were baptized in the entire Ketocton Association in 1782, three hundred and fifty were reported in 1789.[43] The revival did not reach some of the churches in this Association until 1791-2, but for most regions it reached the crest in 1788-9. When it was over, thousands of members had been added to the Baptists in Virginia and "their congregations became more numerous than those of any other Christian sect."[44]

As among the Methodists, one notes the presence of the physical and emotional manifestations among the Baptists with attending results. Semple says that the manner of conducting the general revival was somewhat extraordinary. "It was not unusual to have a large proportion of a congregation prostrate on the floor; and, in some instances, they have lost the use of their limbs. No distinct articulation could be heard unless from those immediately by. Screams, cries, groans, songs, shouts, and hosannas, notes of grief and notes of joy, all heard at the same time, made a heavenly confusion, a sort of undescribable concert. Even the wicked and unenlightened were astonished and said, the Lord hath done great things for this people. At associations and great meetings, where there were several ministers, many of them would exercise their gifts at the same time in different parts of the congregation; some in exhortation; some in praying for the distressed; and some in argument with opposers. At first many of the preachers did not approve of this kind of work. They thought it extravagant. Others fanned it as fire from heaven. It is not unworthy of notice that in those congregations where the preachers encouraged these exercises to much extent the work was more extensive and greater numbers were added."[45] We also see that there were many spurious conversions when Semple adds: "It must also be admitted that in many of these congregations no little confusion and disorder arose after the revival had subsided, . . . many ministers who laboured earnestly to get Christians into their churches were

[43] Semple, p. 384.
[44] Semple, pp. 58-59. A letter published in Rippon's *Baptist Annual Register* and dated February 4, 1790, says that between 4,000 and 5,000 were added to one Association in less than fifteen months time. American Letters for 1790.   [45] *Ibid.*, pp. 57-58.

afterwards much perplexed to get out hypocrites. Perhaps the best conclusion is to avoid either extreme. A stiff formality or an inordinate confusion ought each to be shunned."[46]

Some very significant changes took place among the Baptists after the great revival of 1787-9, which indicate that a complete reversal of social attitudes had occurred in Virginia. These changes will be considered under the results of the Great Awakening.[47] From being persecuted and despised in 1775, they had become respected and influential in 1790. We can better understand this transformation after a study of the part played by the Baptists in the struggle for religious freedom and in the destruction of the Established Church.

It remains only to note that in the midst of the second Baptist revival a union of the two wings of the Church was achieved. This happened in August, 1787. The terms of the union were that the Separates were to accept the Regular Baptist Confession of Faith as containing the great essential doctrines of the gospel, "but to prevent it from usurping a tyrannical power over the consciences of any, we do not mean that every person is bound to the strict observance of everything therein contained. . . ."[48] At the same time, it was agreed that the appellation, Regular and Separate, should give way to the new name of the United Baptist Churches of Christ in Virginia. The union is indicative of the development of a more tolerant spirit in the denomination and of the relaxation in the rigorous discipline which characterized the Separates in the early days of the Baptist movement.

3. The Revival Among the Presbyterians:

Among the Presbyterians the revival of 1787-9 was the first one in Virginia since the time of Davies.[49] It did not occur, however, in the old field of his labours in Hanover County, for

[46] *Ibid.*, p. 58.   [47] See below, Chap. XI.
[48] Fristoe, *History of the Ketocton Baptist Association*, p. 22. Terms of union in Semple, pp. 100-101. See also Leland, pp. 113-114.
[49] "Memoir of William Graham," *Evan. and Lit. Mag.*, IV, 263; Foote, *Sketches of Virginia*, p. 406. References are to Foote's First Series unless otherwise indicated.

here the Baptists now held sway, but, emanating from Hampden-Sydney College in Prince Edward County, it gradually extended into the neighboring southside counties of Charlotte, Cumberland, Campbell, and Bedford east of the Ridge, and among the Presbyterian congregations of Rockbridge and Augusta counties in the Valley.[50] It even exerted considerable influence in certain counties of North Carolina, particularly in Granville and Caswell.[51] Thus the movement complemented the work of the Methodists and Baptists in the spread of evangelical principles throughout the state. Although the latter denominations were first in the field, in the southwestern counties and in the Valley the Presbyterians became preëminently its representatives, as were the Methodists in southeastern and the Baptists in northern Virginia.[52]

The revival at Hampden-Sydney seems to have begun spontaneously among a small band of students. One of these, Cary Allen, had been awakened under the influence of Hope Hull, a Methodist, upon a visit to his home in Cumberland county.[53] Others were probably similarly affected by the preaching of the Methodist, James O'Kelly, and the Baptist, John Williams, who seem to have been labouring in the vicinity of the College when the revival commenced.[54] At any rate Allen, William Hill and one or two other students began to hold prayer meetings at the College.[55] This was a rather strange proceeding among a student

[50] Foote, pp. 406 ff.; R. Davidson, *History of the Presbyterian Church in Kentucky, with a preliminary sketch of the churches in the Valley of Virginia*, pp. 42 ff.   [51] Foote, p. 419.

[52] Foote, Second Series, pp. 169-170, who says that the revival began in the Baptist church in Charlotte and in a little time spread to the Methodists and Presbyterians. See also pp. 412-413, for activities of Baptists and Methodists.

[53] William Hill, "Reverend Cary Allen," *Pres. Quar. Rev.*, IV, 58-59. Hill was himself a student at Hampden-Sydney at the time, was awakened in the revival and became a prominent Presbyterian divine. His accounts of various men and phases of the revival appear in the above periodical. Foote quotes freely from Hill who evidently wrote a good deal about the movement we are studying but I have found nothing beyond the articles in the *Review*. Hill's stepfather had moved to the western counties from Hanover where he had been a member of Davies' congregation.

[54] Foote, pp. 412-13.

[55] "Life and Times of William Hill," *Pres. Quar. Rev.*, II, 41-63, at pp. 44-45.

JOHN BLAIR SMITH

body, the most of whom were indifferent to religious influences, and efforts were made to break up the gatherings.[56] The leaders of the opposition even went to the President of the institution, John Blair Smith, to lodge a complaint against this praying and singing "in a Methodistic manner." This was Smith's first intimation of any seriousness among the students, and, far from suppressing the prayer meetings, he began to meet with them and encourage them. The result was that the College soon became the center of an extensive revival of religion which prevailed through several counties from 1787 to 1789.

Encouraged by the appearance of the revival spirit, Smith began to preach with more earnestness to his congregations and he also organized prayer circles in the neighborhood.[57] He seems to have been a man of striking appearance and much energy.[58] He preached a simple, direct, and animating gospel, often with zeal and fervidness. Under the influence of the revival spirit, his sermons became thoroughly evangelical. "The truth of God was preached plainly, and with reference to an immediate effect. The total depravity of man, his responsibility and guilt, a vicarious atonement, the necessity of repentance and faith in Jesus Christ, the dependence of the sinner upon the spirit of God, and the retributions of eternity, were the great truths exhibited during this season of revivals."[59] Smith was one of the strongest preachers of the day.

The revival spread by its own impetus. From the College the students carried the flame to their own homes, whither they returned to spend their vacations. By 1788 the Awakening was general in Prince Edward, Cumberland and Charlotte counties, and people came from long distances to attend meetings. Says Hill: "Persons of all ranks in society, of all ages, both old and young became the subjects of this work so that there was scarcely a magistrate upon the bench or a lawyer at the bar in Prince Edward or Charlotte but became members of the

---

[56] See Foote, p. 413; "Life and Times of William Hill," *loc. cit.*, 44-45.
[57] Davidson, pp. 42-43; Foote, Second Series, p. 170; S. D. Alexander, *Princeton College during the 18th Century*, pp. 170-171.
[58] Foote, pp. 424 ff.; Alexander, pp. 170-171.
[59] "Life and Times of William Hill," *loc. cit.*, p. 47.

church."[60] It became as rare to find one who was not religious as it had formerly been to find one who was. Frivolities and amusements gave way "to singing, serious conversations, and prayer meetings."[61]

We are fortunate in having a letter written in October, 1788, by the Reverend Robert Smith of Pequea, the father of John Blair Smith, who was present when the revival was at its height and who preached a number of times for his son.[62] He writes: "I have seen nothing equal to it for extensive spread, power and spiritual glory since the years '40 and '41. The work has spread for an hundred miles, but by far the most powerful and general in John Smith's congregations, which take in part of three counties. Not a word scarcely about politics; but all religion in public and private. They run far and near to sermons, sacraments, and societies, which meet every Wednesday and Saturday evenings, and at college on Sabbath evenings also. Numbers of the students have been convinced, and several of them hopefully converted. . . . The blessed work has spread among people of every description, high and low, rich and poor, learned and unlearned, orthodox and heterodox, sober and rude, white and black, young and old; especially the youth, whom it seems to have seized generally. Two hundred and twenty-five hopeful communicants have been added to the Lord's table among John Smith's people in the space of eighteen months chiefly of the young people."

The Presbyterian revival at Hampden-Sydney was not accompanied by the emotional outbursts that characterized the contemporaneous movement among the Baptists and Methodists. As we have said in another connection, the superior training and high intellectual attainments required of their ministry would be sufficient to account for this element of restraint among the Presbyterians and this dominance of the rational over the emotional in their awakening. The control over a revival rests much with the leader and John Blair Smith was

[60] Quoted in Foote, p. 428.   [61] Ibid.
[62] The letter is to a "Lady in Philadelphia" and is published in The Presbyterian for September 27, 1845, and in Foote, p. 422. Another letter to the same party from J. B. Smith is in The Presbyterian of the same date.

opposed to such demonstrations as crying, shouting, leaping and prostrations with which we are already familiar.[63] The tendency to such expressions was common enough among his congregations and he often had to repress them by giving out a hymn or by stopping in the midst of a sermon to compose his people by telling them that God was not the author of confusion but rather of order. He sometimes preached searching sermons in order "to guard his people against delusion."[64]

The presence of the Methodists in the neighborhood no doubt had a reciprocal influence upon the Presbyterians, and William Hill informs us that the new converts often "wished to feel such a load of conviction for sin, as would crush them to the ground; and then such a deliverance as would fill them with ecstatic joy and rejoicing. Many were the attempts that were made to throw away all they had experienced, begin anew, and get religion just in the way that Allen and Le Grand had obtained theirs."[65] In the few cases where sudden conversions accompanied by violent physical exercises did occur, we are told the subjects were put through a long probation of reading and self-examination before being admitted into the Church.[66] Hill informs us: "This was one reason why the subjects of this revival wore so well, and there were so few apostates among them."[67] Certainly the caution, vigilance and judgment displayed by Smith in his conduct of the revival contributed in no small degree to the genuineness and permanency of the work, a feature so frequently commented on by the participants.

In 1789 the area of the revival moved to the westward, with Bedford and Rockbridge counties as the chief centers. It was at its height in Bedford in October, 1789, when the Hanover

[63] Foote, pp. 424-7. The same is to be said of William Graham who stamped his impress on the revival in the Valley.

[64] *Ibid.*, p. 425.

[65] Hill, "Reverend Nash Legrand," *Pres. Quar. Rev.*, III, 601-16, at p. 606. See also his account of Cary Allen, IV, 55-79. These two men had experienced this sort of a conversion.

[66] Hill, *loc. cit.*, III, pp. 605-606; Foote, p. 425.

[67] Hill, *ibid.* Also see Foote, p. 428, who quotes from Hill much to the same effect. *Cf. Watchman of the South*, April 7, 1842.

Presbytery met at Pisgah Church for its session.[68] This being a special occasion, meetings were held both night and day and large crowds attended. The Sunday assembly was held in a large tent in the grove where Drury Lacy preached with great effect.[69]

In August, 1789, William Graham, the rector of Liberty Hall Academy in Rockbridge County,[70] along with Archibald Alexander and James Wilson, two of his students, visited Prince Edward County, at the invitation of John Blair Smith.[71] Although the revival at Hampden-Sydney was now on the wane, it had engendered an ardent spirit which Graham caught and carried back with him to Liberty Hall. Until this time the Valley had not been included in the area of the Awakening and no extraordinary results had attended Graham's preaching at the Academy or to his congregation at Hall's Meeting-house. In fact, vital piety had been very much lacking both among the student body and the people.[72]

On his return from Prince Edward County, Graham attended a sacramental meeting at the Peaks of Otter in Bedford. Here the revival was at full height, as has already been pointed out, and many stories are told of the miraculous works of God. The whole region was aflame and Graham preached with unusual fervency and effect. A delegation of young folks came over from Rockbridge to attend the meeting.[73] They carried the fire home and people were expectant and eager to hear Graham

[68] Hill, "Reverend James Turner," *Pres. Quar. Rev.,* III, 271-2.

[69] Because of his powerful voice Lacy was always one of the prominent preachers at large gatherings. He preached with warmth and animation and his manner of delivery "was better suited to the multitude than the select few," to the plain rather than the cultured. A. Alexander's sketch of Drury Lacy in *Watchman of the South,* January 10, 1839. Alexander was a contemporary of the revival.

[70] On the founding of this academy as well as of Hampden-Sydney see below Chap. IX. The academy was at Lexington, originally in Augusta County, but fell within Rockbridge when the latter county was set off in 1777.

[71] Foote, pp. 421, 466; *Evan. and Lit. Mag.,* IV, 263, Memoir of William Graham; also sketch of same by A. Alexander in *Watchman of the South,* January 4, 1844.

[72] Foote, p. 465; *Evan. and Lit. Mag.,* IV, 261, Memoir of William Graham.

[73] See Foote, pp. 467-8.

upon his return to Rockbridge. Nash LeGrand, who himself
had been converted early in the revival (1787), and had been
licensed to preach in April, 1789, came to assist Graham in the
work at Lexington.[74] The two held meetings in the Academy,
the town and the countryside; many fell under serious convictions and numbers were converted.[75]

Lexington now became the center of a revival which extended up and down the Valley of Virginia and which was even
carried into Kentucky and Tennessee. Churches which had
fallen into a state of torpor were now shaken and revitalized
by an awakening which affected ministers, elders, and members
alike.[76]

In a few places, however, the work of the revivalists was
bitterly opposed by groups of "Seceders." These were emigrants
from Scotland and Ireland who gained the above appellation
from their opposition to the Great Awakening in the Old
World.[77] They revealed the same spirit towards the movement
now under consideration and were strong in some of the Valley
churches. At Winchester, where Le Grand had a church, the
town was divided into two parties. The Irish "Seceders" opposed the work so strongly that the Lexington Presbytery
assigned the church to the two groups alternately. The Irish
minister soon resigned his pulpit, but the opposition to Le Grand
continued to such an extent that he gave up his appointment
and confined himself to his other two congregations at Opeckon
and Cedar Creek.[78] When John Blair Smith came to assist Graham in Rockbridge he preached to the "Seceders" from the text,
"Behold, ye despisers, and wonder and perish" and plainly told
them that they had fallen from grace.[79]

The Awakening of 1787-9 had important consequences for
the Presbyterians of Virginia. It injected a new spirit into the
Church, which had long been without a revival and which was
being rapidly outstripped by the other two denominations up

[74] Hill, "Reverend Nash Legrand," loc. cit., III, 610-611.
[75] Foote, pp. 467-8.
[76] Hill, loc. cit.; Davidson, op. cit., p. 44.
[77] "Life and Times of William Hill," loc. cit., II, 47.
[78] Hill, "Reverend Nash Legrand," loc. cit., pp. 612-13.
[79] "Life and Times of William Hill," loc. cit., II, 47.

to this time the transmitters of the Great Awakening. Once more the Church was infused with the spirit of Davies, the Tennents, and Whitefield, and became aglow with the evangelical zeal that had earlier characterized it. In addition to raising the standard of piety, a large number were brought into the Church and new congregations were formed within the bounds of the Virginia Synod.[80] Moreover, the Presbyterians, unlike the Baptists, were peculiarly fortunate in the number of ministers that were raised in the revival, some of whom, as Nash Le Grand and Drury Lacy, were licensed even before the revival was over and took an important part in it.[81] At both Hampden-Sydney and Liberty Hall the study of theology was greatly stimulated, the first special course for the training of ministers in Virginia being organized at the time by Graham in connection with the Rockbridge Academy.[82] A few years later (1793) Liberty Hall became also a Theological Seminary under the patronage of the Synod.[83]

Finally, we may note that the revival of 1787-8 marks an epoch in the expansion of Presbyterianism in the entire South and Southwest, as evidenced by the formation of the Virginia Synod, composed of the four Presbyteries of Hanover in eastern Virginia, Lexington in the Valley, Redstone in western Pennsylvania, and Transylvania in the Kentucky and Tennessee settlements.[84] The Synod was instrumental in widening the bounds of Presbyterianism by an active missionary policy.[85]

[80] Cf. Foote, p. 428.

[81] Cary Allen, Archibald Alexander, William Hill, Mathew Lyle and James Turner are some of the others who became prominent ministers. In fact a large proportion of a generation of preachers following the revival were converted during the work. As to the Baptists, Leland laments the fact that the revival produced so few for the ministry. "Whether it is because the old preachers stand in their way, or whether it is because the people do not pray the Lord of Harvests to thrust out laborers, or whether it is not rather a judgment of God upon the people for neglecting those who are already in the work, . . . I cannot say; but so it is. . . ." Works, p. 116.

[82] Foote, pp. 469-70, account of A. Alexander, who was one of Graham's pupils.

[83] Ibid., pp. 471-3, for transactions of the Synod. Cf. Evan. and Lit. Mag., IV, 400.

[84] Foote, p. 525; Davidson, op. cit., p. 37.

[85] See Foote, Chap. XXIII.

The new enthusiasm undoubtedly sprang in no small measure from the Great Awakening which we have just been considering.

4. Summary of the Great Awakening in Virginia

Summing up the movement, we see that by the year 1790 evangelical Christianity which found its re-birth in the Great Awakening had, under the impetus of repeated revivals, spread over the entire state. Largely because of its failure to adapt itself to the new Christianity, rather than because of its political connections, the Established Church was all but completely swept away.[86] Its place was now taken by popular or democratic churches, by which we mean those which, by reason of their organization, their doctrines or their appeal, gained their chief constituency from the middle and lower classes. These churches in Virginia were the Presbyterian, the Baptist, and the Methodist. We have also to note that these churches were aggressively evangelical, and measured their numerical strength largely by the degree of their acceptance of the principles of the Great Awakening. If the Established Church eventually rose again from its ashes, it was because it, too, in a large measure, joined ranks with these evangelical churches whose rise had contributed much to its downfall.[87]

As to the geographical aspects of the movement, we note that the center of Presbyterianism, originally in the eastern counties about Hanover, gradually moved to the counties east and west of the Blue Ridge, more especially to those in the Valley, where the racial element with which it was chiefly identified was preponderant. Their place in eastern Virginia, particularly north of the James, was taken by the Regular and Separate Baptists. The latter, who originally planted their first permanent home along the southern border of Virginia, were displaced as the dominant sect in the counties south of the James by the Methodists, who were aided by the Anglican Jarratt. In both the revivals of 1775-6 and 1787-9 the center of

[86] *Cf.* Bassett, "Development of the Popular Churches after the Revolution," *loc. cit.,* pp. 255-7.

[87] *Cf.* Cooke, *Virginia,* pp. 395-6. This took place under the leadership of Bishop Meade.

the Methodist movement was in southeastern Virginia. Thus the revival areas of the various denominations seem to have fairly clear geographical demarcations. Let us not forget, however, that these were merely the regions in which the denominations in question were preponderant. In no place did one group occupy the territory to the exclusion of the others. All three of them were scattered throughout the state and were, according to Leland, numerous. If the Baptists counted 20,000 members by 1790, they were probably the strongest numerically, but any definite comparison in this respect can at best be hazardous. We also know that Virginia was one of the strongest centers of Methodism on the continent, and nowhere, all things considered, was its expansion more phenomenal.

All three of the denominations under consideration made definite and permanent contributions to the life and institutions of the Old Dominion, which is the subject of the remaining chapters of our study. We shall first turn to a consideration of the relations of the Great Awakening to the rise of political democracy and the struggle for religious freedom in which the Baptists, supported by the Presbyterians, took the lead.

CHAPTER VIII

Contributions to the Rise of Democracy

If a study of the rise of dissent in the eighteenth century shows anything, it is the fact that the Great Awakening was one of the secret springs which directed the actions of men and, therefore, was one of the sources of the democratic movement so closely identified with the American Revolution. The evangelical doctrines, when brought to bear upon the great mass of the population, produced a democratic feeling, developed a degree of self-respect, and inculcated ideas of self-government. The very essence of these teachings was to place all men on a plane of exact equality in the Christian Church. Social rank counted for naught with the preachers of the Great Awakening. The Church was open to all alike—to slaves and freemen, to poor and rich, to learned and ignorant—so long as a man professed justification through faith in Jesus Christ. Thus we see in the evangelical groups a great levelling influence at work, which could not fail to have important consequences.

The Great Awakening gave rise to popular forms of church government and thus accustomed people to self-government in their religious habits. The alliance of Church and State, the identification of religious with civil institutions, was found to be detrimental to the cause of religion. The evangelicals regarded God as the sole head of the Church, and although some of them, as the Presbyterians, were willing to recognize legal restrictions on their worship, others, as the Separate Baptists, regarded such restrictions as absolutely repugnant to conscience.

The moral and intellectual uplift which came from the application of the evangelical doctrines imbued men with new ideas, caused them to seek changes, and prepared people for those transformations. Perhaps unconsciously, but none the less in reality, the Great Awakening gradually welded the common people into a democracy which in the end was to change inevitably the temper, if not the form, of government. "The people were coming to themselves and to a knowledge of their rights. For the first time they were learning to take an interest in legislation, in whatever affected their interests as members of society."[1] No longer were they willing to sit by and bow to the will of a ruling few who might endeavor to impose upon them.

The evangelical revival gave to the common people of Virginia their first leadership. The men who preached to them were of their own rank and file, and the very bringing together of great masses of people under the preaching of Whitefield, Davies, Waller, Leland, Williams, Shadford, and the other leaders of the Virginia Awakening developed a certain *esprit de corps*. The long struggle of the Presbyterians and Baptists for recognition created in the dissenters a consciousness of the power of united action. The revivalists were the first to weld together the inarticulate plain people and to bring them to a realization of their strength.

It is a commonly accepted fact that the dissenters were everywhere strong supporters of the Revolution.[2] "The denominations, like the Presbyterian and the Baptist, which were built up by the revival took almost unanimously the patriot side. It was their meeting houses that were burned as nests of rebellion and their pastors that were hunted as instigators of treason."[3] So it was in Virginia; the Presbyterians and Baptists were identified with the republican cause. There was every reason why they should be.[4] The special privileges of the Established

[1] Lovejoy, "The Influence of Methodism," *Meth. Rev.* (So.), Vol. LI, pp. 367-382 at 378 ff. *Cf.* "The Influence of the Reformation on the American Revolution," *Evan. and Lit. Mag.*, VII, pp. 505 ff., 561 ff.

[2] Such books as W. P. Breed, *Presbyterians and the Revolution,* and William Cathcart, *The Baptists and the American Revolution,* aim to show this. E. F. Humphrey, *Nationalism and Religion in America,* 1774-1789 (Boston, 1924), considers the subject of religious elements in the American Revolution, pp. 1-163 and *passim.* Much may be found also in Foote, *Sketches of Virginia,* and in the general denominational histories. The anomalous position of the Methodists in 1776 has been referred to.

[3] Maxson, *The Great Awakening in the Middle Colonies,* p. 150.

[4] See Fristoe, *History of the Ketocton Baptist Association,* pp. 154-155, and T. C. Johnson, *Virginia Presbyterianism and Religious Liberty,* pp. 59, 70, 71. Humphrey, pp. 78 ff., 128. The petitions to the Virginia legislature abound in expressions of loyalty to and support of the Revolutionary cause by these denominations, as will appear further on in this chapter.

Church, maintained by taxation, and the various restrictions placed upon the religious freedom of the nonconformists were repugnant alike to the principles of the Great Awakening and of the American Revolution.[5] Was there any difference between taxation without representation in the state and the compulsory payment of tithes to the Anglican Church by dissenters who could not be represented on the vestries?

The struggles of the Presbyterians and Baptists for toleration in Virginia involved an application of the same principles that later directed the colonies in their revolt against England. Political independence was chiefly cherished by the dissenters in Virginia because they felt that with it would come the overthrow of every vestige of religious oppression.[6] At least, the failure of the War for Independence would mean the failure of the struggle for religious freedom. When the successful war against England did not bring the full destruction of privilege in the Church, the religious struggle continued until it finally resulted in the complete victory of the revolutionary principles in ecclesiastical affairs.[7]

Not many of the leaders of the Great Awakening in Virginia have left us written expressions of their political views. A few of them have, however, and they are very convincing. Among the Baptists of Virginia no one seems to have had more political influence than John Leland. It is commonly maintained that it was Leland's withdrawal from the contest that assured Madison's election to the convention for the ratification of the constitution in Virginia.[8] In he first party alignment under the

[5] Cf. ibid.

[6] See Fristoe, pp. 89-90, 154 ff.; Memorial of the Hanover Presbytery to the Virginia Assembly, October 24, 1776, in Foote, pp. 324 ff. and Humphrey, pp. 78-81.

[7] Cf. Thom, The Struggle for Religious Freedom in Virginia: the Baptists, p. 9 and below, pp. 200 ff.

[8] He was the anti-federalist candidate in Orange County, a strong Baptist center. The Baptists were at first opposed to the Constitution because it did not contain adequate guarantee for religious liberty. Madison's arguments seem to have convinced them of the expediency of the document and Leland withdrew to support Madison. See Smith, "Life and Times of the Reverend John Leland," Bap. Quar., V, 250 and C. F. James, Documentary History of the Struggle for Religious Liberty in Virginia.

new government, Leland was a Jeffersonian Republican and later on became a follower of Jackson.[9]

Leland was a firm believer in the compact theory of government, and in this reflects the Jeffersonian philosophy. In his essay on the *Rights of Conscience,* published in 1791, he asserted: (1) "that righteous men have to part with a little of their liberty and property to preserve the rest"; (2) "that all power is vested in and consequently derived from the people"; (3) "that the law should rule over rulers, and not rulers over the law"; (4) "that government is founded on compact"; (5) "that every law made by legislators inconsistent with the compact, modernly called a constitution, is usurping in the legislators, and not binding on the people"; (6) "that whenever government is found inadequate to preserve the liberty and property of the people they have an indubitable right to alter it so as to answer their purposes"; (7) "that legislators, in their legislative capacity cannot alter the constitution, for they are hired servants of the people to act within the limits of the constitution"; (8) that "upon entering into the social compact" a man does not "surrender his conscience to that society to be controlled by the laws thereof."[10]

Leland was a firm opponent of religious establishments[11] and repeatedly asserted as a fundamental Baptist belief that, religion being a matter between God and the individual (the essence of the evangelical awakening), one's mere opinions were in no way subject to the control of the civil authorities.[12] Under governmental auspices, he pointed out, religion becomes "a principle of state" instead of a "Bible religion" and this is conducive to deism and infidelity.[13] As with the great body of his co-religionists, Leland had nothing but contempt for mere toleration. "Government should protect every man in thinking

[9] Smith, *loc. cit.,* p. 251. See also Leland's *Works,* p. 262, for an indictment of the Federalists, written in 1802.

[10] Leland, *Works,* p. 180.

[11] He gives a list of reasons against establishments in the same essay, pp. 182-3; see also *Works,* pp. 251-2.

[12] *Ibid.,* 181, 118, 251-2.   [13] *Ibid.,* p. 183.

and speaking freely, and see that one does not abuse another. The liberty I contend for is more than toleration. The very idea of toleration is despicable; it supposes that some have a pre-eminence above the rest to grant indulgence; whereas all should be equally free, Jews, Turks, Pagans and Christians. Test oaths and established creeds should be avoided as the worst of evils."[14]

One who reads the political essays in Leland's *Works* is struck with the extent to which he was imbued with Jefferson's ideas of government. Like the great sage of Monticello, he prayed for the day of universal peace when commerce might flourish, "when there shall not be a ship of war in the seas," and when militias might never be needed. He would free the common man from "oppression, personal slavery, religious tyranny," as well as the "intrigues of lawyers" and the "frauds of priests." That government was best which governed least, and, therefore, Leland's ideal included short sessions of the legislature and few laws, a treasury maintained on a frugal basis just sufficient for the exigencies of government, for each man must be "the treasurer of his own earnings." Equitable taxes, economy in expenditures, speedy payment of debts, extension of commerce that would bring a favorable balance of trade, the improvement of the soil, broad educational opportunities—in short, a government based on the honesty, industry and wisdom of the common man, emanating from the people and responsible to them—constituted Leland's ideal.[15] Stinging indeed were his indictments of federalist extravagance and aristocracy.[16] He branded this party as "high toned."

Another Virginia Baptist who left us a summary of his political creed was David Barrow. Before departing to make his home in Kentucky in 1797, Barrow printed a *Circular Letter*[17] in which he enumerates, in twenty-eight points, his

[14] "Virginia Chronicle," *Works*, p. 118.

[15] See *Works*, pp. 259-270, espec. at 269-270. He even favored an amendment to the constitution establishing an elective judiciary. See *ibid.*, pp. 285-300.   [16] *Ibid.*, pp. 262-3.

[17] A copy is in the Va. Bap. Hist. Soc. Taylor, *Virginia Baptist Ministers*, I, 168-170, prints much of it leaving out, however, a very significant

views of government. Like Leland, he regarded government as a necessary evil which, owing to the depravity of man, was better than the state of nature. Nevertheless, government was a civil compact between the people which could be changed at the will of the majority. Barrow believed in "the natural equality of man except in some monstrous cases"; in the right of men to the enjoyment of life, liberty and property and the means of defending themselves if they have not forfeited their right to these blessings by their own evil conduct; in the right of men to make their own laws in person or through their representatives; in the right to hold office by those fairly and freely elected by a majority of the suffrages; in the responsibility of representatives and judges to the people; in annual elections of the representatives; in the abolition of "all religious tests and ecclesiastical establishments"; in the abolition of all privileges held by any group of men; in the liberty of the press and freedom of speech; in "a well regulated militia" as "the best natural defense of a free government"; in trial by jury, fair bail, and reasonable punishments. Finally, Barrow wished the "downfall of all despots and despotism . . . that all the oppressed, in all countries may enjoy the sweets of liberty, and every man of all complexions return to his inheritance. I wish that all Judges and Courts of Justice may be enabled to maintain integrity and exercise impartiality!—I wish success to what few honest Lawyers we have!—But the downfall, or rather the speedy reformation of all pettyfoggers, and knavish characters in this office.—And that all officers, whether civil or military, may not content themselves with empty titles, but hold and exercise their offices, to their own honor and the good of the community."[18]

Such was the political philosophy of two leading Baptists of Virginia who saw fit to write on the subject. There is every reason to believe that Leland and Barrow represented the rank and file of the denomination. Fristoe says: "It is well under-

reference to slavery which Barrow opposed. The political creed is on pp. 8-10 of the *Circular Letter*.

[18] Barrow, *Circular Letter*, p. 12.

stood by our neighbors that the baptists with us are generally republicans," and he proceeds to assign the reasons.[19] Doubtless, too, the opinions of the Baptist ministers counted for much in the politics of the time. We are told of Lewis Conner, who was active in political affairs: "His political opinions were eagerly sought after, and listened to with profound attention by the youth who were growing up around him, while aspirants to office in the county in which he resided never failed to feel themselves much surer of success, if they found the weight of his name and opinions in their scale."[20] At a time when the number of men capable of exerting an active influence in political affairs was comparatively small, the influence of these Baptist leaders must have been considerable, at least in certain counties. Indeed, Fristoe tells us that, "although the Baptists were not numerous, when there was anything near a division among the other inhabitants in a county, the Baptists together with their influence, gave a cast to the scale, by which means many a worthy and useful member was lodged in the house of assembly and answered a valuable purpose there."[21]

We are not without evidences that the Baptists became conscious of their political influence and we have record of at least one church, namely Mathews Church in the county of the same name, which took formal votes to determine whom the members should support for the General Assembly and the national House of Representatives.[22] No doubt, other churches

[19] *History of the Ketocton Baptist Association* (1808), pp. 154-157. That Fristoe referred to the Revolutionary period, is seen in the fact that he cites the arbitrary conduct of the British government in levying taxes without representation, as one of the reasons for the republican tenets of the Baptists.

[20] Taylor, *Virginia Baptist Ministers*, I, 191-2.

[21] *History of the Ketocton Baptist Association*, p. 90.

[22] "Resolved, on motion, that Thomas Smith be barred the interest of our brethren, and that Mordecai Cook and Mann Page be voted for as representatives to our next General Assembly." "On motion, who should have the vote of this Church, as a member to Congress, John Page and Francis Corbin, resolved that John Page should have the vote in preference." McGill (compiler), *Hist. of the Churches of the Rappahannock Association*, pp. 34-35. *Cf.* above, p. 89 and n. 86, for similar action by the Presbyterians in the earlier period.

took similar action, especially during the struggle for religious freedom, when vital interests of the denomination were at stake, for Fristoe tells us that "the business then was to unite as an oppressed people in using our influence and give our voice in electing members of the State legislature—members favorable to religious liberty and the rights of conscience."[23] Later we shall see the influence exerted on politics by the Baptist Associations through their General Committee during this same period.

On other matters, also, the denomination did not hesitate to express its opinion. Such was the case when the constitution first appeared in Virginia and was opposed by many Baptists because it did not contain sufficient guarantees for religious liberty. The General Committee which met at Williams' Meetinghouse, Goochland, in 1788, expressed itself to this effect, but, probably through the influence of Madison, the Baptists were led to support the plan for a more effective national government, hoping to secure an early amendment to the constitution, which would secure their desired object.[24] We shall see that such a declaration of religious liberty was inserted in the Virginia constitution of 1776 by Madison,[25] and that the same principle was proposed by Virginia for incorporation into the Federal Constitution.[26]

Although we have been speaking mostly of the Baptists in connection with the rise of political democracy in Virginia, it is to be remembered that the Presbyterian and Methodist churches, judged from the standpoint of constituency, were likewise popular churches, and in rank and file, Republican in politics. If the Methodists fell under a cloud owing to the Anglican affiliations of Asbury and some of the leading ministers, this denomination soon outlived the charges of Toryism.

[23] Fristoe, p. 90.

[24] Semple, *History of the Baptists in Virginia*, p. 102; *cf.* "Address of the Baptists to President Washington, August 8, 1789," and the latter's reply, in Semple, pp. 484 ff.

[25] See below, pp. 203-4; *cf.* Humphrey, *Nationalism and Religion in America*, p. 362; Eckenrode, *Separation of Church and State in Virginia*, p. 44.

[26] Humphrey, pp. 470 ff., espec. 479.

It is hard to believe that the great bulk of Methodists were not similar to their Baptist and Presbyterian rivals, although, because they were Anglican in origin, they had far less reason to express themselves on political matters than did the other two evangelical groups. The attitude of the authorities had much to do with this, and therefore we can see why the Baptists who had suffered from mobs, bonds, fines, and prisons should be the most outspoken and forceful in expressing their political views, and the Methodists, least.[27] Originating as a revival group within the Established Church, we could hardly expect the Methodists to join in the attack against the mother institution. This is not proof, however, that they did not represent the same undercurrent of democracy as their more outspoken Baptist and Presbyterian friends. Indeed, the exalted position generally given the individual in the evangelical churches seems to afford sufficient basis for this belief.

In church government and organization, the denominations which we have been studying contributed to the growth of liberalism. This was particularly true of the Baptists, whose churches were thoroughly democratic.[28] Fristoe said: "Our religious education agrees with, and perfectly corresponds with, a government by the people,"[29] while we are told that the simple organization of a small Baptist church in the neighborhood greatly impressed Jefferson as embodying "the true principles of civil government."[30] Not only did every Baptist church select its own officers, but in regular monthly meetings all of the business of the church was transacted, every member often having

[27] *Cf.* Address to Washington, *loc. cit.*

[28] "We believe that the Church of Christ has full power to govern itself. Her officers . . . are not to be imposed upon her by any other authority beside, but are to be chosen by the unanimous suffrage of her own members; by the common consent or universal vote of the whole assembly. She has the power to receive whom she pleases by the same suffrage and to exclude . . . to reprove, or censure, or suspend, or excommunicate. . . ." David Thomas, *The Virginian Baptist,* p. 17.

[29] Fristoe, p. 157. See also church constitutions in the MS. Record Books cited below.

[30] See *Religious Herald,* April 6, 1871, April 20, 1871, July 16, 1874.

an equal vote.[31] In these meetings members were tried, disciplined, or excommunicated; representatives to the Associations were chosen; elders and deacons were elected;[32] financial business was transacted; in short, every matter which came before the church was handled in the monthly meetings, and members were expected to be present.[33]

There was no authority in the Baptist organization which could bind the individual church in any matter whatever. However, as a matter of expediency and mutual benefit—as a bond between the churches—Associations were formed.[34] The Associations were composed of delegates from the churches within their designated bounds, and held their meetings annually. The powers of the Associations were wholly advisory. They could in no way infringe upon the absolute independence of the churches,[35] or, as we read in one constitution, they had "no power to Lord it over God's heritage, nor shall they have power to infringe any of the internal rights of any church in the union."[36] The Associations, nevertheless, did much for the wel-

[31] There was no uniformity as to voting, some churches admitting, as Thomas seems to indicate, all members; others admitted all the males, while some restricted voting to free males. See Semple, p. 130. A number of MS. Church Books of the eighteenth century are in the Va. Bap. Hist. Soc. In these one sees in operation the government of the Baptist churches.

[32] On the church officers, see Thomas, pp. 27-28. The elders assisted in church administration while deacons cared for secular concerns. Only ministers could administer the sacrament.

[33] Repeated absence without good excuse was likely to result in expulsion, and there are many such cases in the Church Books. Thus Boarswamp Church, which restricted voting to free males, required a suitable reason for the first offence; for the second, the member was to be admonished; the third absence was to be regarded "as an open violation of the Articles of our discipline and shall be dealt with in such a manner as the church or a majority of the free male members shall think proper." The records show that these rules were enforced. MS. Record Book, Boarswamp Church, Va. Bap. Hist. Soc.

[34] Thomas, *Virginian Baptist*, p. 36; Fristoe, pp. 16-17; Semple, p. 62.

[35] *Ibid.* Also the constitution of any Association, *e.g.* the second constitution of the Roanoke Association, article 3, May, 1793. MS. Va. Bap. Hist. Soc.

[36] Second Roanoke Association Constitution (1793), art. 3. *Cf.* Leland, "Virginia Chronicle," in *Works*, p. 113.

fare of the churches, and their annual gatherings were also occasions for the holding of great religious meetings.[37]

In order to secure more unity of action in waging the contest for religious freedom, a General Committee[38] was organized in 1784 to represent the collective interests of the Associations.[39] The General Committee was made up of not more than four delegates from each district Association. Here again the Baptists were very jealous of setting up any body which could be supreme over the churches, and the General Committee never claimed to be more than the mouthpiece of the Baptists at large.[40] In no way did it trench upon the independence of the churches, or the liberties of the Associations. Thus in the Circular Letter issued by the Committee in 1793 we read: "And whereas doubts have arisen (as we're informed) . . . concerning the *committee*, lest in time it should become dangerous to the liberties of the Associations and Churches, whose *external* interest and concerns *only* it means to meddle with, and such rights to guard and protect, in *this point of view*, you will look at us, and not as a body either possessing, or exercising power over the *liberty* and *independence* of the Churches." Thus the Baptist organization was thoroughly in accord with the principles of government by and for the people. Unquestionably, in its practical workings, it actually contributed to the development of the ideal of democracy in politics as well as in social relations.

The Presbyterians and Methodists were not as democratic in their church government as the Baptists. The former placed the control of the affairs in the hands of the elders and pastors,

---

[37] Semple, p. 63. Richard Dozier notes "abt. 2,000 people" on Sunday, June 4, 1786, and "abt. 1,600 people" on the next day at an Association meeting in Northumberland. MS. copy "Text Book" of Richard Dozier, Va. Bap. Hist. Soc.

[38] Fristoe, p. 87. This had been preceded by a General Association. See Semple, p. 91.

[39] *Ibid.*, pp. 92, 94-95. The General Committee dissolved in 1799 after the battle for religious freedom was over. Minutes for 1799, p. 4; Semple, p. 112.

[40] See Minutes of the General Committee for 1791, 1792, 1793 and especially the Circular Letters for those years. Va. Bap. Hist. Soc.

who constituted the local Session, and who also represented the congregation in the Presbytery and in the Synod. Their system was, therefore, a representative form of government.[41] While the congregations had the right to choose their pastors, it remained for the Presbytery to pass upon the qualifications of the latter.

The Methodist organization was thoroughly centralized, with the Bishops and Conferences as the directing powers.[42] As we have noted, the Bishops assigned the preachers, and the churches as such had no representation in the Conferences.[43] However, the significant fact with all the evangelical groups is that each emphasized the worth and equality of the individual. Is not this the real essence of democracy? In all of them each member had the right to express himself freely—a thing lacking in the old Established Church. Thus, the Methodist classes and bands were small units in which every member was expected to take an active part by praying, testifying, or exhorting. In fact, no Church placed more emphasis on the activity of the individual, and the more gifted were bound to have an opportunity to assume some sort of leadership by being chosen to head a class or band, or by being pressed into the ranks of the lay ministry. Even with their centralized organization, then, the Methodists were essentially a popular Church in which there were decided democratic influences operating upon the members.

The application of the political ideals of the dissenters, and the growth of their political consciousness, is best seen in connection with the struggle for religious liberty. This movement, says Thom, "was really a part of the greater struggle for political freedom, with which it was so nearly coincident in time. Much the same causes led to each; the logic of both was

[41] *Encyc. Brit.,* article on "Presbyterianism"; Charles Hodge, *Const. Hist. of the Pres. Church.* The Session corresponded in a general way to the monthly meeting of the Baptists.

[42] See J. J. Tigert, *Const. Hist. of Amer. Epis. Methodism;* J. M. Buckley, *Const. and Parl. Hist. of the M. E. Church.* Conferences met annually and in 1792 the quadrennial General Conference began.

[43] Lay representation was not instituted for many years, and the preachers, being itinerants, represented no particular churches.

the same; and there was no time at which the religious struggle was not largely political, and not clearly seen to be so by the leaders of thought."[44] The details of this struggle have been well told by others, and it is not so much our purpose here to repeat them, as to show the relation of the conflict to the great evangelical movement which we have been studying.[45] It was a phase of the internal revolution, which everywhere was contemporaneous with the revolt against Britain. It was a chapter in the great conflict between liberal and conservative forces, which accompanied the American Revolution and, we believe, was but the logical application of the democratic ideas that were born in the Great Awakening.

That the Baptists should assume the lead in the battle for religious freedom and equality is easily understood in the light of the foregoing chapters. The severe persecutions to which they were subjected engendered in them a bitterness towards the Established Church, and besides, absolute freedom of conscience was a part of their religion.[46] Their political philosophy, as expressed by men like Leland and Barrow, emphasized the principle of equality, which was the very antithesis of compulsory support of a Church. In addition, there was a strong irritation caused by the social distinctions we have already noted, which led the upper classes to despise the lower, and the latter to hate the former, and which fanned the zeal of the Baptists in their

[44] Thom, *The Struggle for Religious Freedom in Virginia: the Baptists* (J. H. U. Studies, XVIII), p. 9.

[45] The best study is by Eckenrode, *The Separation of Church and State in Virginia*. Thom, *op. cit.*, has developed the study with particular reference to the Baptists, as has C. F. James, *Documentary History of the Struggle for Religious Liberty in Virginia*. Johnson, *Virginia Presbyterianism and Religious Liberty*, endeavors to emphasize the contributions of the Presbyterians. Jernegan develops the problem in *Parallel Source Problems in United States History* and hereafter referred to as *Source Problems*. In connection with this discussion I have examined every one of the available religious petitions in the Virginia State Library archives.

[46] See Thomas, *Virginian Baptist*, p. 17, for a statement on this as a Baptist belief. Leland and many others repeated it with force. It was common to all evangelicals. Although not all sought to achieve it in the laws, they practiced it in their relations to others. All of them placed religion on the basis of a free choice. We have seen how absolutely catholic the Methodists were, for instance.

attack upon the Establishment.[47] More than any other group in Virginia, the Baptists made popular the idea of religious liberty, until Leland could write in 1790 that it "has been so canvassed for fourteen years, and has so far prevailed, that in Virginia, a politician can no more be popular without the possession of it, than a preacher who denies the doctrine of the new birth. . . ."[48]

The spread of democratic feeling in the colony of Virginia was given an added impetus by the democratic basis of the quarrel with England, namely, the right of all Englishmen to tax themselves.[49] The demand of the dissenters for full equality before the law was in keeping with the trend of the times, but the Revolution brought an opportunity which might not have come in decades of peace. We have plenty of evidence that the dissenters fought the Revolution for more than independence from England.[50] Thus the Baptists reminded the Assembly in 1783 that "while we were opposing our enemies in the field, we were petitioning our rulers at the helm of legislation, to set us free from the yoke of religious oppression, which we long groaned under from the former government. . . ."[51] About the same time the Presbyterians informed their legislators that "love of liberty and political equality" were the "principles which engaged us and carried us through the late glorious contest," and that "we cannot help expressing our sorrow to see how slowly and with what seeming reluctance equal justice is done, and all denominations of Christians in the state are put in possession of their constitutional rights."[52] There are numerous

[47] Cf. Thom, op. cit., pp. 42, 44.

[48] "Virginia Chronicle," in Works, p. 123. Incidentally the quotation shows how popular the evangelical teachings had become after the post-Revolutionary revivals.

[49] Cf. Eckenrode, op. cit., p. 41. Fristoe cites this as a reason why Baptists favored the Revolution, History of the Ketocton Baptist Association, p. 154.

[50] Especially in the religious petitions from 1775 on which run into the hundreds. Many of these are printed in Eckenrode in full or part.

[51] MS. petition, Powhatan County, November 6, 1783. The same sentiment is repeatedly expressed in others from 1775 on. Cf. Memorial from Hanover Presbytery, October 24, 1776. See also Journal of House of Delegates, October 16, 22, Nov. 1, 9, 1776, and scores of religious petitions in the Archives of Va. State Library.   [52] MS. petition, October 31, 1787.

expressions of exactly the same sentiment from many counties which show how in the minds of a large body of the inhabitants religious, and even political equality were expected as the reward of the common blood shed in the war.[53]

It is interesting indeed to note the tone of some of these petitions. They reveal a consciousness of the political strength of the dissenters, who regarded their requests not as favours to be granted, but as rights which they could claim as men and voters. Thus the militia and freeholders of Augusta County, strong Presbyterian territory, demanded equal liberty for all denominations not "as the pittance of courtesy but . . . as their patrimony which cannot be withheld from them without the most flagitious fraud, pride and injustice, which if practiced may shake this continent and demolish provinces."[54] Similarly, in a Baptist petition for full equality we read: "We do not ask this, Gentlemen, as a favour which you have a privilege either to grant or withhold at pleasure, but as what we have a just claim to as freemen of the Commonwealth, and we trust it is your glory to consider yourselves not as the masters but servants of the people, whom you have the honour to represent, and that you will not fail in any instance, to recognize the natural rights of all your constituents."[55]

In these petitions the dissenters appear as an articulate political group conscious both of their rights and their strength. Hawks, the Episcopalian historian, says: "The Baptists were not slow in discovering the advantageous position in which the political troubles of the country had placed them. Their numerical strength was such as to make it important to both sides to secure their influence; they knew this, and therefore determined to turn the circumstance to their profit as a sect."[56] To a slightly lesser extent was this true of the Presbyterians. The explanation seems to be that whereas the Baptists fought for complete sepa-

[53] *E.g.,* MS. Rockbridge petition, December 1, 1784, and in Eckenrode, p. 97; MS. Pittsylvania petition, November 7, 1785, and many others.

[54] Purdie's *Virginia Gazette,* October 18, 1776. In this we recognize the signatures of the Presbyterian leaders.

[55] MS. Baptist petition, May 31, 1783.

[56] *Ecclesiastical Contributions, Virginia,* p. 137.

ration of Church and State, the Presbyterians were more concerned with merely the removal of religious disabilities.[57] The Regular Baptists who, prior to the Revolution were willing to submit to the Act of Toleration, now joined the Separates in overthrowing the Establishment.[58]

As early as 1772 the Baptists began to memorialize the Assembly for the same indulgence in religious matters "as Quakers, Presbyterians, and other Protestant Dissenters enjoy." Identical petitions came from Lunenburg, Mecklenburg, Sussex, and Caroline, while a stronger one from Amelia asked "that Liberty of Conscience may be secured to them."[59] The result was the drawing up of a Toleration Act in 1772 which, however, was so objectionable that it never passed.[60] Both Baptists and Presbyterians strongly expressed disapproval of the bill which was printed and circulated. The dissatisfaction of the dissenters was best expressed in a long memorial drawn up by Hanover Presbytery in November, 1774, and presented to the House on June 5, 1775.[61] The principal objections were: (1) The bill did not grant the right to itinerate which was necessary to adequately meet the religious needs of the dissenters; (2) it did not allow night meetings which were sometimes necessary— a provision which was a reflection on the dissenters; (3) it required that church doors be open at all times, which implied "a suspicion of our loyalty, and will fix a stigma upon us to after ages, such as we presume our honorable representatives will not judge that we have anyhow incurred"; (4) it did not permit the baptism of slaves—a provision absolutely contrary to the evangelical principles and to the "laws of Christ."

The Hanover memorial also voiced certain positive demands, namely: (1) that the same penalties be inflicted on those who disturbed their meetings as upon those who disturbed the Establishment; (2) for freedom in speaking and writing upon

---

[57] *Religious Herald,* July 25, 1872.

[58] C. F. James in *Religious Herald,* February 7, 1889.

[59] Eckenrode, pp. 38-39; Thom, pp. 44-45; James, *Doc. Hist.,* pp. 33-34.

[60] Eckenrode, pp. 39-40; Thom, 45 ff.; James, 35 ff.

[61] MS. Records of Hanover Presbytery, October 15, 1773; *Jour. of House of Burgesses,* June 5, 1775. The memorial is given in Johnson, *op. cit.,* pp. 65-69. It was probably written by Caleb Wallace. See W. H. Whitsitt, *Life and Times of Judge Caleb Wallace,* p. 34 and Eckenrode, p. 40.

all religious subjects; (3) for the right to hold property for the support of their schools and churches; (4) that nothing in the Act of Toleration be so expressed as to render us suspicious or odious to our countrymen; (5) "to have and enjoy the full and free exercise of our religion, without molestation or danger of incurring any penalty whatsoever." There is much significance in the tone of the memorial which one finds well expressed in the statement: "We are petitioning in favor of a Church that is neither contemptible nor obscure. . . ."

The Baptists had the same objections to the bill as the Presbyterians[62] and, furthermore, asked "that an Act of Toleration may be made giving the Petitioners and other Protestant dissenting Ministers liberty to preach in all proper places, and at all seasons, without restraint."[63] The bill in question never became a law. "The colony was now on the verge of revolution and the great controversy with England drew attention from other subjects. Besides, the time had passed for toleration. The dissenters had practically won toleration before, and, with a revolution on hand, they would be satisfied with nothing short of complete liberty."[64] Semple tells us: "This was a favorable season for the Baptists. Having been much ground under the British laws, or at least by the interpretation of them in Virginia, they were to a man favorable to any revolution by which they could obtain freedom of religion. They had known from experience that mere toleration was not a sufficient check, having been imprisoned at a time when that law was considered by many as being in force."[65]

The sixteenth article in Declaration of Rights of the Virginia constitution of 1776, as amended on motion of Madison, declared that "all men are equally entitled to the free exercise of religion, according to the dictates of conscience. . . ."[66] Madi-

---

[62] *Jour. of House of Burgesses,* May 12, 1774; Thom, pp. 46-47; Eckenrode, p. 39.

[63] *Jour. of House of Burgesses,* May 16, 1774; Thom, p. 47; Eckenrode, p. 39.

[64] Eckenrode, p. 40.   [65] Semple, p. 85.

[66] *Source Problems,* p. 237; Eckenrode, pp. 43 ff. for discussion of the article. The whole Bill of Rights is often printed in source books. See also Gaillard Hunt, *James Madison and Religious Liberty,* Am. Hist. Ass'n. Rep., 1901, I, 166-7.

son's amendment was of fundamental importance, as the original proposition declared merely for toleration and even permitted magistrates to arrest those who disturbed the peace "under color of religion."[67]

It was one thing to express the principle of religious liberty in a Declaration of Rights and another thing to write it into the laws of the state. In the eyes of the dissenters this involved the placing of all denominations on an absolutely equal basis, the complete separation of Church and State, the repeal of all laws which gave precedence to the Establishment in anyway whatsoever.[68] This was the only sort of liberty consistent with the new form of government that had been established. For the purpose of securing these objects petitions and memorials poured in upon the Assembly from all parts of the state.[69] The most notable of these was a petition circulated by the Baptists and signed by about ten thousand people who, no doubt, represented all opinions.[70]

From the Methodists and Anglicans came counter petitions in favor of the Establishment.[71] The Anglicans argued on the basis of justice, wisdom, and policy. It would be unjust and a violation of good faith to deprive the clergy of their livings which were guaranteed to them in the laws when they entered the ministry. Wisdom proved "that a religious establishment in a State is conducive to its peace and happiness." The virtues of

[67] *Source Problems,* p. 236. Mason's intention in the original article was doubtless for full religious liberty but the wording was unfortunate. See James, pp. 62 ff., who contends for Baptist influences on Madison, and Johnson, pp. 76 ff., who gives credit to the Presbyterians. Hunt, *loc. cit.*

[68] Eckenrode, p. 45.

[69] See Eckenrode, Thom and James for many extracts. The *Evan. and Lit. Mag.,* IX, 30 ff. prints the five Presbyterian memorials from 1776 to 1785.

[70] *Cf.* Fristoe, *op. cit.,* p. 91; Eckenrode, p. 48 and note; James, p. 69. Eckenrode examined this petition but I could not find it in the Archives. Fristoe says that even some Episcopalians who thought that the dissenters had been unjustly treated signed it.

[71] *Jour. of House of Delegates,* October 28, 1776; James, pp. 75 ff.; Eckenrode, pp. 47 ff.; *Source Problems,* pp. 239 ff. The Methodist petition was signed by George Shadford "in Behalf of the whole Body of the people commonly called Methodists in Virginia, consisting of near, if not altogether, three thousand members."

Christianity can best be propagated in this way. On grounds of policy, equality among all denominations must inevitably lead to strife for supremacy amongst the most powerful. Finally, the memorialists were convinced that a majority of the inhabitants favored a continuance of the Established Church and that the question should be submitted to the people.[72]

The weight of opinion was against the Established Church, and, moreover, Jefferson had launched his great program of reforms which included full religious liberty and separation of Church and State.[73] However, this could not be achieved at one blow, since the Assembly was controlled by Anglicans.[74] What happened was the passage, on November 19, 1776, of a series of resolutions[75] providing for freedom of opinions and the destruction of the Established Church. The resolutions were followed by an act of December 9 which repealed all laws restraining freedom in religious opinions and exempted dissenters from all contributions for the support of the Established Church.[76] Most significant of all, it suspended the levy for the support of the Anglican clergy until the summer of 1777, on the ground that the exemptions allowed dissenters might make the support of the Church too burdensome on its members in some parishes. Hence, for the present, it would be better to place it on a voluntary basis. The matter of a general assessment for the support of all churches was postponed.

The act of December 9 really spelled the end of the Establishment.[77] To free half the taxpayers from the support of the state religion meant the end of such support.

From 1776, annually until 1779, the salaries of the Anglican clergy were suspended.[78] An effort was then made to pass Jefferson's bill for religious freedom but it failed despite wide-

[72] However, Thomas Jefferson records that two-thirds of the people had become dissenters by the time of the Revolution. See *Notes on the State of Virginia* (1781), ed. Baltimore, 1800, p. 159.

[73] Eckenrode, pp. 46 ff.; D. S. Muzzey, *Thomas Jefferson*, p. 61.

[74] See Thom, pp. 60-61, who quotes Jefferson, and *Source Problems*, pp. 243-244.

[75] Given in Eckenrode, pp. 49-50, and James, p. 79; Thom, pp. 58-59.

[76] Eckenrode, pp. 52-53; Hening's *Statutes at Large*, IX, 164.

[77] Eckenrode, p. 53. See Hawks, pp. 145-146, for effects of the law on the clergy.   [78] Eckenrode, pp. 54, 55, 56.

spread support from Baptists and Presbyterians and even some from Anglicans and Methodists.[79] In its stead was passed, on December 13, 1779, a bill which permanently deprived the established clergy of their means of support which had been suspended since 1776.[80]

The act of December 13 removed the last prop from under the Establishment. The only hope of its supporters now lay in securing a general assessment for the support of *all* denominations. This question was not settled until 1785, and it produced a great deal of agitation in the state. The crisis did not come until after the Revolution had ended, and the movement for a reëstablishment of state patronage of religion represents an effort to check the liberal tendencies which had been engendered by the Great Awakening and had been popularized by the struggle with England.[81]

Patrick Henry and James Madison were leaders of the opposing forces. The former, although a firm believer in religious and civil liberty and usually a supporter of the dissenters in their battles for equality, nevertheless upheld a general assessment to sustain religious teachers as a measure conducive to the stability of the new government.[82] This view was in harmony with Henry's growing conservatism. Madison who represented Orange County, a strong Baptist district, headed the popular party.

From the scores of petitions, remonstrances, memorials, and newspaper articles which appeared for and against the plan for a general assessment we can merely indicate a few lines of opinion which were expressed time and again.

In the first place, it was pointed out that religion being an indispensable adjunct of civil government and essential to the

[79] MS. petition, Amherst County, November 1, 1779, purports to be from "Church of England-men, Presbyterians, Baptists and Methodists." Cf. *Jour. of House of Delegates*, November 1, 1779. Dixon and Nicholson's *Virginia Gazette*, September 11, 1779, contains a criticism of Jefferson's bill in which it is attacked as unsocial and selfish and in violation of the social compact that was made by the majority.

[80] Eckenrode, pp. 61-62, 64; Thom, p. 67.

[81] Cf. Eckenrode, *The Revolution in Virginia*, pp. 296-7.

[82] *Religious Herald*, March 5, May 7, 1874; Eckenrode, *Separation of Church and State*, p. 81; *Revolution in Virginia*, p. 297.

prosperity and happiness of society, it was the duty of the legislature to encourage it.[83] Only in this way could it be assured that religion would continue to flourish in all parts of the state, and many of the petitions called attention to a general neglect of religion and morality.[84]

Religion being so necessary to the good government of a free state, it should not be left "to the accidental coming of some traveling preacher" but should be regularly performed by "fixed" teachers with stated support,[85] "it being highly unreasonable to suppose that any set of men could devote their time or fortunes to the attainment of education unless they should expect to be enabled to preserve a decent and respectable rank in life."[86] A general assessment, it was pointed out, "affords the most probable means of procuring a succession of learned ministers and rescuing the most excellent of all religions from that contempt into which the ignorance of its teachers must ever expose it."[87]

As to the constitutionality of a general tax for the support of religious teachers, it was argued that since each person was to support the denomination of his choice and that no sect was to be given preference in the law, it did not violate the Bill of Rights. It was held to be no valid objection to the plan that some people were opposed to the compulsory support of all religion, for were not men compelled to serve in the army against their consciences?[88] Moreover, religion was recognized as being beneficial to society, and "whatever is to conduce equally to the advantage of all should be borne equally by all."[89]

[83] MS. Essex petition, November 2, 1785; Warwick, May 15, 1784; Surry, November 14, 1785, and others. Dixon and Nicholson's *Virginia Gazette,* September 18, 1779, article by "A Social Christian."

[84] E.g. Amherst petition, November 27, 1783; Essex, November 2, 1785; Westmoreland, November 2, 1785; Lunenburg, November 8, 1783, and others. See also *Virginia Gazette or American Advertizer,* November 22, 1783.

[85] Dixon and Nicholson's *Virginia Gazette,* September 18, 1779.

[86] MS. Essex petition, November 2, 1785. The same idea is expressed in many others.

[87] MS. Surry petition, November 14, 1785.

[88] *Virginia Gazette or American Advertiser,* November 8, 1785.

[89] *Ibid.,* Isle of Wight petition, November 4, 1784; Eckenrode, pp. 83-84, and others.

While one can see that the primary object of a general
assessment was to save the Establishment, many, no doubt, saw
the reasonableness of a scheme whereby all titheables should
pay for the support of religion, being allowed to select the denomination to which they would contribute. In this way there
would be assured a steady supply of qualified ministers of the
gospel, and no community would suffer from the neglect of
religion on account of its inability to support a pastor. However, with the establishment of the Methodist Episcopal Church
on an independent basis and the incorporation of the Protestant
Episcopal Church, both in December 1784, there was less
reason for a general assessment on the grounds of scarcity of
ministers.[90]

With the great body of dissenters the plan for publicly supported religious teachers was regarded as an attempt to set up
an Establishment in a slightly different guise than formerly.[91]
At a time when the bill seemed certain to pass, the Hanover
Presbytery sent a memorial to the legislature requesting that
the plan be one on a "liberal" basis, that is, that public worship
and instruction be maintained not as a spiritual system, for
religion is not subject to human legislation, but only as a means
of promoting the social good. Every man was to have the right
to attach himself to any Christian religious society which he
chose to support, and provision was to be made for the incorporation of such societies.[92] It is only fair to say that this action
of the Presbytery did not represent the voice of the denomination, that the rank and file expressed themselves strongly against
the assessment plan,[93] and that a few months later, in May
1785, the Presbytery itself voted unanimously against the

[90] This was the burden of an Amherst petition, December 10, 1785, in
which many of the signers had at first favored the bill but now had changed
their minds.

[91] Virginia Gazette or American Advertizer, November 8, 1785.

[92] Memorial of Hanover Presbytery, October, 1784, in James, pp. 231-5,
Johnson, 100-104, Foote, Sketches of Virginia, First Series, 336-8, MS. Recs.
Hanover Presbytery, October 28.

[93] Memorial of Presbyterian Convention at Bethel, May, 1785, given in
Foote, pp. 342-4 and James, 236-40; Johnson, p. 110. Petition of Augusta
session to the Presbytery, May, 1785, in MS. Recs. Hanover Presbytery,
May 19; Johnson, p. 107.

scheme.[94] The original action of the Presbytery seems to have been dictated by a desire to secure as liberal terms as possible in a bill whose passage seemed at the time inevitable.[95]

In scores of petitions which poured upon the Assembly, particularly in the fall of 1785, thousands of dissenters—Baptists, Presbyterians, Quakers, and now even Methodists—attacked the bill for providing religious teachers.[96] Over and over again one reads the political philosophy of the Great Awakening in these remonstrances, the most able of which was the memorial prepared by James Madison, which was widely circulated as a broadside, and came in with signatures from many counties.[97] Religion, or the duty we owe the Creator, is a matter of conviction alone and precedes the claims of civil society. Man enters civil society always with a saving allegiance to the supreme authority of Christ. The right of freedom of conscience, being an unalienable gift of nature, is not the subject of legislation. The legislature cannot take it away without destroying the constitution.[98] If it can do so it "may control the freedom of the press, may abolish the trial by jury, may swallow up the executive and judiciary powers of the State; . . . may annihilate our very right of suffrage and erect themselves into an independent and hereditary assembly. . . ."[99] The same authority which can establish Christianity to the exclusion of all other religions, might, by the same logic, establish some particular sect of Christians over all others.

[94] Foote, p. 341; MS. Recs. Hanover Presbytery, May 19, 1785. Eckenrode, pp. 89 ff., for discussion of the Presbyterian position.

[95] The Memorial of 1784 was drawn up by J. B. Smith and William Graham. Johnson, p. 105.

[96] Eckenrode, p. 111, estimates that not fewer than 10,000 at the least signed the anti-assessment petitions. About 1,500 names were signed to the Presbyterian memorials alone, and other Presbyterians signed the undenominational petitions. The number of Baptist signers must have been very large. Thom, p. 56, says that it was their custom to send in petitions by counties rather than as a denomination to make a stronger impression on the legislature. Leland, "Virginia Chronicle," in *Works,* p. 113, says that the Methodists now being an independent denomination "vigorously opposed the assessment." Cf. Ambler, *Sectionalism in Virginia,* p. 40.

[97] Many copies of this are in the Virginia archives as it was presented from Albemarle, Orange, Louisa and other counties. It is printed by Semple, Appendix, pp. 500-509.

[98] A Rockingham petition, November 18, 1784, quotes Locke on this. See Eckenrode, pp. 95-96.   [99] Madison's memorial.

It was pointed out by the champions of religious freedom that the Christian religion needs no establishment for its support and that, indeed, religious establishments have in all ages been a bane to its purity and excellency. It would only confirm the suspicions of the enemies of Christianity "that its friends are too conscious of its fallacies to trust to its merits."[100] The bill was regarded as contrary to the gospel and utterly repugnant to the spirit of Christianity. Those who are truly pious will gladly contribute to the support of religious teachers; those who are not will not be made better by being compelled to pay tithes. The Church of Christ being a spiritual body, the Quakers pointed out, it "is no more dependent on human Literature or Pecuniary Provisions for learned Teachers, than that the Salvation of Souls depends on Human learning and knowledge."[101] Moreover, the assessment bill was regarded as the first step in the direction of intolerance, "a snake in the grass, or as a first link which draws after it a chain of horrid consequences, and that by degrees it will terminate in who shall preach, when they shall preach, where they shall preach, and what they shall preach."[102] Must not the legislature under the proposed scheme "assume the prerogative of judging who are, and who are not worthy to receive the public benefice. And, of consequence, our religious principles, as well as practices must be subject to their censure; and stand, or fall according to their determination."[103] Many believed that the plan for supporting all sects was worse than a single Established Church, for by releasing ministers from the support of their congregations the pulpits of all would be exposed to mercenaries.

There are many strong expressions that the bill for an assessment was contrary to the principles of republicanism and a violation of the Declaration of Rights.[104] "To compel a man to furnish contributions of money for the propagation of opin-

[100] Madison's memorial.

[101] MS. petition, November 14, 1785, partly quoted in Eckenrode, 111.

[102] MS. Accomac petition, October 28, 1785.

[103] MS. petition, Orange County Baptist Association, 1785, November 17, 1785. Cf. Religious Herald, July 25, 1872.

[104] MS. petition, Cumberland, October 26, 1785; Caroline, October 27, and others.

ions which he disbelieves and abhors, is sinful and tyrannical; that even the forcing him to support this or that teacher of his own religious persuasion is depriving him of the comfortable liberty of giving his contributions to that particular pastor, whose morals he would make his pattern, and whose powers he feels most persuasive to righteousness. . . ."[105] "We think it a grievance," reads another petition, "that a law should be made in favour of any set of men whatever which commands our money or property from us contrary to our consents. . . ."[106] Such a law should not be enacted without the clearest mandate from a majority of the people and "the representation must be made equal, before the voice either of the representatives or of the counties will be that of the people."[107]

The struggle for an assessment bill was part of the great reaction in Virginia, an effort of the conservatives to check the tide of democracy that had been engendered to a considerable extent by the evangelical revivals. The movement was supported, in the main, by the tidewater and southside counties where the Established Church still had many friends. The midland counties were divided, the Baptists probably accounting for the opposition, while the western counties, where Presbyterianism was the leading religious interest, were strongly opposed to the plan.[108] We have noticed that even the Methodists, now that they had their separate church organization, joined the ranks of the liberals in this contest.[109]

The removal of Henry from his dominant position in the House of Delegates by his election to the governorship, the widespread publicity given to the issue by the circulation of Madison's memorial, the decision of the Hanover Presbytery, in deference to the opinion of its constituency to absolutely oppose assessment, and the crystallization of opinion among the Baptists, are regarded by Eckenrode as the causes which turned the tide against assessment when its passage seemed assured.[110]

[105] MS. Nansemond petition, October 27, 1785.
[106] MS. Campbell petition, October 27, 1785.
[107] Madison's memorial.
[108] Eckenrode, pp. 86 ff., who thoroughly analyses the vote on the several resolutions.   [109] See above, p. 209.   [110] Eckenrode, pp. 94 ff.

Not only did the plan of the conservatives to reunite Church and State fail, but any such efforts in the future were made impossible by the passage of Jefferson's bill for religious freedom, which had failed in 1779. This act, passed in December, 1785, guaranteed "That no man shall be compelled to frequent or support any religious worship, place, or ministry whatsoever, nor shall be enforced, restrained, molested or burdened in his body or goods, nor shall otherwise suffer on account of his religious opinions or beliefs; but that all men shall be free to profess, and by argument to maintain, their opinion in matters of religion, and that the same shall in no wise diminish, enlarge, or affect their civil capacities."[111] It was further declared that the rights asserted being "of the natural right of mankind," any attempts hereafter made to repeal them would be "an infringement of national right." The Act for Establishing Religious Freedom was the logical outcome of the application of the evangelical principles to politics. It was the result of the spread of democratic ideas among the mass of people, who had been made conscious of their strength and taught to act together by the leaders of the Great Awakening.

With the passage of the Act of 1785 the real struggle for religious freedom was over. Unhappily, however, religious strife continued. In December, 1784, the conservatives had secured the passage of an act for incorporating the Protestant Episcopal Church.[112] This law gave to the Episcopalians the glebes, churches, chapels, plate, books, and other property which belonged to the Established Church. Moreover, it gave to them full corporate powers to acquire and dispose of property, and provided for the election of vestries by the members. The Church was also given full power to regulate its own affairs in convention.

To the dissenters the incorporating act was a violation of the principle of religious liberty as well as the section of the Bill of Rights which prohibits rewards or emoluments except for services rendered the state. In the fall of 1786 petitions

[111] Given in Hening, XII, p. 84; Thom, pp. 79-80 note; *Source Problems*, p. 264.
[112] *Journal of House of Delegates,* December 22, 1784; the act is in Hening, XI, 532-7; Eckenrode, pp. 101-2, analyses the vote.

again began to rain in upon the Assembly demanding the repeal of the obnoxious act. The underlying argument of the petitioners was that the property which had been confirmed to the Protestant Episcopal Church, was public property which had been taken as taxes from the people and ought to be returned to them.[113] It was repugnant to the principles of the Revolution that any one denomination should be given special favours, and the idea that all should stand on the same level was repeated again and again. One petition even advanced the statement that the discrimination in favour of the Episcopal Church tended to destroy the "fundamental compact" of society.[114] Probably 5,000 people signed the petitions for the repeal of the incorporating act, while half as many signed counter-petitions.[115] The latter were drawn up almost wholly in the eastern and southside counties where the Anglican Church still had considerable support.

In January, 1787, with scarcely a struggle, the incorporating act was repealed and for the first time all churches in Virginia stood upon exactly the same basis before the law. All of them "were now absolutely independent of the civil power as to doctrine, discipline and means of support. . . . The State had abandoned the effort to regulate society by means of religion; the principle of religious liberty was completely ascendant."[116] The repeal was largely a victory for the liberal and dissenting elements in the eastern counties, since the Episcopal Church was practically extinct beyond the Blue Ridge and the western counties were but little concerned. The victory showed that the liberal party was now predominant in all parts of the state.

If the repeal of the incorporating act severed all connection between Church and State in Virginia, it still left the glebes in the possession of the Episcopalians.[117] To the non-Anglicans it was contrary to the Bill of Rights that property which had been

[113] See Eckenrode, Chap. VI, who quotes from many petitions.
[114] Chesterfield petition, Eckenrode, pp. 122-3.
[115] Eckenrode, pp. 120, 125.   [116] *Ibid.*, p. 129.
[117] The act contained a clause, "Saving to all religious societies the property to them respectively belonging, who are hereby authorized to appoint . . . trustees who shall be capable of managing and applying such property to the religious uses of such societies."

purchased with public money should remain in the possession of any religious body, and a war for the confiscation and sale of this ecclesiastical property for the benefit of all citizens was immediately begun.[118] This was the last phase of the religious struggle in the Old Dominion, and it was the Baptists who, by sheer persistence, pushed it to its logical conclusion.

Beginning in the fall of 1787, petitions for the sale of the glebes were sent up to the Assembly, and for the next decade the Journal regularly records the reading of such requests. After 1790 practically all of these came from the Baptist General Committee, the other denominations seeming to have lost either their interest or their aggressiveness.[119] The underlying argument was that the Protestant Episcopal Church was not the successor to the old Anglican Establishment and therefore had no right to property which had been bought by men who were ancestors of Presbyterians, Baptists and Methodists. To permit them to retain the glebes was a mark of political favour contrary to justice, to the inalienable rights of all men, and to the fourth and sixteenth sections of the Bill of Rights which declared respectively against special emoluments except for public services and for freedom of religion.[120]

In defence of their position the Episcopalians asserted that the dissenters "voluntarily quit all Claim . . . to any Part of the Church Property, upon the Condition that they should be exempted in future from contributing to the Support of the Church and her Clergy. . . ."[121] In reference to the Baptists they continued: "Yet we understand that one Denomination . . . still persevere in petitioning your honorable House. . . . To add Weight to their Petition, they solicited the Methodists . . . and the Presbyterians . . . to assist them in obtaining Subscribers to their Memorial and Petition, but we are informed that both refused to concur with them. Being thus disappointed, they re-

[118] Eckenrode, Chapter VII.
[119] *Journal of House of Delegates*, November 8, 1791, October 10, 1792, November 25, 1794, November 17, 1795, November 17, 1796, December 9, 1797, December 15, 1798.
[120] See Pres. Memorial of 1787 in Eckenrode, pp. 131-2. The same arguments appear in many other petitions.
[121] MS. petition, Amelia, November 4, 1790, and Lunenburg, November 19.

doubled their own Diligence, and used every Artifice and Deception to get as many Subscribers as possible, by which means they prevailed on many of the In-cautious and Uninformed of other Denominations, nay even of the Episcopalians, to subscribe; who, when better informed, wished to erase their names. This being the Case, the number of Subscribers ought to have little weight." The language of the Baptists was branded as menacing and disrespectful" and their reasoning "false and inconclusive."[122]

The persistence of the Baptists finally bore fruit. When it appeared that a bill for the sale of the glebes would pass, the conservatives of both the House and Senate tried to save the property for the Episcopalians by having the matter declared to be a judicial one.[123] The effort failed, and on January 24, 1799, a bill passed by which the glebes reverted to the state.[124] In fact every statute, good or bad, dealing in any way with religious sects was repealed, and the religious rights of the Virginians were left to rest upon four sources, viz., the principles of the Revolution, the Declaration of Rights, the Constitution, and Jefferson's Bill for Religious Freedom.[125]

It only remained to decide the method of disposing of the glebes. This was not done, however, until 1802, during which interval petitions continued to filter in upon the Assembly. Finally a law of January 20, 1802, ordered vacant glebes and those that would become vacant to be sold by the overseers of the poor, who were to use the money for the support of the poor or any other purpose, save a religious one, which a majority of the voters might decide.[126] The act did not affect church edifices or church yards, certain specified private donations, nor any property acquired by the Episcopalians since 1777.[127] Says Dr.

[122] The Baptists compared their treatment since the Revolution with that of the colonies by the British Parliament prior to it.

[123] Eckenrode, pp. 145 ff.

[124] Shepherd, *Statutes at Large,* II, 149.

[125] Howison, *History of Virginia,* II, 395-6; *cf.* preamble of the act of 1799.

[126] Shepherd, *Statutes,* II, 314-316.

[127] Some of the provisions of the law were grossly violated (see Hawks, 235-6, Howison, II, 399), and the public profited little from the sale of the church property (Eckenrode, p. 148).

Hawks: "The warfare begun by the Baptists seven-and-twenty years before, was now finished."[128] Let us not forget, however, that in the struggle they had many allies.

In one other way the democratic influences of the Great Awakening were manifested in Virginia. Coming from the same region, namely, the midland and western counties, and, no doubt, from the same elements in the population that had waged the battle for religious freedom, was a strong movement to amend the constitution of 1776. The constitution, on the whole, represented a triumph of conservative principles, although the fact was not apparent, perhaps, at the time it was adopted.[129] In carving out the senatorial districts and in giving all counties equal representation regardless of size, the tidewater was given a disproportionate influence in the legislature.[130] Also no provision was made for amending the constitution, extending the suffrage, or reapportioning representation.

Expressions of discontent with the constitution of 1776 appeared in some of the religious petitions during the struggle against assessment and for the repeal of the incorporating act. Thus a petition from Rockbridge (1784) expressed disappointment that their "most essential Rights" remained "tottering and uncertain and they still must be so whilst they have no better a basis to rest upon than our present Constitution. . . ."[131] The Memorialists asked that a convention be called "for the express purpose of forming a Constitution that may define and secure the valuable Rights of the Citizens to them and their Posterity." Madison's Memorial declared that "the representation must be made equal before the voice either of the representatives or of the counties will be that of the people,"[132] while similar sentiment was expressed in an Augusta petition of 1786.[133]

---

[128] *Ecclesiastical Contributions, Virginia*, p. 233.

[129] Ambler, *Sectionalism in Virginia*, pp. 29-30; Eckenrode, *Revolution in Virginia*, p. 165.

[130] Jefferson, *Notes on the State of Virginia*, pp. 161-2, makes some interesting comments on this. The tidewater was given as many senators (12) as from the fall line to the Ohio and 71 representatives to 78 for the same region. The senatorial districts were marked out by the convention that made the constitution, so really was a part of it.

[131] December 1, 1784, in Eckenrode, p. 97.

[132] In Semple, at p. 107.   [133] In Eckenrode, p. 124.

After the struggle for separation of Church and State was virtually over, petitions directed against the undemocratic character of the Constitution kept coming in from the western counties.[134] Hundreds of names were attached to them and the agitation continued throughout the decade of the 'nineties. The opinion was expressed again and again that the constitution of 1776 was at best "a temporary expedient," "an ordinance of an ordinary Legislature" framed and introduced without proper authority, but to which circumstance made compliance necessary. It was pointed out repeatedly that Virginians "are deprived of the privileges which the citizens of other states enjoy as their indubitable rights," that the acts of a numerous body of tyrants are no different than those of a single tyrant, that "the constitution of every free government ought to be the act of the people who compose the government, and ought consequently to be paramount and not subordinate to either the Legislature, Executive, or Judiciary." Some thought that the present frame of government was "too complex in its Structure and too aristocratic in some of its Features to accord well with the Simplicity and Equality of the democratic Principle it was intended for," and that it was now time "to lay aside royal Form under republican Name."

The particular defects were in connection with the system of representation, the suffrage, the lack of a clear definition of powers and the fact that the constitution was not the act of the people and that therefore the latter had no security beyond the integrity of their representatives—"a security weak and unstable even at the present day and what at some future period . . . (may) end in the subversion of that liberty, for the acquisition of which they neither withheld their treasure or their blood." Beneath these petitions one can see a real discontent, as well as a confidence that the common people were thoroughly capable of shouldering the full responsibilities of government.

---

[134] *E.g.* Augusta, Loudoun and Louisa, 1792; Culpeper and Madison, 1793; Monongalia, Augusta, Berkeley, Rockbridge, 1795; Berkeley, Shenandoah, Frederick, Pittsylvania, 1796; Rockingham, Berkeley, Bedford, Hampshire, 1797. Most of these can be found in the Virginia archives, and from them I take the quotations which follow.

Undoubtedly the Great Awakening was one of the great contributing factors to the development of democracy in Virginia. The very nature of the evangelical movement and its teachings worked for democracy, both in society and politics, because it was democratic in its influences on the individual. This is exemplified in the writings of the leaders, in the forms of church government and organization which were evolved, in the practical application of the principles of the Great Awakening as seen in the struggle for religious freedom, and in the movement for the amendment of the Constitution of 1776. By the end of the eighteenth century Virginia was democratic in her political philosophy, despite the survival of certain aristocratic forms. In the election of 1800 the state gave Jefferson an overwhelming majority.[135] While there were other contributing forces to this revolution in the Old Dominion, certainly one cannot say that the least of these was the rise of evangelical Christianity and the development of the popular churches.

[135] See Ambler, p. 79. Jefferson received 13,363 out of 20,797 votes.

SAMUEL STANHOPE SMITH

CHAPTER IX

The Founding of Colleges

It remains for us in these concluding chapters to consider certain other effects of the Great Awakening on the life of Virginia and to point out the contributions made by the three denominations which represented the evangelical movement. These results we may treat conveniently as educational, humanitarian, and social. In this chapter we are concerned only with the first of these.

The Great Awakening gave a strong impetus to both ministerial and secular education in Virginia. In this movement the Presbyterians stand forth as by far the greatest contributors in the period under consideration (1740-1790), although before it was over the Baptists and Methodists had taken incipient steps towards founding institutions of learning.

The Presbyterian ministers from the very beginning brought with them to the New World the traditions of a liberal education. Despite the early lack of a sufficient number of preachers, the denomination never entertained a thought of introducing men into the ministry who had not received adequate training in an institution of higher learning, save, perhaps, in the case of a few exceptionally useful men.[1] Even during the Great Awakening when, due to the revivals, there was a rapid expansion in membership and a consequent shortage of ministers, the Presbyterians never relaxed in their standards of a trained ministry. The result was that other denominations, like the Baptists and Methodists in Virginia, who emphasized gifts of heart as more essential than gifts of mind, sometimes to the utter neglect of the latter, often outstripped the Presbyterians in gaining converts.

Preparatory to being admitted into the ministry, candidates for orders in the Presbyterian Church were compelled to undergo various trials consisting of the preparation of an exegesis in Latin on some assigned subject, the delivery of trial

[1] Alexander, *The Log College*, p. 10; Miller, *Life of the Reverend John Rodgers*, p. 22.

sermons and lectures, examinations in various branches of learning including, usually, Latin, Greek, and Hebrew; some of the sciences, as physics and astronomy; rhetoric, logic, philosophy, and theology.[2] This required a preparatory education in the classics, sciences, and divinity. The result was a group of men of high educational attainments. During the Great Awakening, as we have already noted, the New Side group in the Presbyterian Church put much emphasis on personal piety and one's religious experiences, which they thought were overlooked by the Old Side in its emphasis on high educational attainments. Before being ordained the candidates for the ministry were placed on probation and a new series of trials preceded final ordination.

That the examinations and trials were approached with no little trepidation and only after hard study and application by the candidates, one can easily appreciate by reading Philip Fithian's *Journal and Letters*. We also hear of some who were not very successful in their endeavors. Thus, in the case of Samuel Shannon, the Hanover Presbytery "under the most serious consideration, in connexion with the length of Time he has prosecuted his studies, do advise and judge it most expedient for Mr. Shannon to decline further Views to the gospel Ministry; at the same Time we also think it our Duty to declare that we hope and expect Mr. Shannon will prove himself a useful Member of Society in some other Calling. . . ."[3] It appears that Shannon later appeared before the Presbytery, was licensed as probationer, and some years later ordained.[4]

In their regard for ministerial training, the Presbyterians did not overlook lay or secular education. The Synod of New York and Philadelphia, to which Hanover Presbytery was first attached, enjoined congregations "to pay a special regard to the good education of children, as being intimately connected

---

[2] There are many examples of the trials of candidates in the MS. Recs. of Hanover Presbytery. See also Foote, *Sketches of Virginia*, First Series, pp. 351, 352-3, 410, 491-2; *Evan. and Lit. Mag.*, II, 476.

[3] MS. Recs. Hanover Presbytery, October 27, 1780, pp. 115-16.

[4] *Ibid.*, October 26, 1781, pp. 148-9, and November 25, 1784, p. 179, for licensure and ordination respectively.

with the interests of morality and religion; and that . . . every congregation be required to endeavor to establish one or more schools in such place or places as shall be most convenient for the people; that they be particularly careful to procure able and virtuous teachers; that they make the erection and care of schools a part of their congregational business, and endeavor to induce the people to support them by contributions, being not only the most effectual, but, in the end, the cheapest way of supporting them. . . ."[5] The Synod in particular urged that effectual provision be made for the education of poor children. Ministers were given to understand that regular and rigid inspection of church schools was "an indispensable part of their duty." The early ministers themselves sometimes performed the additional rôle of teachers, even setting up schools in their homes if regular school houses were lacking.[6]

In 1790, John Leland, commenting upon the various sects in Virginia, was struck by the attention given by the Presbyterians to education and remarked that "it may be said in truth that they have the best art of training up children in good manners, of any society in the state."[7] No doubt, if we could make a study of the reciprocal influences of the various denominations under consideration, we should find that the greatest contribution of the Presbyterians lay in the example of their dignified and educated ministry and their attention to the education of their children.[8] The time came when their less careful Baptist and Methodist contemporaries had to follow their example in founding schools and theological seminaries or be considered "queer."

The earliest schools of the Presbyterian Church in America and in Virginia were the famous Log Colleges. We have already

[5] *Recs. of Pres. Church,* May 23, 1785; *Watchman and Observer,* November 27, 1845.

[6] Peyton, *Augusta County,* pp. 42-3. Rev. John Craig's school was the first one in Augusta county. For others see Foote, *Sketches of Virginia,* 392, 351. Rev. John Brown conducted a classical school at New Providence in Augusta and Rev. John Todd, one east of the Blue Ridge in Louisa.

[7] "Virginia Chronicle," in *Works,* p. 101.

[8] *Cf. Pres. Mag.,* II, pp. 1-5, "Reciprocal Influences of the Evangelical Denominations."

had occasion to mention the most famous of these and the
parent institution, namely, the Reverend William Tennent's
school which was opened in 1727 at Neshaminy in Pennsylvania.[9] As we have noted in another connection, Tennent's
school turned out a group of men eminent for their piety, zeal,
and qualities of leadership, and also contributed heavily to the
Great Awakening.[10] It was the first college wholly under the
auspices of the Presbyterian Church and despite the limitations
of a single teacher for all the branches, it became famed for the
high quality of its curriculum, particularly its classical course.[11]

Tennent's Log College became the germ of Princeton College and, directly or indirectly, the mother of many institutions,
including Hampden-Sydney and Washington College in Virginia.[12] With the growing infirmities of its founder, it became
apparent that the Log College would become extinct, and still
the need was great for a higher institution of learning where
candidates might prepare for the ministry. The fact that the
Old Side Philadelphia Synod was engaged in the work of establishing a school at New London stimulated the New Side group
to greater exertion. The result was the founding of the
College of New Jersey, commenced at Elizabethtown in 1746,
later removed to Newark, and finally, in 1756, established at
Princeton.[13]

Those who took the leading part in establishing the new institution were all friends of the Log College and most of them
had received their training within its humble walls. Under its
first charter, issued in 1746, Gilbert Tennent, William, Jr.,
Samuel Blair, and Samuel Finley, all alumni of the Log College,
were members of the Board of Trustees,[14] while the first two

[9] See above, p. 12. The classical account is Archibald Alexander, *Biographical Sketches of the Founder and Alumni of the Log College.* See also,
Murphy, *The Presbytery of the Log College,* and Foote, *Sketches of Virginia,* First Series, 389-90.   [10] See above, pp. 12, 52 ff.

[11] Murphy, pp. 67, 161; *cf.* Foote, p. 390.

[12] Alexander, Chap. VII, *passim.*

[13] E. R. Craven, "The Log College of Neshaminy and Princeton University," *Jour. Pres. Hist. Soc.,* I, 308-314, corrects some previous misconceptions in John MacLean, *History of the College of New Jersey,* due to lack
of evidence. See also J. DeWitt, in *Princeton Sesquicentennial Celebration,*
Part III, for relation of the Log College to Princeton.

[14] Craven, *loc. cit.,* p. 312.

presidents, Jonathan Dickinson and Aaron Burr, were members of the New Side Synod of New York. Samuel Davies regarded the new institution as merely the continuation of Tennent's school and in 1753, as we have seen, he and Gilbert Tennent were sent to England to raise funds for Nassau Hall.[15] Three years later Whitefield wrote of the Log College: "This is now increased to a large College now erecting in the New Jerseys."[16]

In a very real sense then there is a continuity between the Log College and Princeton, for it was Tennent who convinced the Presbyterians of the Middle Colonies that they need not depend upon either New England or the universities of the Old World for an educated ministry. Above all, he taught that evangelical feeling and missionary zeal were necessary in the training of its ministry if the Church were to fulfill its mission. Princeton was a product of the great revival; it was born of the inspiration of the Great Awakening and after the reunion of the two Synods, in 1758, it became the approved college of the Presbyterian denomination.[17]

Tennent's school at Neshaminy was the mother of Samuel Blair's famous academy at New Londonderry or Fagg's Manor, Pennsylvania.[18] Blair received his literary and theological training at the Log College, became pastor of the church at Fagg's Manor in 1739, shortly after which his community became the center of the remarkable revival of which we have already spoken.[19] Blair was not long in Fagg's Manor before he opened

[15] See above, p. 91.

[16] Quoted from his *Journal* by Craven, *loc. cit.*, p. 312.

[17] Alexander, p. 83; Foote, p. 226. In 1743 the Old Side group developed plans for a school of their own. Rev. Francis Alison was appointed master of a school at New London which was designed as a preparatory school from which it was planned scholars would pass on to Yale. In 1752 Alison was called to Philadelphia to take charge of an academy which soon (1755) attained collegiate rank under his headship. It later developed into the University of Pennsylvania. Until the reunion, the Synod of Philadelphia directed their candidates to this college for their training. The academy at New London died out with the removal of Alison and with the establishment of Princeton and the University of Pennsylvania the plan of the Synod to found a college of its own was checked. At the time of the reunion, Princeton was the only Presbyterian institution of higher learning. On the Old Side plan see Foote, pp. 224 ff.; Alexander, 86 ff.; Craven, *loc. cit.*, 310.

[18] Alexander, pp. 171-2; Murphy, pp. 87-89; Miller, pp. 17 ff.; Foote, p. 159.   [19] See above, p. 8.

a classical and theological seminary similar to the Log College. It grew rapidly and the attainments of its alumni are sufficient evidence of the thoroughness of the training they received. The names of Samuel Davies, John Rodgers, James Finley, Robert Smith, and Alexander Cumming adorn the roster of its students.[20]

Samuel Finley, another alumnus of Tennent's school, became the founder of a famous academy at Nottingham, Maryland. This was opened about the time Blair's school was closed by the death of its founder in 1751. James Waddell, one of the leaders in Virginia, received his training under Finley's teaching, as did other celebrities including Governors Martin of North Carolina and Henry of Maryland, Dr. Benjamin Rush of Philadelphia and his eminent brother, Judge Jacob Rush, and Ebenezer Hazard of Philadelphia, who was noted for his collections of historical documents.[21] Finley was an accomplished scholar and a great teacher. Few students were better versed in the classics than those who came from his school. As a scholar and teacher he even exceeded Samuel Davies, whom he followed in the presidency of Nassau Hall.

From Blair's school at Fagg's Manor the Reverend Robert Smith, father of John Blair and Samuel Stanhope Smith, went as pastor to Pequea, Pennsylvania in 1751 and opened a classical school to prepare students for Princeton.[22] In addition to his two sons who became eminent as teachers, preachers, and college presidents in Virginia, David Caldwell of North Carolina, prominent in the Mecklenburg convention and the Revolution, John McMillan, the great western missionary and founder of a school which became the nucleus of Jefferson College, are two other notables who received their training in Smith's academy. James Waddell went from Nottingham to become assistant teacher at Pequea and later went to Virginia to aid in the upbuilding of Presbyterian education.[23]

[20] Murphy, p. 89; Alexander, pp. 171-2; Miller, p. 19; Foote, p. 159.
[21] Alexander, p. 206; Murphy, p. 97.
[22] J. N. Beam, "Dr. Robert Smith's Academy at Pequea, Pennsylvania," *Jour. Pres. Hist. Soc.*, VIII, 145-161; Foote, p. 409.
[23] Murphy, p. 89; *Watchman of the South,* September 19, 1844.

It is only in the setting of this general background that we can fully appreciate the contributions of the Presbyterians to the educational uplift of Virginia. The Great Awakening brought home the need of a type of evangelical training which was sponsored by the revivalist wing of the Church. In response to the demand, the Log Colleges sprang up, each one sending out its preachers and teachers to spread the revival afar and found other Log Colleges in new regions. Thus, with the New Side Presbyterians the Awakening and education went hand in hand and in Virginia two famous institutions were the result: Hampden-Sydney College and Liberty Hall Academy.

Prior to the founding of Liberty Hall Academy, the forerunner of Washington College (now Washington and Lee), and of Hampden-Sydney, a classical school was maintained by the Reverend John Todd in Louisa County, and one west of the Ridge, in Augusta, was conducted by the Reverend John Brown.[24] It will be recalled that Todd was an associate of Samuel Davies. The young James Waddell came to assist Todd for a while as a teacher and, in his later years, he himself opened a school when he made his home in the same county.[25] Brown was a graduate of Nassau Hall and in 1753 he accepted a call to the united congregations of Timber Ridge and New Providence.[26] Near his residence at the latter place he established his grammar school, which was afterwards merged into Liberty Hall.

In 1771, the Presbytery of Hanover took up the subject of establishing an institution of learning on a broader and more permanent basis than the grammar schools of Todd and Brown. "Presbytery being very sensible of the great expediency of erecting a Seminary of learning somewhere within the bounds of the Presbytery do recommend it to all the members to take the matter into consideration, and report their thoughts at our next, respecting the best method of accomplishing it."[27] The

[24] Foote, *Sketches,* p. 392.
[25] *Ibid.,* p. 379, and Ford, *Scotch-Irish,* p. 379; *Watchman of the South,* September 19, 1844.
[26] S. D. Alexander, *Princeton College during the Eighteenth Century,* p. 5.
[27] MS. Recs. Hanover Presbytery, October 9, 1771.

matter was deferred, however, until October 13, 1774, when it was agreed to locate the Seminary in Augusta County and for the present to place it in charge of William Graham, "a gentleman properly recommended," and under the superintendence of Reverend John Brown.[28] The congregations were asked to make contributions for a library and apparatus for the school.

Having been joined by Samuel Stanhope Smith as probationer, the Presbytery at the same time recommended the establishment of a second school east of the Ridge.[29] Smith is spoken of as "a gentleman who has taught the languages for a considerable time in the New Jersey College, with good approbation," and who, if properly encouraged, could be induced to take the school.[30] The congregations of Cumberland, Prince Edward, and Briery in particular were asked to start a subscription for the above purpose. The subscriptions for the institution succeeded beyond expectation, thirteen hundred pounds being reported on February 1, 1775, and "considerable additions are expected."[31]

It was agreed to locate the second academy in Prince Edward County where one hundred acres of land had been donated for the purpose.[32] Twelve trustees were selected by the Presbytery, which also reserved the right to choose the rector and assistants. Samuel S. Smith was chosen first rector[33] and tuition was fixed at four pounds per annum, to be divided among the rector and assistants.[34] Smith retained his position until he was called to a professorship at Princeton in 1779, when his brother, John Blair Smith, succeeded him.[35] Hampden-Sydney was the name given to the Prince Edward academy and the Presbytery refers to it under that name in 1776.[36]

[28] MS. Recs. Hanover Presbytery, June 3, 1773, October 16, 1773, October 13, 1774.

[29] Ibid., October 13, 1774. Calendar of Board Minutes of Hampden-Sidney College, 1776-1876 (comp. A. J. Morrison), contains a narrative of its founding based on the sources. See also Foote, pp. 393 ff.

[30] MS. Recs. Hanover Presbytery, October 13, 1774.

[31] Ibid., February 1, 1775.

[32] Ibid., February 2, 1775.

[33] Smith was also installed as pastor of the united churches of Cumberland and Prince Edward. Foote, p. 398.

[34] MS. Recs. Hanover Presbytery, February 3, 1775.

[35] Ibid., October 28, 1779.   [36] Ibid., May 6, 1776.

The Presbytery announced, that, although under Presbyterian auspices, the Seminary would be conducted on a most liberal catholic plan and that care would be taken "that no undue influence be used . . . to byas (bias) the judgment of any; but that all of every denomination shall fully enjoy his own religious sentiments, and be at liberty to attend that mode of publick worship, that either custom or conscience makes most agreeable to them, when and where ye may have opportunity of enjoying it."[37]

Announcement that Hampden-Sydney Academy would open on November 10, 1775, with a well equipped library and set of scientific apparatus, appeared in Dixon and Hunter's *Virginia Gazette* for October 7, 1775. "The Rates, at the utmost, will not exceed 10 pounds Currency per Annum to the Steward, and 4 pounds Tuition Money; 20 shillings of this being always paid at Entrance." Again the catholicity of the plan was emphasized, and it was announced that the system of education would be patterned after the College of New Jersey, "save that a more particular Attention shall be paid to the Cultivation of the English Language than is usually done in Places of public Education."[38]

The announcement of the projected Academy called forth an attack upon Smith from a Churchman who signed himself "Luther."[39] "Luther" ridiculed the so-called catholic basis of the school, pointing out that it was controlled by a denomination whose doctrines were not only repugnant to those of the Church of England, but "submersive of morality" and "of the most

[37] *Ibid.,* February 3, 1775; *cf.* April 14.

[38] Dixon and Hunter's *Virginia Gazette,* October 7, 1775. An abbreviated copy of a subscription blank in the Calendar of Board Minutes announces that Smith "proposes to teach Geography in greater perfection, than, he is well assured, it is done in the major parts of our Institutions of Learning; and so to render it an excellent handmaid to the extensive and useful study of History; which with the science of Chronology shall be attended to. Mathematical learning he has made himself master of; and designs to teach those who choose, Arithmetic and Algebra; and Geometry applied particularly to surveying. This will prepare the way for the study of Natural Philosophy in all its branches; after which he will instruct them in the important studies of Eloquence, Criticism, and the science of Morals." Pp. 12-13, dated November 12, 1774.

[39] Dixon and Hunter's *Virginia Gazette,* November 18, 1775.

pernicious tendency," having reference to their predestinarian views. "If this school should meet with that encouragement which Mr. Smith seems to intimate in his advertisements, we might reasonably expect, in a few years, to see our senate house, as well as pulpits, filled with Dissenters; and thus they might, by an easy transition, secure the establishment in their own favour." He urges all Anglicans to withhold their subscriptions until the school is put in charge of Anglican Masters.

Smith replied to his antagonist that while the plan for the institution was matured by the Presbyterians, the trustees who had the power of visitation and management were "chiefly members of the Church of England," thus showing the liberality of the Presbytery. He scored "Luther" for his narrow principles and branded him as an anonymous scribbler, leaving the public to judge the school on its own merits.[40]

On December 9, 1775, the choice of Philip Halcombe as Steward was announced in the *Gazette*. "The Steward is appointed to furnish good and wholesome Diet to the Students; one Half of the Meat at least to be fresh, and one Half of the Bread to be made of the fine Flour of Wheat." He will also "furnish Servants to keep the Rooms clean and in good Order, for which Services he is to receive at the Rate of eight Pounds Currency per Annum, forty Shillings of this always to be paid at the Beginning of the Year, to enable him to procure good Provisions, and at a cheap Rate." Students must furnish their own beds, buy their own candles and do their own washing, however. "For some Years they will be permitted to take their wood off the Land belonging to the Academy, gratis." It was announced that books might be rented from the library at a moderate rate.

Hampden-Sydney opened its doors in January, 1776. Besides the rector, the first faculty consisted of two assistants, John Blair Smith and Samuel Doak, both graduates of Princeton.[41]

---

[40] *Virginia Gazette,* December 9, 1775.

[41] John Springer, also a Princeton graduate, had been engaged originally but was delayed in coming and Doak was hired to fill his place. Recs. Hanover Presbytery, November 8, 1775, May 4, 1776. See also Alexander, *Princeton College during the Eighteenth Century.* Doak soon went to Tennessee to become a great factor in its educational development. He founded a Log

The large attendance, which soon passed the hundred mark, made the employment of a third teacher, David Witherspoon, necessary.[42] The unexpected enrollment made it necessary to build cabins and huts for accommodations, and the crowded conditions led to the organization of a lottery in 1777, "for the purpose of raising 1260 pounds to be laid out in erecting additional buildings to the academy."[43]

The Academy had scarcely begun its existence when work was disorganized by the outbreak of the Revolution. In the fall of 1777, a student company of soldiers, having been organized with John Blair Smith as captain, marched to Williamsburg to meet an expected invasion of the British.[44] The students were soon discharged, but some of them entered the army permanently. The depreciation of paper money also endangered the welfare of the college, making the problem of boarding the students a difficult one.[45] As the war was carried to the South, the student body became depleted by reason of the number who left to enter the ranks, and at the time of Cornwallis's invasion school activities were entirely suspended for a period.

It was during the war, in 1779, that John Blair Smith succeeded to the presidency of the Academy, combining, like his predecessor, the offices of pastor, teacher and rector.[46] The war left Hampden-Sydney with its student ranks thinned and its finances embarrassed. Nevertheless, there was strong confidence

College known as Martin Academy and later as Washington College, the first such institution in the Mississippi Valley. He carried the first library across the mountains in sacks on pack horses for use of his rising college. Merriam, *Higher Education in Tennessee*, p. 227; Foote, p. 398; Alexander, *Princeton College*, pp. 184-5.

[42] MS. Recs. Hanover Presbytery, May 4, 1776; Foote, pp. 398, 400.

[43] See the interesting letter of George Craghead, one of the students of this first year in Foote, p. 400 and Calendar of Board Minutes, September 26, 1776.

[44] "The Student Company of Hampden-Sydney," *Va. Mag. of Hist. and Biog.*. XVII, 442; Foote, p. 401, quotes from Craghead's letter.

[45] See Foote, p. 401, quoting Craghead. Cal. Board Mins., December 11, 1777 ff. for the difficulties in providing board.

[46] Foote, p. 399. Smith served as President until 1789 when he devoted himself wholly to the ministry. In 1791 he accepted a charge in Philadelphia and in 1795 became head of Union College in New York. Drury Lacy served as acting President of Hampden-Sydney until Archibald Alexander was elected to the headship in 1796. Foote, pp. 406, 407, 436-7.

in the future and in 1783 a charter from the legislature gave it full collegiate standing with all the attendant privileges.[47]

With the return of peace, the recovery was rapid and the college was again soon filled to capacity. On September 22, 1786, the first collegiate degrees were conferred, when eight students were awarded the A.B. degree.[48] The college also offered the Master's degree for two years of post-graduate work.[49] The first advanced degree conferred was, however, an honorary one granted the Reverend Hanry Pattillo, of North Carolina, on April 25, 1787.[50] It was in this same year that Hampden-Sydney became the center of the great post-Revolutionary revival. This revival was a part of the great inter-denominational Awakening which marked the final triumph of evangelical Christianity in Virginia, and it left Hampden-Sydney throbbing with a new zeal for its mission.

In 1774, it will be remembered, the Presbytery decided to take under its patronage Brown's school in Augusta County, with William Graham as tutor.[51] This was the beginning of the development of a permanent institution of learning west of the Blue Ridge. A year later John Montgomery, "late from Prince Town College," was appointed as Graham's assistant and a hundred and fifty pounds was appropriated for the purchase of books and apparatus.[52] In May 1776, a permanent site for the Academy was selected at Timber Ridge, the reason being that Graham had accepted a call from the congregation there and the Presbytery wished to entrust the care of the school to him.[53] Land was donated for the purpose and the neighbors offered to build a log house, a story and a half high, to accom-

[47] Foote, p. 403; Cal. Board Mins., June 5, 1783, p. 27. The laws and ordinances for the regulation of the College are in the Board Minutes, pp. 29-32.

[48] Foote, p. 405; Cal. Board Mins., September 22, 1786, p. 34.

[49] Regulation no. 9, in Cal. Board Mins., p. 29.

[50] Foote, p. 405; Cal. Board Mins., June 28, 1787, p. 35.

[51] This school changed its location a number of times between New Providence, Mount Pleasant, and Fairfield. At this time it seems to have been at Mount Pleasant, the highest point of the Ridge, a short distance above Fluvanna cut. It was about a mile from Fairfield and Brown's house. See Foote, pp. 443, 444.

[52] MS. Recs. Hanover Presbytery, October 27, 1775, May 4, 1776; Alexander, *Princeton College during the Eighteenth Century*, p. 189.

[53] "Memoir of William Graham" in *Evan. and Lit. Mag.*, IV, 254-5. MS. Recs. Hanover Presbytery, May 4, 1776 and May 6, 1776.

modate the school. In addition the Presbytery was assured "of the probability that fire Wood and Timber for the Buildings, will be furnished gratis, for at least Twenty years."[54] Twenty-three trustees were named and the Presbytery reserved for themselves the right of visitation and of choosing the rector and assistants.[55]

Purdie's *Virginia Gazette* of November 8, 1776, announced that "Liberty Hall, is now established for the liberal education of youth, on Timber Ridge, in Augusta county, where all the most important branches of literature, necessary to prepare young gentlemen for the study of law, physick, and theology, may be taught to good advantage, upon the most approved plan. The education and morals of youth being the great objects in view, those peculiarities which form the complexion of any party shall have no place in the scheme." Tuition was announced to be four pounds and board nine pounds, one third of the latter payable in advance.[56] "The students are to provide their own beds, washing, and candles; firewood will be gratis." Graham solicits the support of the public, in assuring them that they "will never find cause to call in question their catholick principles in conducting this Academy."

The war brought hard times to the Augusta Academy, as it did to its sister institution in Prince Edward. A volunteer company under Graham was formed which stood ready to answer the call to duty. The greater part of the students eventually were drafted into service and the Academy became so depleted that in 1779 it closed its doors.[57] Graham had been forced to seek additional means of support on a farm near Lexington and, for a time, had endeavored to visit the Academy two or three days a week, but the arrangement proved unsatisfactory, and students sought Graham in his home instead, where he kept up a sort of private school.[58]

Following the surrender of Cornwallis, the Presbytery, in October, 1782, applied to the legislature for for an act of in-

[54] MS. Recs. Hanover Presbytery, May 6, 1776; Foote, p. 448.

[55] "Memoir of William Graham," *loc. cit.*, p. 255.

[56] This amount is inserted in ink in the advertisement changing the original six pounds, ten shillings which was printed.

[57] Foote, 450 ff.; "Memoir of William Graham," *Evan. and Lit. Mag.*, IV, pp. 256 ff.   [58] Foote, p. 457; *Evan. and Lit. Mag.*, IV, 258.

corporation which was granted to "the Rector and Trustees of Liberty Hall Academy" with the right to confer degrees.[59] The Timber Ridge institution was not revived, however. A small frame building erected on a site, part of which lay on Graham's lands, became its successor.[60] Graham was continued as rector and the first tutor elected was James Priestly, noted for his proficiency in the classics.[61]

In 1789 Liberty Hall Academy became the center of the great revival which had begun at Hampden-Sydney and which now spread up and down the Valley under the preaching of Graham and others. As at its sister institution, the Awakening came to Liberty Hall at a time of religious depression following the war, and, in a sense, marked the beginning of a new epoch in its history.[62]

It remains only to say that Graham continued in the rectorship of the Academy until 1796, when personal and financial reasons led to his resignation.[63] The fearlessness with which he expressed his political views also created enemies and made his position untenable.[64] Before his resignation, however, came Washington's endowment of the institution, which thereupon changed its name to Washington Academy.[65] Meanwhile a new set of buildings replaced the old ones which had been destroyed by fire.

[59] Foote, p. 458; *Evan. and Lit. Mag.*, IV, 260; *Journal of House of Delegates,* December 28, 1782.

[60] This was near Lexington which had, in 1777, become the seat of the new county of Rockbridge.

[61] Foote, pp. 458-9; *Evan. and Lit. Mag.*, IV, 260-1. Priestly became the first president of Cumberland University at Nashville, Tenn.

[62] See *Evan. and Lit. Mag.,* IV, 261.

[63] See Foote, p. 463, 475-7; *Evan. and Lit. Mag.,* IV, 402, note on his salary as rector. When the assistants were paid, often little was left for the rector, sometimes nothing.

[64] An instance of this is his part in the erection of the state of Frankland. See Foote, pp. 463-4, 476, 560. His letter of resignation is in *Evan. and Lit. Mag.,* IV, 404-5. Graham took up lands on the Ohio where the careless system of surveys involved him in a lawsuit which ruined him financially. Indeed, it was on a journey to Richmond on legal business which subjected him to the exposure which caused his death in that city on June 8, 1799. Foote, p. 486; *Evan. and Lit. Mag.,* IV, 406-8.

[65] Foote, pp. 479-85, for the negotiations in the matter of endowment. In 1813 the institution became Washington College and, after the Civil War, Washington and Lee University.

We have thus seen that in a very positive way, evidenced by the establishment of two colleges that still exist, to say nothing of various smaller schools, the Presbyterians contributed to the educational upbuilding of Virginia. Their efforts should be all the more appreciated when we realize that the only other college in the colony was William and Mary, founded in 1693. It is also clear that the inspiration and leadership that was behind these sprang directly from the Great Awakening.

Neither the Methodists nor the Baptists gave such a direct impetus to education in Virginia in the period of the Great Awakening as did the Presbyterians. Probably the reason for this was that they did not lay such stress upon an educated ministry as did the Presbyterians. The Methodists, however, had all of the traditions of a trained clergy behind them. John Wesley held the degree of M.A. and did everything possible to encourage his preachers to study. In England he made very extensive use of the press in spreading the revival. Kingswood in England was early established by him as a preparatory school for boys. In like manner Coke and Asbury, the first two American bishops, were deeply interested in educational projects[66] and the plan for an institution of learning was conceived even before the Christmas Conference of 1784 severed connection with the Established Church.[67] The enterprise was officially endorsed by the Conference, subscriptions were taken, and Cokesbury College at Abingdon, near Baltimore, opened its doors in December, 1787.[68]

The Methodists of Virginia no doubt did their part in making Cokesbury College a reality, for it was a denominational undertaking and was partly supported by private subscriptions

[66] E. C. Brooks, "Francis Asbury an Educational Reformer," *Meth. Rev. Quar.* (So.), Vol. LXV, pp. 341-52; Thomas Coke, *Journal,* November 14, 1784, and *passim.* Asbury was chiefly interested in secondary schools for training the people rather than in theological seminaries.

[67] Asbury, *Journal,* I, p. 291. The subscription for an American Kingswood was begun by John Dickens in 1780 when he and Asbury were travelling in North Carolina.

[68] Description of Cokesbury in *Arminian Mag.* (Amer.), I, 590 (1789) ; also Lee, *History of the Methodists,* pp. 116-17; A. W. Cummings, *Early Schools of Methodism,* p. 27; Thomas Ware, *Sketches of the Life and Travels of Thomas Ware,* pp. 112-113.

and yearly collections on all the circuits.[69] More than this can be said of them, however, for even before Cokesbury was established Ebenezer Academy in Brunswick County, Virginia (the very heart of Southern Methodism), came into existence. Just when this institution opened its doors we do not know, but there is good reason to believe that it was the earliest school established under Methodist auspices and probably it was founded sometime between 1780 and 1784.[70] It was still flourishing when Lee wrote his *Short History of the Methodists* in 1809.

Among the Methodists, too, the printing and distribution of books, tracts, sermons and other literature, in which they surpassed all other denominations in the state, became a factor of ever increasing importance in the educational uplift of the masses. As we have already seen, the pioneer in this work was Robert Williams, of Virginia.[71] The inspiration for these efforts came from the evangelical revival.

It was not until 1788 that the Baptists of Virginia took up the design of establishing a seminary of learning.[72] Although the project was advocated for some years, it did not materialize before the end of the century. The social attitude towards the Baptists, and their deep seated antipathy towards the Established Church with its trained clergy, along with the success of their own revival, caused the denomination to overlook the value of education. After the battle for religious freedom was won and the Established Church was swept from the field, and after the Baptists had established themselves socially and had become both numerous and popular, they quickly realized the need of educating their ministers and their children.[73] This was a part of the social revolution which we shall consider in our final chapter.

[69] Cummings, pp. 22 ff. for the plan and scope of the enterprise.

[70] O. S. Baketel, "The First Educational Institutions of the M. E. Church," *Meth. Rev.* (N. Y.), Vol. XCVII, pp. 404-8; Cummings, p. 38.

[71] See above, p. 146.

[72] Semple, *History of the Baptists in Virginia,* p. 104.

[73] Circular Letter, Roanoke Association, 1789, 1791, in MS. Minutes; Circular Letter of the General Committee of Correspondence, October, 1808, in Minutes for that year. Also see below, Chapter XI.

CHAPTER X

THE EVANGELICALS AND SLAVERY

The Great Awakening brought with it a changed attitude towards the slaves, which we may denominate its humanitarian influences. In all of the evangelical churches with which we have been concerned, the doors were thrown wide open to this class. Indeed, a feature of the revivals was the strong appeal made to the blacks alike by the Presbyterians, Baptists, and Methodists. The reception of the slaves to communion was in sharp contrast to the exclusiveness of the Established Church where, for social reasons, difficulties were apt to be placed in the way of baptizing slaves.[1] Then, too, the vigorous emotional appeal made by the evangelical churches had a strong attraction for the slaves as compared with the formal and rational presentation of the gospel from the Anglican pulpits.[2]

No one took more interest in the welfare of the Negroes than did Samuel Davies. In 1755, he had about three hundred of them who regularly attended his ministry, of whom about a hundred had been baptized after careful catechizing.[3] Benjamin Fawcett, the noted English dissenter, who in 1756 wrote *A Compassionate Address to the Christian Negroes in Virginia*, says that the first account he ever heard of considerable numbers of Negroes embracing the gospel was under Samuel Davies in Virginia.[4]

If the slaves were to be christianized, they could not well be left in ignorance. Hence Davies took a deep interest in

[1] An example of this is seen in a long letter written by the Rev. James Maury to Commissary Dawson complaining of this very thing. In one instance a group of slaves who had come forward for baptism were ordered to retire by the church warden, in spite of Maury's desire to administer the sacrament. There was objection to baptizing them on week days as this would take them from their work. Dawson MSS. October 10, 1759.

[2] See F. M. Davenport, *Primitive Traits in Religious Revivals*, Chap. V on "The Religion of the American Negro."

[3] Foote, *Sketches of Virginia*, First Series, pp. 284-5; Letter to R. C., March, 1755, in *Evan. and Lit. Mag.*, IV, pp. 540-1; Letter to John Wesley, 1755, cited below, n. 5.

[4] *Compassionate Address*, p. 33.

teaching them to read and spell.[5] Through the coöperation of
John Wesley and other English friends, and the instrumental-
ity of the London Society for promoting Religious Knowledge
among the Poor, he endeavored to keep the slaves and poor
whites supplied with books.[6] He found the Negroes eager to
learn and willing to apply themselves, and many of them made
excellent progress.[7] Besides the Bible, Watts's *Psalms and
Hymns* was the book that he particularly desired, for he found
that the Negroes "above all the human Species" loved to sing.
They sometime spent the entire night in his kitchen singing
their religious songs.[8]

In no part of his ministry was Davies more successful than
in his efforts to further religion and education among the blacks.
The same may be said of his colleagues, Todd and Wright.
The former had about two hundred Negroes in each of his three
Hanover preaching places in 1757, and he often preached especially for them. He, too, supplied them with religious books and
they learned to hold their own meetings.[9] Over in Cumberland
County, Mr. Wright did a similar work and set up two or
three schools for the instruction of the blacks.[10] This work of
the Presbyterian New Lights attracted the attention of the
Quaker, John Woolman, in a trip through Virginia in 1757.[11]

Davies saw nothing in the institution of slavery that made
it inconsistent with the Christian religion. Indeed, he pointed
out that it was a part of the order of Providence that some
should be masters and others servants. Christianity did not

[5] See the little volume of *Letters from the Reverend Samuel Davies and
others showing the state of religion in Virginia. . . .* London, 1761. Also see
his letters to John Wesley in Wesley's *Journal,* IV, 125-6 (July, 1755) and
IV, 149-50 (March, 1756). Cf. M. W. Jernegan, "Slavery and Conversion
in the American Colonies," *Amer. Hist. Rev.,* XXI, 523.

[6] *Ibid.* and Foote, pp. 284-5.

[7] Letter to R. C., March 2, 1756, *Evan. and Lit. Mag.,* IV, 544-9; to Mr.
C., February 7, 1757, in the volume of letters, also those to Wesley.

[8] Letter to Wesley, March, 1756, *loc. cit.;* Foote, p. 289.

[9] Todd to Mr. C., February 3, 1757, in the *Letters from Davies and Others.*

[10] Davies to R. C., March 2, 1756, *loc. cit.,* p. 548.

[11] *Journal of John Woolman,* p. 215 (Harvard Classics ed.). Woolman
says: "Some of our Society and some of the society called Newlights, use
some endeavors to instruct those they have in reading; but in common this
is not only neglected, but disapproved." This disapproval, however, was
gradually overcome as we shall see.

destroy this relationship, but only regulated it.[12] Fawcett, too, in his *Compassionate Address,* made it plain that physical bondage is by no means incompatible with spiritual freedom and showed the slaves how they could be instruments of good work. "If it pleases God to favour you with good and gentle Masters, your obedience to them will not only be easy and pleasant, but you ought to bless and praise God for them. If, on the other hand, your Masters are froward and thereby render your obedience the more difficult, do not therefore cease to pray even for such Masters." Thus were the slaves encouraged in the Christian life and taught the virtues of duty, obedience and contentment.

The Great Awakening also brought a humanitarian influence to bear upon the masters of slaves. Davies' little book on *The Duty of Christians* was particularly addressed to this class. The masters were reminded that Christ died for all men and that Saint Paul esteemed it worth while to labour for slaves and servants. Davies made it clear that no master could be a good Christian and entirely neglect the spiritual welfare of his slaves, even the meanest of whom were immortal. He pointed out how it was to the actual advantage of masters to instruct their slaves in religion, as it made them more faithful, honest and diligent. A good Christian is never a bad servant, for Christianity teaches obedience.[13]

Davies' efforts were not without results. Although he met with some opposition in his work among the blacks, he wrote that they "are freely allowed to attend upon my ministry, and some times my private instructions, even by such masters as have no religion at all, or are Bigots to the established church."[14] His work even excited emulation among the masters to teach their slaves and he was encouraged "that the generality of my people who are proprietors of four or five hundred negroes, will make a conscience of teaching them to read."[15]

[12] Davies, *The Duty of Christians to propagate their Religion among Heathens, Earnestly recommended to the Masters of the Negro Slaves in Virginia,* London, 1758.

[13] Davies, *The Duty of Christians,* pp. 16, 17, 19, 22, 23, 27 ff.

[14] See above, p. 96 and note 116 for example; also Letter to J. F., March 2, 1756, in *Letters.*   [15] Letter to Mr. C., Feb. 7, 1757, in *ibid.*

Davies' position with respect to the relation of the Church to slavery was really typical of the attitude of his denomination. The first official pronouncement of the Presbyterians on the matter came in 1787, when the Synod of New York and Philadelphia "earnestly recommend it to all the members belonging to their communion to give those persons who are at present held in servitude such good education as may prepare them for the better enjoyment of freedom. . . ."[16] The Synod saw that much needed to be done to educate and instruct the slaves before emancipation would be practical, but recommended "that masters, wherever they find servants disposed to make a just improvement of the privilege, would give them a *peculium,* or grant them sufficient time and sufficient means of procuring their own liberty at a moderate rate, that they may render them useful citizens; and, finally, they recommend it to all their people to use the most prudent measures, consistent with the interest and the state of civil society, in the counties where they live, to procure the final abolition of slavery in America."[17] It was content to prepare them for the day of freedom.

There were, however, some among the Presbyterians, as David Rice, who found only condemnation for the institution of slavery.[18] To Rice the slave was as much a creature of God and entitled to his liberty as was his master. He was by nature free and no legislature had the right to reduce him to perpetual servitude. Such a system was inconsistent with justice, good policy, and the very principles on which our government was founded. Rice opposed it both on moral and economic grounds and believed that there was absolutely no scriptural justification for it. Moving to Kentucky, Rice became a member of the convention which framed the first constitution of the state and he

[17] In 1818 the General Assembly took a strong stand in condemning *Slavery,* pp. 53-54, prints the action.

[17] In 1818 the General Assembly took a strong stand in condemning slavery as totally irreconcilable with Christianity and urged the members "to increase their exertions to effect a total abolition." Barnes, pp. 54-56. The inevitable consequence of this position was the schism in 1838.

[18] David Rice, "Slavery Inconsistent with Justice and Good Policy" (1792), in Bishop, *History of the Church in Kentucky,* pp. 385-418.

advocated a provision for gradual emancipation.[19] It cannot be said that Rice represented the views of his Church. He rather expressed the sentiment of the frontier, but he typifies a strong movement that made great headway, even in Virginia, among the Methodists, and which also sprang from the teachings of the Great Awakening.

As with the Presbyterians, the Baptists received many slaves into the Church, regarding them as worthy as their masters in spiritual affairs.[20] Some of the leaders believed that slavery was pregnant with enormous evils and that the Church should condemn the institution.[21] It was Leland who introduced the resolution adopted by the Baptist General Committee in 1789: "Resolved that slavery is a violent deprivation of the rights of nature, and inconsistent with a republican government; and we, therefore recommend it to our brethren, to make use of every legal measure to extirpate this horrid evil from the land and pray Almighty God that our honorable legislature may have it in their power to proclaim the great Jubilee consistent with the principles of good policy."[22] During his fourteen years of residence in Virginia, Leland never owned a slave.[23]

The Baptist, David Barrow, also came to the conviction that slavery was iniquitous, contrary to the laws of God and nature, and inconsistent with a republican form of government, and he manumitted his slaves in 1784.[24] Since he was unable to properly support his family and provide for the education of his children without holding slaves, he preferred to remove to Kentucky. His farewell wish to all masters was that they "may consider how inconsistently they act, with a Republican Gov-

---

[19] He wrote his pamphlet just before the convention met and Asbury wrote to him commending him upon his views. See S. G. Ayers, "Francis Asbury and his Presbyterian Friends," *Meth. Rev. Quar.* (South), XLVI, p. 467.

[20] MS. Church Record Books list many slaves among the members.

[21] See Smith, "Life and Times of the Reverend John Leland," *Bap. Quar.*, V, p. 251; Barrow, *Circular Letter*, pp. 4-5, 13.

[22] Leland, *Works*, p. 51; Semple, p. 105; *cf.* Minutes of the General Committee, 1790, p. 7, for a slight variation in phraseology.

[23] Leland, *Works*, p. 51.

[24] Barrow, *Circular Letter*, pp. 4-5.

ernment and whether in this particular, they are doing as they would others should do to them!" He prayed for the day of deliverance of "the poor, oppressed, naked, hunger bitten slaves" and bade them have patience and strong hearts. To the kind master, he expressed his sympathy, but pointed out that slaves are daily liable to fall into bad hands and that the only safe remedy was emancipation.[25]

The resolution of the General Committee was the nearest approach to any official sentiment of the United Baptist Churches of Virginia in the matter of slavery. However, the General Committee was at best an advisory body with no power to bind either the Associations, or the churches. Among the latter there was no unanimity of sentiment, and, under the Baptist plan of organization, the matter of slavery was really one for each church to decide. In 1787 the Ketocton Association "determined that hereditary slavery was a breach of the divine law."[26] They then appointed a committee "to bring in a plan of gradual emancipation, which was accordingly done. It excited considerable tumult in the churches, and accordingly in their letters to the next Association they remonstrated so decidedly that the Association resolved to take no further steps in the business."[27]

The action of the Roanoke Association in 1790 on the resolution of the General Committee is typical. While "not unanimously clear" in their minds whether God intended some to be slaves, "yet the subject with us is so very abstruse and such a set of complex circumstances attending the same, that we suppose neither the general committee nor any other Religious Society has the least right to concern therein as a society, but leave every individual to act at discresion in order to keep a good conscience before God, as far as the laws of our land will admit; and that it is the indispensable duty of masters to forbear and surpress cruelty, and do that which is just and equal

[25] *Ibid.,* p. 13. In his quotations from the *Circular Letter,* Taylor, *Virginia Baptist Ministers,* omits the significant reference to slavery doubtless because of the feeling at the time he published his volumes (1860).

[26] The Ketocton Association embraced a group of northern and western counties including Loudoun, Fairfax, Prince William, Stafford, Fauquier, Shenandoah, Frederick. See Fristoe, pp. 386-387.

[27] Semple, p. 392.

to their servants."[28] Similarly, in 1792, the Strawberry Association expressed the opinion: 'We advise them (the General Committee) not to interfere in it."[29] The next year the General Committee itself resolved, "that the subject be dismissed from this committee, as believing it belongs to the legislative body."[30]

We note, then, that among the Baptists there was no unanimity of opinion regarding slavery. Some Associations opposed the institution "as contrary to the laws of God and nature" and favored emancipation, while others believed it outside the province of any religious society to consider.[31] Under the Baptist form of organization, the matter must necessarily be left to the conscience of the individual or, at best, to each church.[32] Regardless of the lack of official action on the part of the denomination, we note that many humanitarian influences sprang from the Great Awakening. Some of the leaders, as Leland and Barrow, developed strong anti-slavery views which, no doubt, helped to mould opinion. In some cases, slaves were actually emancipated. In addition to the example of Barrow, it is said that Robert Carter of Nomini Hall, owner of several hundred slaves, gradually liberated all of them after joining the Baptists.[33] Finally, the Baptists contributed to the general uplift of the slaves by receiving them into the Church,[34] by giving them opportunity to exercise their gifts,[35] and by bringing about more humane treatment of them.[36]

[28] MS. Mins. Roanoke Association, June, 1790, pp. 39-40.

[29] MS. Mins., May, 1792.   [30] Minutes of General Committee, 1793, p. 4.

[31] Portsmouth Association, Minutes 1796, p. 5; see also Dover Association, Minutes, October, 1797.   [32] See Semple, pp. 246, 122.

[33] Semple, p. 178; Rippon's *Baptist Annual Register,* "American Letters," 1791, mentions 442 slaves liberated by Carter.

[34] A church at Williamsburg composed wholly of blacks was received into the Dover Association in 1793. Semple, p. 126.

[35] Slaves were not always given a vote in the monthly business meetings but sometimes were. Semple, p. 130. Pettsworth or Gloucester Church once chose a colored pastor. Semple, p. 170. Upper King and Queen Church advised the Negroes to be careful of exercising their gifts in their meetings and no one was to preach without consent. MS. Church Record Book, June 19, 1790. The Association at Burrus's meeting house in 1788 asked the question: "What is to be done with a slave that appears to be useful in the ministry?" The answer was: "Such a person to be encouraged but not ordained." We shall see in our next chapter that slaves actually preached to congregations of whites.

[36] *E.g.,* MS. Mins. Bap. Association at Burrus's meeting-house, 1788, resolved that it is not allowable to separate man and wife who were slaves

It has been suggested that the predestinarian views of the Presbyterians and Baptists generally reconciled those churches to the existence of slavery, although many private individuals opposed it.[37] The Methodists, however, made a strong effort to eradicate slave-holding altogether from their membership and so doing almost brought a schism in the Church.[38] The English preachers were, from the outset, zealous opponents of slavery, and quite naturally they infused their opinions in the societies among which they travelled. The publication of Wesley's *Thoughts Upon Slavery,* in 1774, did much to give definite shape to the growing anti-slavery sentiment in the young Church.[39] This little work was a severe indictment upon both slave trader and slave holder. Wesley could see no basis, legal or natural, for slavery. "It cannot be that either war or contract can give any man such a property in another as he has in his sheep and oxen, much less is it possible that any child of man should be born a slave. Liberty is the right of every human creature as soon as he breathes the vital air; and no human law can deprive him of that right, which he derives from the law of nature."[40]

The first two American Bishops, Coke and Asbury, were strong opponents of slavery, regarding it as sinful, and they were soon joined by other leaders, as Jesse Lee, Freeborn Garrettson, and Philip Gatch.[41] The latter emancipated his nine

unless one had used every endeavor to retain them together. The penalty for violation was to be excommunication.

[37] T. E. Bond, "The M. E. Church South," *Meth. Quar. Rev.* (N. Y.), Vol. XXXI, pp. 282-302, at 300-301.

[38] On the whole subject see L. C. Matlack, *History of American Slavery and Methodism from 1780 to 1849,* and his *Anti-Slavery Struggle and Triumph in the M. E. Church* (1881) which carries the history further. My references are to the former volume. See also Daniel De Vinné, *The M. E. Church and Slavery* (1857).

[39] Published in Anthony Benezet's *Views of American Slavery taken a Century Ago* (1858), and other places. My references are to Benezet's volume.

[40] *Ibid.,* p. 98. Wesley's position is in contrast to Whitefield's who advocated slavery and used slaves on his Georgia plantation. See W. E. Lecky, *England in the Eighteenth Century,* III, 102.

[41] See their respective biographies for numerous references to the subject of slavery. On Lee see D. Curry, "Rev. Jesse Lee," *Meth. Quar. Rev.* (N. Y.), Vol. XXXII, pp. 58-80, at 78-79; L. M. Lee, *Life and Times of*

FREEBORN GARRETSON

slaves in December, 1780, and repugnance towards the institution was partly responsible for his removal into the Northwest Territory in 1798.[42]

As slavery did not exist in England, there was no written rule against it in Wesley's "General Rules," and these applied also to the American societies.[43] The great revivals in Virginia drew many slaveholders into the Church, and after 1776 the southern element was for a time preponderant in the councils of the denomination. The great increases in membership were in the South; most of the preachers were assigned to slaveholding states. It was customary to hold the Conference there, and in 1779-80 there was a temporary schism due to the ordinance controversy.[44] For a while during the Revolution, Asbury was in confinement in the North and unable to exercise his influence; and by 1780, many members and a good number of the travelling and local preachers in the Methodist Church were slaveholders.

In 1780 a Conference of seventeen ministers held at Baltimore by Francis Asbury, took the first action respecting the holding of slaves. Two questions were asked: "Ought not this Conference to require those Travelling Preachers who hold slaves to give promise to set them free?" An affirmative answer is appended.[45] The second question dealt with the laity and was framed as follows: "Does this Conference acknowledge that slavery is contrary to the laws of God, man, and nature, and hurtful to society; contrary to the dictates of conscience and

Jesse Lee. On Garrettson see his _Life_ compiled by Bangs. On Gatch see his _Memoirs,_ edited by McLean. Matlack mentions the views of these leaders.

[42] The deed is printed in his _Memoirs,_ p. 93. At this time Gatch lived in Powhatan County.

[43] Sherman, _History of the Revisions of the Discipline_ (3rd ed.), pp. 128-130. The General Rules were drawn up in 1743 and were retained by the Methodists in America without alteration although they were not inserted in the _Discipline_ until 1789. _Discipline_ for 1789, sec. 35. Townsend, _et al., New History of Methodism,_ II, 502-5.

[44] De Vinné, _op. cit.,_ pp. 11-13, presents these facts on the introduction of the slavery question into the Church. Also quoted in Matlack, p. 24.

[45] Minutes 1780, Question 16, Matlack, pp. 14 ff. prints the extracts. Sherman, pp. 230-4 prints the various actions on slavery from 1780 to 1860. It was customary for the early Conferences to frame their decisions in the form of questions and answers, but the action was binding.

pure religion, and doing that which we would not others should
do to us and ours? Do we pass our disapprobation on all our
friends who keep slaves, and advise their freedom?"[46] Again
the answer was "Yes."

It must be noted that while the above action was mandatory
in respect to the itinerants, it was merely advisory for the laity,
although slavery is condemned in no uncertain terms. Probably it was felt that reform must commence with the preachers
before it could be carried to the people and that the latter would
hesitate to uphold a system "contrary to the laws of man, and
nature, . . . and pure religion." But men, even preachers, were
not to be so easily convinced of the evils which the Conference
presumed and many resented the language that was used in the
Minutes.[47] Philip Gatch, however, emancipated his slaves at this
time, and perhaps others did likewise.

That the advice of the Conference respecting the holding
of slaves was not generally effective is proven by the necessity
for repeated action on the matter by that body. First, in respect
to the local preachers, the Conference of 1783 asks: "What shall
be done with our Local Preachers who hold slaves contrary to
the laws which authorize their freedom in any of the United
States?"[48] It was decided to try them for another year, but if
they persisted in holding slaves "it may be necessary to suspend
them." Hitherto nothing had been said concerning the local
preachers and evidently they had neither heeded the mandate
to the itinerants nor the advice to the laity. The Conference was
cautious in its action, however, and it is plain that the issue
must have been regarded as a delicate one which might easily
disrupt the Church.

Little, apparently, was accomplished by the rule of 1783,
even in the states north of the Potomac. Again, in 1784, it was
asked: "What shall we do with our Local Preachers who will

[46] Minutes, 1780. Question 17.
[47] W. W. Bennett, *Memorials of Methodism in Virginia*, p. 133, quotes
Lee as follows but gives no reference as usual: "the preachers in this case
went too far in their censures, and their language in their resolves was calculated to irritate the minds of the people and by no means calculated to
convince them of their errors."   [48] Minutes 1783, Question 10.

not emancipate their slaves in the States where the laws admit it?" "Try those in Virginia another year and suspend the Preachers in Maryland, Delaware, Pennsylvania and New Jersey."[49] Deference is thus given to the stronger public sentiment which prevailed in Virginia, but the local preachers in the North must mend their ways at once.

Still firmer action was taken against the itinerants, among whom slavery apparently lingered. In answer to the question, "What shall be done with our Travelling Preachers that now are, or hereafter shall be, possessed of slaves, and refuse to manumit them where the law permits?" it was decided: "Employ them no more."[50] Again the Conference was careful not to contravene the laws of states that did not permit emancipation. The existence of these laws was a serious obstacle to the program of the Methodist Church, for to compel preachers or members to dispose of slaves other than by liberating them might result in cruel injustice to the latter and thus prove worse than the evil itself.[51]

Up to this time (1784), nothing further than the advisory action of 1780 had been officially done to persuade the private members to get rid of their slaves. Here there was need for great caution lest offence be given to the societies, but the Conference now made a rule that under no circumstances should a member be permitted to sell a slave, nor should any one buy a slave except to emancipate him. The penalty for violation by any one who had been previously warned was to be expulsion from the Methodist society.[52]

The Christmas Conference of 1784 determined to forever purge the newly born American Church from the taint of slavery. Drastic indeed was the action that was taken.[53] The institu-

---

[49] Minutes 1784, Question 13. There had been no law against manumission in Virginia but in 1782 an act was passed granting the right specifically.
[50] *Ibid.*, Question 22.
[51] See Bond, *loc. cit.*, pp. 296-7.   [52] Minutes 1784, Question 12.
[53] The proceedings of the Christmas Conference do not appear in the regularly printed Minutes but are found in the form of the First Discipline and are reprinted in Tigert, *Const. Hist. of the M. E. Church,* Appendix vii. The designation First Discipline is apt to confuse the student. The extracts dealing with slavery are in Matlack, pp. 15-16, and in Sherman, pp. 231-2.

tion was pronounced "contrary to the golden law of God . . . and the inalienable rights of mankind as well as every principle of the Revolution. . . ." Immediate and effective action "to extirpate this abomination from among us" was declared necessary and a scheme of emancipation was drawn up.[54] Persons refusing to comply with the rules were given the option of withdrawing from the Methodist societies within twelve months after they had been notified to free their slaves, or else they were to be excluded. No slaveholders were to be admitted to membership unless they previously signed a deed of emancipation. Exception was made, at least in letter, to the states which had laws against emancipation, and special consideration was given Virginia, although its statutes allowed manumission.[55] "And respecting our brethren in Virginia that are concerned, and after due consideration of their peculiar circumstances, we allow them two years from the notice given, to consider the expedience of compliance or non-compliance with these rules."[56] The ban on the buying and selling of slaves for any other reason than freeing them was continued, nor could any one give away slaves for the purpose of keeping them in bondage.[57]

Thus was Methodism within a few years to part company with slavery as far as was humanly possible. The arm of its authority was to extend down through the circuits into every region where the superior voice of the State did not command a halt. There was to be no compromise with this greatest evil of all ages. Could Methodism effect its purpose without being driven from the slave states?

[54] First Discipline, Question 42. Slaves between the ages of 40 and 45, not later than the forty-fifth year of age; those between 25 and 40 must be freed within five years; those between 20 and 25, not later than the thirtieth year; those under 20, not later than the twenty-fifth year. All infants born after these rules were to be free.

[55] De Vinné, pp. 16-17, holds that even where the law forbade emancipation the Conference never intended to grant any person a dispensation to continue in sin. The obligation was morally binding everywhere and the animus of the rule was that masters should at least disclaim all right of property in their slaves and discard all authority which the laws give over them, thus morally if not actually freeing them. The moral obligation could not be measured by geographical lines and there were to be no exceptions. This, of course, is merely the opinion of De Vinné and submitted by him without substantiating evidence.

[56] Tigert, *op. cit.*, p. 556.   [57] First Discipline, Question 43.

David Sherman says that the Methodists desired "to circumscribe, repress, and extirpate slavery, but to do it in such a way as not to exclude practical effort for the salvation of both master and slave. The problem was a difficult one; perhaps no people could have solved it better. The difficulties in the solution arose from the very success attained with both classes."[58] It was impossible to enforce the rules because of the offense they gave to the southern members and the strenuous opposition they created from the local and even some of the travelling ministers. The attitude of Virginia was soon given expression. When Coke came there in the spring of 1785 and began to denounce slavery and exhort for emancipation, he was threatened with mob violence, and bills of indictment were presented against him in at least two counties.[59]

At the Conference held in Virginia, in May, 1785, a strong effort was made to secure the repeal of the obnoxious slavery rules, but Coke and his supporters threatened to refuse to appoint preachers for those circuits in which the regulations were disregarded, and the rules stood.[60] Moreover, a petition to the Virginia Assembly entreating a law for emancipation was framed and distributed on the circuits for signatures.[61] Thus were the Methodists responsible for the abortive emancipation movement which found expression in a number of petitions which were presented to the legislature in the fall of 1785.[62]

[58] History of the Revisions of the Discipline, (3rd ed.), p. 230 note.

[59] Coke, Journal, April 1, 8, 11, 23, 1785, and second visit, section iii. See also Matlack, pp. 17-19; Samuel Drew, Life of Thomas Coke, p. 138.

[60] In 1782 it was decided to hold two Conferences each year, one in the North and one in the South. The former, being of longest standing, was given precedence in the making of rules which were binding on the South. Lee, History, pp. 78-79; Coke, Journal, May 1-4, 1785.

[61] Coke, Journal, May 1-4, 1785. See also Leland, "Virginia Chronicle," in Works, p. 113.

[62] Journal of House of Delegates, November 8, 1785, records the presentation of five identical petitions purporting to be from "electors" of the state. A total of 104 signers appear on the petitions themselves. November 10, four identical petitions were presented from Halifax, Amelia, Mecklenburg and Pittsylvania—strong Methodist territory. A counter petition from Brunswick of the same date says that "we are credibly informed that petitions are secretly handed about for subscription, by persons . . . pretending to be moved by religious principles and taking for their motive universal charity." Brunswick was the heart of Virginia Methodism and the counter

Coke and Asbury even visited General Washington at Mount Vernon in the endeavor to secure his approval of the petition, but the latter would not commit himself definitely in the matter.[63] Eckenrode considers this movement for emancipation as very significant of the progress of liberalism in Virginia—a manifestation of the growing democratic ideals in politics and society.[64]

Within one month after the failure of the Virginia Conference to secure a repeal of the slavery rules, the Baltimore Conference suspended them indefinitely.[65] In naïve words, Coke records: "We thought it prudent to suspend the minute concerning slavery, on account of the great opposition that had been given it, our work being in too infantile a state to push things to extremity."[66] The regulations did not remain in the Minutes six months. To have enforced them would have disrupted the Church and the Methodists were not willing to go that far as yet. The most the Conference did at this time was to express its continued antipathy for slavery in the following *nota bene:* "We do hold in deepest abhorrence the practice of slavery; and shall not cease to seek its destruction by all wise and prudent means."

Whether or not the suspension of the slavery rules was intended to be permanent, the fact remained that they were never

petition would seem to indicate that the Methodists were very busy there. The above petitions are in the Virginia archives. The Methodists also circulated a petition in North Carolina to secure the repeal of the law against emancipating slaves. Asbury even visited the Governor in its behalf and according to Coke "gained him over" but the legislature did not take the desired action. See Coke, *Journal,* April 19, 1785; Samuel Drew, *Life of Thomas Coke,* p. 139. The Quakers were the only other denomination which consistently supported the emancipation movement. Prior to 1765 they confined their efforts to amelioration rather than emancipation, but in 1768 it was made a breach of discipline for a Friend to purchase a slave. Occasionally the Quakers petitioned for emancipation. See S. B. Weeks, *Southern Quakers and Slavery,* pp. 201 ff.; MS. petitions from Quakers November 29, 1780, and May 20, 1782, as examples of their attitude.

[63] Coke, *Journal,* May 26, 1785.

[64] *The Revolution in Virginia,* p. 298.

[65] Minutes for 1785; Lee, *History,* p. 102; De Vinné contends that the suspension was not intended to be permanent but simply to give opportunity to think matters over. Again this is merely his opinion.

[66] *Journal,* June 1, 1785.

successfully revived and the crisis of a half century later was settled only by a division of the Church.[67]

Meantime, another trend is observable in the emphasis placed upon the spiritual welfare of the blacks. The Conference of 1787 required the preachers to leave nothing undone "for the spiritual benefit and salvation of the negroes, . . . and for this purpose to embrace every opportunity of inquiring the state of their souls, and to unite in society those who appear to have a real desire of fleeing from the wrath to come, to meet such in class, and to exercise the whole Methodist discipline among them."[68] The demand that the slaves be not given too unlimited freedom even in religious gatherings is seen in the requirement that their class leader must always be white.[69]

We have thus seen that the Great Awakening was the source of real humanitarian influences favoring the slaves. All three of the evangelical churches we have been studying opened the doors wide to the slaves and counted many hundreds of them among their members.[70] Much was done to educate the blacks and to ameliorate the conditions of their bondage, while considerable numbers of them were emancipated as a direct result of the revivals.[71] One of the denominations of the Great Awakening placed itself officially on record as opposed to the institution of slavery and made a heroic effort to bring about its abolition. Even among the Baptists and Presbyterians who did not as a church oppose slaveholding, there were individuals who preached strongly against it and used their influence ac-

[67] See De Vinné, pp. 48, 49, 53, and Tigert, p. 218, for opposing views. The former contends that the moral obligation still continued. See Matlack for the later history. No action was taken in the General Conference concerning slavery from 1785 to 1796.

[68] Minutes 1787, Question 17.

[69] First Discipline, Question 41.

[70] We are given the statistics for the Methodists. In 1786 there were 1,890 slaves in a total membership of 18,000, or about one in ten. The proportion is the same for Virginia. Bennett, p. 233.

[71] In addition to the instances already given, Philip Bruce says that at the time of the revival of 1787-8 the Methodists manumitted upwards of a hundred slaves at a single session at the court in Sussex County. Letter to T. Coke, March 25, 1788, in *Arminian Mag.* (Amer.), 1790, II, 563. No doubt there were other similar instances only it would not be possible for us to identify the denominational standing from the court records. Bruce's statement is, therefore, very significant.

cordingly. More than this, Christianity was used to teach many practical virtues to the slaves and to impress upon the masters their obligations towards their servants. Finally, we must not overlook the great spiritual uplift which came to the blacks from the evangelical movement.

CHAPTER XI

Religion and the Social Revolution

By the end of the eighteenth century a social revolution had occurred in the Old Dominion. In the same manner that it contributed to the development of democratic ideas in politics, the Great Awakening was a factor in the social upheaval. Both of these transformations were merely the result of the application of democratic principles to the relationships of life and they are more or less inseparable.[1]

Class lines and social distinctions were very pronounced in Virginia in the middle of the eighteenth century.[2] The presence of a ruling group was firmly grounded in the traditions of the colony and Jarratt tells us that the consciousness of a difference between gentle and simple folk was universal.[3] We have also seen that the Established Church was identified with the dominant order, and was, therefore, restricted in its appeal and exclusive in constituency.

By the end of the century all this had changed. Jarratt, who had become a gentleman himself by that time, lamented in his later years the passing of the old order and the break down of the social distinctions between the gentle and plain people. "In our high Republican times," he wrote in 1794, "there is more levelling than ought to be consistent with good government. I have as little notion of tyranny and oppression as any man but a due subordination is essentially requisite in every government."[4] He confessed the theoretic supremacy of republican institutions, but the want of a clear distinction between the governing class and the governed was to him a great defect of the later age. He would return to the good old days of royal government when in practice laws were better executed, and government was more peaceably administered, and the gentle folk were held in due respect as superiors by the common man. It was his opinion that things had gone to the extreme.

[1] The evidence for the social changes is much more elusive as men did not consciously express themselves on this as they did in political matters.
[2] See above, Chapter II.   [3] *Autobiography,* p. 14.   [4] *Ibid.,* pp. 14-15.

[251]

Jarratt's lack of sympathy for the social upheaval that had occurred in his generation was due, doubtless, to his faithful adherence to the Established Church. Nevertheless, because he was an evangelical he contributed to the very changes which later disturbed him. We see this in his revival which, he tells us, began among the middle class of people, not that he believed that conviction had made no headway among those below but because the lower classes were shy in conversing with clergymen, "whom they supposed to stand in the rank of gentlemen and above the company and conversation of plebeians."[5] Jarratt remembered his own former timidity in approaching the gentle folk and his great embarrassment in their presence. The same attitude was possessed by "the poorer sort, in Bath, at that day."[6] They hesitated to approach their minister because they were curbed by the traditional respect for the upper members of society, in which rank the clergy were counted. However, Jarratt soon began to hold prayer meetings in private homes— "a great novelty in a minister of the church." These meetings were of great significance not only religiously but socially, for it was in them, says Jarratt, that "the poorer sort, who at first may be shy in speaking, soon wore off their shyness and spoke as freely as others."[7]

Here we see in actual operation the gradual pushing upward of the lower classes which brought about the social revolution. It was a characteristic of the evangelical revival and was repeated on a much larger scale among the denominations which yielded to its influences. We see it at work among the Baptists and Presbyterians and in the Methodist classes and bands. The evangelical churches, as we have seen, emphasized the importance and worth of the individual and developed a self-respect

---

[5] *Autobiography*, 91.

[6] This was in the 'sixties before the Baptist and Methodist revivals had made their impressions.

[7] *Autobiography*, p. 92. Richard Dozier, MS. copy, "Text Book" records several instances of negroes preaching in the Northern Neck. *E.g.* May 26, 1782 (to 400 people); December 25, 1787, a Negro "who rides with Mr. Asberry" (Bishop Asbury) preached "in a clear and most wonderful manner"; April 27, 1789 "Negro Jacob, a slave," "a most wonderful preacher." For slaves to preach before whites in the Northern Neck is surely significant of a tremendous overturn. See below, note 46, on Dozier's "Text Book."

which, however much it might be resented, demanded the right to be heard. This applied even to the black man. Certainly the "levelling" process which Jarratt lived to deplore was a by-product of the Great Awakening, although it received added impetus from the American Revolution.

There was no exclusiveness in the evangelical churches and the bringing together for religious worship of men and women from all social ranks on an equal plane must have been a powerful leaven in the transformation of society. The Methodist class meeting alone was an irresistible influence against class distinctions.[8] The preaching of free grace for all mankind was another great leveller of society, but, whether Arminian or Calvinistic, the evangelical churches endeavored to reach every individual. Important, too, as a social influence was the development of a ministry which came direct from the people and appealed to their thoughts and emotions in a way that was adapted to their habits of speech and life. This was particularly true of the Baptists and Methodists, while a special feature of the latter organization was the lay ministry.

We can best see the change that had come over Virginia in connection with the Baptists. It will be recalled that prior to 1776 these people were regarded as poor, ignorant, lowly and the meanest of the mean. Their preachers were without learning or patronage, generally very poor, plain in their dress, unrefined in manners, awkward in their address.[9] In short, as the old lady told Benedict, the Baptists were regarded as "outlandish" and "deformed in some way or other" and "hardly any of them looked like other people."[10] In the popular mind a very definite social stigma attached itself to the name Baptist. The cropped heads of the Baptist men, the plain dress of their women, their "odd tones" and the "disgusting whoops" excited at first ridicule and contempt, and then resentment that such a people should want a hearing along with the gentle folk.

[8] See W. P. Lovejoy, "The Influence of Methodism," *Meth. Rev.* (So.), Vol. LI, pp. 375-8.

[9] Semple, *History of the Baptists in Virginia,* pp. 43-44 and above pp. 113-114.

[10] See above, p. 116.

By the end of the century significant changes had occurred among the Baptists. Says Semple: "Their preachers were become much more correct in their manners of preaching. A great many odd tones, disgusting whoops and awkward gestures were disused. In their matter, also, they had more of sound sense and strong reasoning. Their zeal was less mixed with enthusiasm, and their piety became more rational. They were much more numerous and, of course, in the eyes of the world more respectable. Besides, they were joined by persons of much greater weight in civil society; their congregations became more numerous than those of any other Christian sect, and, in short, they might be considered, from this period, as taking the lead in matters of religion in many places of the State. This could not but influence their manners and spirit more or less. Accordingly a great deal of that simplicity and plainness, that rigid scrupulosity about little matters which so happily tends to keep us at a distance from greater follies, was laid aside. Their mode of preaching, also was somewhat changed. At their first entrance into the State, though not incoherent in their method and language, they were quite correct in their views upon all subjects of primary importance. No preachers ever dealt out to their hearers the nature of experimental religion more clearly and more warmly. As their respectability increased, the preachers and their hearers found a relish for stronger meat, which, to a proper extent, was very suitable; but it too often happened, in indulging this, that party spirit and even vanity had too much influence. To dive deeply into the mysteries of the Gospel, to tell or to make a plausible guess about what happened before the world was made or what will happen before it shall end, looked more wise and excited more applause than to travel on in the old track."[11] The result was that some of the preachers fell into errors; Arminianism made its inroads; practical piety was not as strongly urged as in former days; and discipline was relaxed.

Similar testimony comes from the pen of Fristoe, who lived through the entire period[12] and, in 1808, at the age of sixty,

[11] *Ibid.,* pp. 59-60; 1810 ed., p. 39.
[12] He was born in Stafford County in (1748?), began to preach at the age of nineteen and was chosen moderator of his Association at the age of

wrote: "There is a considerable difference between thirty and forty years past and present time as to the conduct of the populace towards our ministers—prejudices are much conquered, and their judgments better informed—so that preachers of late are not held up in contempt as formerly; whether it arises from want of zeal for God, honesty and faithfulness to man, and a want of circumspection in life and conversation, or whether it arises from an opposite behaviour, we will not with confidence assert."[13] The "cant word" that the Baptists "are an ignorant and illiterate set—and of the poor and contemptible class of the people," was no longer true.

In addition to the statements of Semple and Fristoe, a number of things may be mentioned as indicative of the change in the Baptists. One of these was the attention which they began to give to the more adequate support of their ministers. In their intense antipathy towards the Establishment with its paid clergy, the early Baptists became shamefully negligent of support of their own preachers.[14] The denomination wished to escape any possible charge of having hireling ministers since they freely charged the parsons with preaching for mercenary motives. In addition, the poverty of the early Baptists was a real obstacle to be overcome. In his account of church after church, Morgan Edwards states, "No estate, no salary except presents" to such and such an amount.[15] The result was that many preachers, without competent support and having large families, suffered from actual want and not a few abandoned the pulpit for the farm. Many finally emigrated to the more fertile valleys of Kentucky.[16]

Even at the end of the century, the Baptist ministers still suffered from this neglect, but at least the early prejudices

twenty-six, and wrote its history in 1808. He died in 1828. See Semple, pp. 405-6. Beale's note, p. 406, gives the date of Fristoe's birth at about 1742.

[13] *History of the Ketocton Baptist Association*, p. 59.

[14] *Ibid.*, p. 57.

[15] MS. Materials Towards a History of the Baptists in Virginia.

[16] Taylor, *Virginia Baptist Ministers*, I, *passim*, for many examples of lack of support. Semple, p. 456, refers to Kentucky as "the cemetery of Virginia Baptist preachers" so great was the exodus there. Fristoe, p. 226 n., estimates (1808) that half the preachers who were raised in Virginia migrated to the West.

against a salaried ministry were passing.[17] In addition to some churches making provision for the compensation of their pastors, the Associations sometimes devoted Circular Letters to the subject.[18] Thus the Roanoke Association, in 1793, urged adequate support of ministers that the latter may devote more time to study and improvement of their minds. It is ordained "that they who preach the Gospel shall live of the gospel, and if it be barbarous and inhuman to muzzle an ox in your employment, surely it is more so when you neglect to support the hands of your minister. The frivilous *(sic)* arguments of poverty; ought not to be mentioned." Everyone should give to the Lord, it was urged, in order "to avoid roberry." *(sic)*[19]

It is significant also that by 1790 the Baptists were beginning to pay attention to education, both ministerial and secular. The design of establishing a seminary of learning which was proposed by the General Committee in 1789, has already been referred to.[20] The scheme was pushed for about seven years, finally failing for lack of funds. One expediency of such a seminary was: "Our brethren of other denominations around us Could no longer curse us for not knowing the Law, or discard and Reprobate a great deal of our Teaching for not knowing our Mother tongue, much less the original languages, and if we (in this as we ought in everything), do it with a single eye to The glory of God, and the advancement of the Redeemer's interest Then shall we have sufficient to hope we shall meet with heavens approbation."[21] Apparently the Baptists felt the need of a more educated ministry in order to keep the respect of other denominations. The Circular Letter of the General Committee

[17] See Fristoe, p. 56.

[18] MS. Upper King and Queen Church Record Book, September 19, 1789; MS. Morattico Church Book, 1797, p. 35, also pp. 17, 21; MS. Albemarle Church Book (no date cited). Circular Letter, Portsmouth Association, 1796, on "Duty of Churches to their Ministers," in Minutes. MS. Minutes Roanoke Association, Circular Letter, October, 1789, pp. 27-30; *ibid.*, October, 1793, pp. 95-97; also Minutes, June, 1790, p. 36.

[19] *Ibid.*, Roanoke Association, October, 1793, pp. 95-97.

[20] See above Chapter IX and Circular Letter of Baptist General Meeting of Correspondence, held in Chesterfield County, October 22, 1808 (Va. Bap. Hist. Soc.).

[21] MS. Circular Letter, Roanoke Association, in Minutes, May, 1789.

Ro. B. Semple

of Correspondence in 1808 deals with the utility of human learning and asserts: "we solemnly declare, that from a general acquaintance among our brethren in different parts of the state, it is our opinion that nine tenths of them value human learning among the most precious of our earthly things."[22] The Committee urges that while some few "out of the way of information, observing the abuses of education and learning" may depreciate the latter, it "cannot think it charitable or libearal *(sic)* to saddle a whole society with sentiments holden only by a few of the most obscure." Certainly this sounds different from the earlier accounts of the Bapists. They had come to a new evaluation of standards.

Not only was ministerial education urged, but also the training of children. The Circular Letter of the Roanoke Association in June, 1791, was given over wholly to this subject. No longer must Baptists "let their poor, ignorant children run wild," as Benedict was informed they did in the early days, but they must be trained for careers of usefulness in Church and State. "In a word if you would wish to see your children useful and valuable, you must be thorough in their education."[23]

In 1788, the first proposal for writing a history of the Baptists in Virginia was made in the General Committee.[24] The ultimate result was Semple's work, which was published in 1810. The denomination had become conscious that it had a respectable past and a history worth giving to the world. One purpose of such a work was to prove to our "countrymen we are the plain, honest people we have ever profest to be."[25] Moreover some misconceptions of the early Baptists must be cleared up. "We do not doubt but the pen of our historian will point Back far and clear enough to convince the impartial inquirer that we with propriety disown any affinity with the Madmen of Münster, which has been so often attempted to be Fixed upon us by abusive pen, and rancurous tongues."[26] If the early Baptists

[22] P. 7.
[23] In MS. Minutes, pp. 70-73.
[24] Semple, p. 103, and Preface to original edition.
[25] MS. Circular Letter, Roanoke Association, May, 1789, in Minutes.
[26] *Ibid.*

did not resent connection with the Anabaptists of Münster, such was not the case by 1790.

A denomination which had become strong and popular must be careful of those who represented it before the world. Thus the Roanoke Association warned the churches: "Guard against heretical principals and stragling preachers, that cannot evince by proper certificates and credentials they are in orderly standing in their respective churches."[27] Were not the Baptists themselves regarded as stragglers and heretics but a generation before? Now, however, they were established socially. The same Association severed connection with "some disorderly persons that called themselves baptist attached to one James Younger as their Minister equally if not more disorderly than either of them."[28] The Association resolved to be careful of admitting churches into the union in the future. This would seem to indicate that the Baptists were looking upon some much as they themselves were commonly regarded in the earlier days, namely, as a disorderly set. Equally significant was the recommendation of the Strawberry Association, in 1791, that candidates for ordination be examined by a "presbytery of ministers who are of the ablest" in order "to prevent the further spread of non Qualifyed ministers being ordained."[29] Was it that the call of God no longer sufficed to give one license to preach? If so, the Baptists had reached a new standard of values.

Semple mentions that in the great revivals of 1787-9 the Baptists became the most numerous denomination in the state and "they were joined by persons of much greater weight in civil society."[30] Rippon's *Baptist Annual Register* for 1790 informs us that since the Revolution "a great number of rich planters" had joined the Baptists.[31] One of these was Councillor Carter of Nomini Hall, whom we have mentioned more than once in this study. He remained a Baptist for about fifteen years, after which he embraced Arminianism and later the doctrines of Swedenborg.[32] Of him Asbury wrote in his Journal for Sun-

[27] MS. Circular Letter, October, 1789, Minutes, p. 30.
[28] MS. Minutes, May, 1789, pp. 8-9.
[29] MS. Minutes, October, 1791.   [31] *American Letters,* 1790, p. 107.
[30] See above, p. 254.   [32] Semple, pp. 178-9.

day, December 19, 1790: "visited Counsellor Carter, and spent the evening in much peace and love. He has the manner of a gentleman, the attainments of a scholar, and the experience of a Christian. He is a very social gentleman—a Baptist."[33] Carter took a prominent part in Baptist affairs in the Northern Neck and belonged to Morattico church in Richmond County. For some time he served in the capacity of clerk to his church and a number of manuscripts in his own handwriting have been preserved.[34] In May, 1787, he was sent with Lewis Lunsford as a delegate to the Association.[35] Richard Dozier frequently records sermons preached at "Nominy Hall,"[36] which evidently became a regular place of visitation for Baptist preachers.

The social revolution cannot be understood apart from the bettering of the economic status of the Baptists. The early poverty of the denomination has been mentioned frequently enough in this study. By the end of the eighteenth century, however, the Baptists counted a large proportion of small farmers with estates ranging from a hundred to a thousand acres, many of whom owned slaves.[37] Just to what extent this was a result of the great overturn of property and wealth during the Revolution, we cannot say.[38] We do know that many landowners came into the Church in the great post-Revolutionary revivals but

[33] Quoted in *ibid.*, note.

[34] Va. Bap. Hist. Soc. Among these is a plan of church government, dated September 29, 1788, for submission to the churches.

[35] MS. Church letter, May 5, 1787. A MS. record of a church meeting, March 14, 1789, indicates that in 1788 Carter and some thirty others secured dismission to form Yocomoco Church in Northumberland. Semple does not mention this church but has Wicomico Church organized from Morattico in 1804.

[36] MS. (copy) "Text Book" of Richard Dozier (Westmoreland County), Va. Bap. Hist. Soc.

[37] The land tax lists are available from about 1790 on. In a few instances the Baptists can be checked up from the membership lists which appear in some of the extant Church Books. As best the check must be very incomplete but sufficient to see the large sprinkling of landholders and slaveholders in the few churches where the membership lists are available. Boarswamp Church is a good example as it has a fairly complete record of members (Henrico County). A difficulty is that not all members lived in the county where the church was located and it is not easy to check them. Nevertheless, the results I obtained were gratifying.

[38] See Eckenrode, *The Revolution in Virginia*, pp. 119 ff. on this phase of the Revolution.

doubtless the denomination profited from the great confiscations, which, says Eckenrode, "paved the way for the rise of numerous small farmers to affluence" and constituted "one of the most important social results of the Revolution."[39] At any rate, their presence in the denomination was significant of a change in the economic and social status of the Baptists.

Another phase in this upheaval in Virginia society was the great change in social attitudes which came with the evangelical revival. Pastimes and customs that were once universal in the colony were now frowned upon. The Baptists condemned swearing, quarrelling, superfluity in dress and apparel, intemperance of all sorts, "playing or dancing wanton tunes," horse racing "as it is commonly carried on," the use of cards and dice "and the like instruments of folly, and, in brief, all those exercises and entertainments of pastime and merriment commonly termed recreations."[40] On the contrary, private worship, personal piety, and strict observance of the Sabbath were encouraged. Examination of the conduct of members was a regular part of the business of the Baptist churches, and members were frequently censured or excommunicated for breach of discipline.[41]

Possibly the Methodists were even greater sticklers on conduct than the Baptists. The class rules forbade indulgence in evil of every kind, particularly swearing, drunkenness, fighting, giving or taking usury, unseemly conversation, and even the wearing of gold or costly apparel.[42] On the matter of simplicity in dress, the First Discipline was very firm and ordered all who

[39] *The Revolution in Virginia*, pp. 187, 190.

[40] Thomas, *The Virginian Baptist*, p. 20. See also Fithian, *Journal and Letters*, pp. 117-118 (1774), who says the Baptists are "quite destroying pleasure."

[41] The MS. Church Record Books abound in such instances. Thus Broad Run Church excommunicated Henry Watkins "for Playing the Violin and Associating in the company of wicked men" (July 27, 1778). Others were disciplined for intemperance, for not attending worship, for wife beating, Sabbath breaking, lying, superfluity in apparel, fighting, etc. Upper King and Queen Church condemned "cock't hatt—curl'd and powered hair, also hair tied by man—likewise two stocks the one white and the other Black at the same time—Gold to be worne by none—high crown'd caps—Rolls, Necklaces, Ruffles, Stays and Stomagers" (September 16, 1780).

[42] Given in Lee, *History of the Methodists*, pp. 30-33.

indulged in superfluous ornaments to be excluded from the societies. "Give no tickets to any that wear High Heads, enormous Bonnets, Ruffles or Rings," are the words of the rule.[43] The Methodists gained a reputation for their strictness in conduct which became synonymous with their name.[44] With them it was the test of godliness, and the rules were vigorously enforced.

Naturally, this change in manner of living at first brought reproach upon the evangelicals. Davies tells us that one who joined the Presbyterians was more ridiculed than people ever were "for Drinking, Swearing, and other vicious Extravagancies, if they went to Church." If persons were sober and thoughtful, he continues, and held family worship, and refrained from excesses, if they were guilty "of such unfashionable things as 'Reading and Praying' they are soon branded with the opprobrious Name of New Lights. . . . Satyrs, etc. are published in the Gazette, to alarm the World of these Dangerous Animals."[45] However, the unfashionable became ordinary, the stigma and opprobrium wore off, and Virginia became evangelical. One can scarcely realize the far reaching upheaval involved in this transition, which made even the aristocratic Northern Neck willing to listen to the gospel, although expounded by black men.[46] Is it any wonder that in this process,

[43] First Discipline, Question 18.
[44] Gatch, *Memoirs*, p. 86 for example.
[45] Davies, *Impartial Trial*, p. 27.
[46] See above, note 7. Richard Dozier, of Westmoreland County, kept a record of the preachers and texts of the sermons he heard in various churches and homes in the Northern Neck, from 1771 to 1811. He therefore lived through the entire period during which the Baptists were getting established. He records the texts and preachers of over seven hundred sermons during this period. Occasionally he makes a comment on the preacher but it is usually the text that interests him. Dozier was a Baptist but now and then he listened to a sermon by a Methodist or a Presbyterian. We learn from the "Textbook" that three, four, and five hundred people were an average sized audience with occasionally many more, as at an Association meeting. In the poem, written as a Preface, Dozier says:

> "When I am dead and in my grave,
> This book, my children you will have
> To see what wonders have been done,
> For me thro' Christ, God's only Son."

In eight other stanzas he comments upon various preachers who must have especially impressed him. A MS. copy of this interesting document is owned

the Established Church, with its restricted appeal and easy morals, was swept from the field?

Thus were new values created by the Great Awakening and a new attitude towards life developed. If popularity brought with it a relaxation in discipline and if, with the development of a broader spirit of toleration, some of the early plainness and simplicity wore off, still Virginia never returned to the old *mores* of the mid-eighteenth century. The religious life of her people continued to be dominated by the popular churches, whose rise to a position of influence came with the Great Awakening.

Although the Great Awakening was primarily a revival of personal religion, from it sprang many forces which made for the betterment of society. In its effects upon the individual it was democratic, and it applied this principle to all relations of life—religious, political, and social. The rise of democracy was preceded and foreshadowed by the rise of religious dissent, which did much to crystallize the ideas and forces back of the American Revolution. The application of the principles of the Awakening, reinforced by the ideas of the Revolution, brought complete religious liberty to Virginia. From it also sprang educational and humanitarian influences evidenced by the establishment of educational institutions, and a more humane attitude towards the slaves. Lastly, in its very nature, the evangelical revival contributed mightily to the social upheaval which had occurred in Virginia by the close of the eighteenth century.

by the Va. Bap. Hist. Soc., the original, apparently, having been lost. Dr. George W. Beale, who revised Semple's history, owned the copy from which the above society obtained theirs. This information is from Dr. Garnett Ryland of the Virginia Baptist Historical Society.

BIBLIOGRAPHY

I. Bibliographical Guides

Allison, W. H. *Inventory of Unpublished Material for American Religious History in Protestant Church Archives and other Depositories.* Washington, 1910.

Archibald, F. A. *Methodism and Literature.* New York, 1883. Contains much bibliographical information on American Methodism.

Bowerman, G. F. *A selected Bibliography of the Religious Denominations of the United States.* New York, 1896. Very brief and now much out of date.

Cavender (pseud.), C. H. *Catalogue of Works in refutation of Methodism from its origin in 1792.* Second ed. revised. New York, 1868.

Evans, Charles. *American Bibliography.* 8 vols. Chicago, 1903. Indispensable; extends to 1793.

Green, R. *Anti-Methodist Publications issued during the Eighteenth Century.* London, 1902. Catalogues 606 items.

Johnston, W. D., and Mudge, I. G. *Special Collections in Libraries in the United States.* Washington, 1912.

Mode, P. G. *Source Book and Bibliographical Guide for American Church History.* Menasha, Wisconsin, 1921.

Nagler, A. W. *Pietism and Methodism,* Nashville, 1918. Contains valuable bibliography on both these subjects.

Swem, E. G. *A Bibliography of Virginia.* Richmond, 1916. Lists thousands of books and items in the Virginia State Library.

Torrence, W. C. *A Trial Bibliography of Colonial Virginia.* (Va. State Lib. Bull.) Richmond, 1910. This volume covers the period 1754-1776.

Townsend, W. J., and others. *A New History of Methodism.* 2 vols. London, 1909. The latest and best on the subject written on the plan of the Cambridge Modern History. Volume II contains extensive bibliography.

Turner, J. B. *Catalogue of Manuscript Records in the Presbyterian Historical Society.* (Jour. Pres. Hist. Soc., Vol. VIII.) Later accessions listed in subsequent years.

Tucker, R L. *Separation of the Methodists from the Church of England.* New York, 1918. Contains extensive bibliography on English Methodism.

Virginia Newspapers in Public Libraries. (Va. Mag. Hist. and Biog., Vols. IX-X.) An indispensable guide.

II. Books, Sermons, Pamphlets and Items Printed Separately

A Collection of Hymns for the use of the people called Methodists. Seventh ed., London, 1791. Preface by John Wesley dated 1779.

Alexander, Archibald. *Biographical Sketches of the Founder and Alumni of the Log College*. Philadelphia, 1851.

Alexander, S. D. *Princeton College during the Eighteenth Century*. New York, 1872.

————. *The Presbytery of New York 1738-1888*. New York, 1887.

Ambler, Charles H. *Sectionalism in Virginia from 1776 to 1861*. Chicago, 1910.

Anderson, J. S. M. *The History of the Church of England in the Colonies*. 3 vols., London, 1856. Vol. III, 1700-1800.

Anon. *American Husbandry*. London, 1775, 2 vols.

Archibald, F. A. *Methodism and Literature*. New York, 1883.

Asbury, Francis. *Journal*. Volume I, from August 7, 1771 to December 29, 1778, Philadelphia, 1792. Volume II, from January 1, 1779 to September 3, 1780, Philadelphia, 1802.

Asplund, John. *The Annual Register of the Baptist Denomination in North America to November 1, 1790.*

Atkinson, John. *The Beginnings of the Wesleyan Movement in America and the establishment therein of Methodism*. New York, 1896.

Atkinson, John. *Centennial History of American Methodism*. New York, 1884.

Baird, Robert. *Religion in America*. New York, 1856.

Baird, S. J. (ed.). *A Collection of the Acts, Deliverances, and Testimonies of the Supreme Judicatory of the Presbyterian Church from its Origin in America to the Present Times with notes and documents*. Philadelphia, 1856.

Bangs, Nathan. *A History of the Methodist Episcopal Church*. 2 vols., New York, 1838.

———— (ed.). *The Life of the Reverend Freeborn Garrettson compiled from his Printed and Manuscript Journals and other authentic documents*. Fifth ed., New York.

Barclay, W. F. *The Constitution of the M. E. Churches in America*. Nashville, 1902.

Baring-Gould, S. *The Evangelical Revival*. London, 1920.

Barnes, Albert. *The Church and Slavery* (Presby.). Philadelphia, 1857.

Barrow, David. *Circular Letter . . .* Southampton County, Virginia, February 14, 1798. Norfolk.

Beardsley, F. G. *History of American Revivals*. New York, 1904.

Beecher, W. J. and Mary A. *An Index of Presbyterian Ministers, 1706-1881*. Philadelphia, 1883.

Belcher, Joseph. *George Whitefield . . . with Special Reference to his Labours in America*. New York, 1857.

Benedict, David. *A General History of the Baptist Denomination in America and other parts of the world*. 2 vols., Boston, 1813.

————. *Fifty Years among the Baptists*. New York, 1860.

Bennett, W. W. *Memorials of Methodism in Virginia*. Second ed., Richmond, 1871.

Bishop, R. H. *An Outline History of the Church in the State of Kentucky containing the Memoirs of Reverend David Rice.* Lexington, 1824.

Bitting, C. C. *Notes on the History of the Strawberry Baptist Association of Virginia, 1776-1876.* Baltimore, 1879.

Bolivar, Christian. *The Scotch Irish Settlers in the Valley of Virginia.* Richmond, 1860.

Breed, W. P. *Presbyterians and the Revolution.* Philadelphia, 1876.

Briggs, C. A. *American Presbyterianism.* New York, 1885.

Buckley, J. M. *History of the Methodists in the United States.* New York.

————. *Constitutional and Parliamentary History of the Methodist Episcopal Church.* New York, 1912.

Burk, John D. *The History of Virginia.* 4 vols. Petersburg, 1804-1816.

Burkhead, L. S. (ed.). *Centennial of Methodism in North Carolina.* Raleigh, 1876. Contains articles of general interest.

Burkitt, L., and Read, Jesse. *History of the Kehukee Baptist Association.* Halifax, N. C., 1803.

Caldwell, John. *An Impartial Trial of the Spirit operating in this part of the world; by comparing the nature, effects and evidences, of the present supposed conversion with the work of God.* Boston, 1742. Williamsburg, 1746.

Campbell, Charles. *History of Virginia.* Richmond, 1847.

Cathcart, Wm. *The Baptists and the American Revolution.* Philadelphia, 1876.

Channing, E. *History of the United States.* Vol. III, New York, 1912.

Chapell, F. L. *The Great Awakening of 1740.* Philadelphia, 1903.

Cleveland, C. C. *The Great Revival in the West, 1797-1805.* Chicago, 1916.

Coke, Thomas. *Journal,* Nashville, 1896.

————. *Extracts of the Journals . . . of the five visits to America.* London, 1793.

————. *Sermon Preached at Baltimore . . . at the ordination of the Reverend Francis Asbury, to the Office of Superintendent.* Baltimore, 1785.

Cooke, John Esten. *Virginia: A History of the People.* Boston, 1883.

Creamer, David. *Methodist Hymnology.* New York, 1848.

Cross, A. L. *The Anglican Episcopate and the American Colonies.* Cambridge, Mass., 1902.

Cummings, A. W. *Early Schools of Methodism.* New York, 1886.

Davenport, F. M. *Primitive Traits in Religious Revivals.* New York, 1905.

Davidson, R. *History of the Presbyterian church in the state of Kentucky; with a preliminary sketch of the churches in the Valley of Virginia.* New York, 1847.

Davies, Samuel. *A Sermon on Man's Primitive State; and the first covenant.* Philadelphia, 1748.

————. *A Sermon preached before the Reverend Presbytery of New Castle, October 11, 1752.* Philadelphia, 1753.

————. *An Appendix Proving the Right of the Synod of New York to the Religious Liberties and Immunities allowed to Protestant Dissenters by the Act of Toleration.* Williamsburg, 1748.

———— and others. *Letters from the Reverend Samuel Davies and others; showing the state of religion in Virginia.* London, 1761.

————. *Little Children Invited to Jesus Christ . . . With an Account of the late remarkable religious impressions among the students in the College of New Jersey.* Fifth ed., Boston, 1765.

————. *Miscellaneous Poems chiefly on Divine Subjects.* Williamsburg, 1751.

————. *Religion and Patriotism . . . A sermon.* Philadelphia, 1755.

————. *Sermons.* 3 vols., New York, 1841 (ed. Albert Barnes).

————. *The Crisis: . . .* London, 1757.

————. *The Curse of Cowardice. . . .* London, 1758.

————. *The Duty of Christians to propagate their Religion among Heathens, Earnestly recommended to the Masters of Negro Slaves in Virginia.* London, 1758.

————. *The Duties, Difficulties and Rewards of the Faithful Minister. . . .* Glasgow, 1754.

————. *The Impartial Trial, impartially Tried, and convicted of Partiality: . . .* Williamsburg, 1748.

————. *The substance of a letter . . . to Mr. Bellamy . . . concerning the state of religion in Virginia. . . .* Letter dated Hanover, June 28, 1751.

————. *The vessels of mercy, and the vessels of wrath . . . A sermon.* New Kent, Virginia, August 22, 1756.

————. *Virginia's Danger and Remedy. Two discourses. . . .* Williamsburg, 1756.

De Vinné, Daniel. *The Methodist Episcopal Church and Slavery.* New York, 1857.

Doddridge, Joseph. *Notes on the Settlement . . . of the Western Parts of Virginia . . . from 1763 to 1783.*

Eckenrode, H. J. *The Separation of Church and State in Virginia.* Richmond, 1909.

————. *The Revolution in Virginia.* Boston, 1916.

Engles, Wm. (ed.). *Records of the Presbyterian Church in the United States of America, 1706-1788.* Philadelphia, 1841.

Faust, A. B. *The German Element in the United States.* 2 vols., Boston, 1909.

Fawcett, Benjamin. *A Compassionate Address to the Christian Negroes in Virginia.* London, 1756.

Fithian, Philip. *Journal and Letters, 1767-1774.* Princeton, 1900.

Foote, W. H. *Sketches of Virginia,* First Series. Philadelphia, 1850.

————. *Sketches of Virginia,* Second Series, Philadelphia, 1855.

Ford, H. J. *The Scotch Irish in America.* Princeton, 1915.

Fristoe, Wm. *History of the Ketocton Baptist Association.* Staunton, Va., 1808.

Garrettson, Freeborn. *Experience and Travels.* Philadelphia, 1791.

Gatch, Philip. *Memoirs.* Compiled by John McLean. Cincinnati, 1854.

Gillett, E. H. *History of the Presbyterian Church in the United States.* Philadelphia, 1873.

Gillies, John. *Historical Collections Relating to . . .the Success of the Gospel.* London, 1845. First published in 1754.

————. *Memoirs of Reverend George Whitefield.* Middletown, 1836.

Grissom, W. L. *History of Methodism in North Carolina.* Nashville, 1905.

Hampden-Sydney College. *Calendar of Board of Minutes, 1776-1876* (comp.) by Alfred J. Morrison. Richmond, 1912.

Hanna, C. A. *The Scotch Irish.* New York, 1902.

Hawks, F. L. *Contributions to the Ecclesiastical History of the United States.* Vol. I is a History of the Protestant Episcopal Church in Virginia. New York, 1836.

Hays, G. P. *Presbyterians.* New York, 1892.

Hening, W. W. *Statutes at Large being a Collection of all the Laws of Virginia, 1619-1792.* 13 vols. Richmond and Philadelphia, 1809-1823.

Hodge, Charles. *Constitutional History of the Presbyterian Church in the United States.* In two parts. Philadelphia, 1851.

Howe, Henry. *Historical Collections of Virginia.* Charleston, 1849.

Howell, R. B. C. *The Early Baptists of Virginia.* Philadelphia, 1864.

Howison, R. R. *A History of Virginia.* 2 vols. Philadelphia, 1846 and 1848.

Hufham, J. D. *The Baptists in North Carolina.* N. C. Baptist Historical Papers, 1897-1898.

Humphrey, E. F. *Nationalism and Religion in America, 1774-1789.* Boston, 1924.

Ireland, James. *Life.* Winchester, Va., 1819.

Jackson, Thos. (ed.). *The Lives of Early Methodist Preachers chiefly written by Themselves.* Vol. III contains the autobiographies of Thomas Rankin and George Shadford.

James, C. F. *Documentary History of the Struggle for Religious Liberty in Virginia.* 1900.

Jameson, J. F. *The American Revolution Considered as a Social Movement.* Princeton, 1926.

Jarratt, Devereux. *An argument between an Anabaptist and a Methodist on the subject and mode of baptism. . . .* Fredericksburg, Va., 1814. Reprint.

————. *A brief narrative of the revival of religion in Virginia. In a letter to a friend.* . . . Fourth ed., London, 1779. The same in Asbury's *Journal*, I, pp. 157 ff.

————. *Life of Devereux Jarratt.* Baltimore, 1806. This is the famous autobiography which was originally written as a series of letters to Coleman.

————. *Justification, in a Letter to a Friend.* Richmond, 1790.

————. *Sermons on Various Important Subjects in Divinity. Adapted to the Plainest Capacities and Suited to the Family and Closet.* 3 vols., Philadelphia, 1793 and Raleigh, N. C., 1805.

————. *Sermon preached before the convention of the Protestant Episcopal Church in Virginia,* at Richmond, May 3, 1792. Richmond, 1792.

————. *Thoughts on some important subjects in divinity; in a series of letters to a friend.* Baltimore, 1806.

Jefferson, Thomas. *Notes on the State of Virginia.* First Hot-Pressed Edition, Philadelphia, 1801.

Johnson, T. C. *Virginia Presbyterianism and Religious Liberty in Colonial and Revolutionary Times.* Richmond, 1907.

Jones, Hugh. *The Present State of Virginia.* London, 1724.

Journal of the House of Delegates of the Commonwealth of Virginia 1777-.

Kercheval, Samuel. *A History of the Valley of Virginia.* Second ed., Woodstock, Va., 1850.

Kuhns, Oscar. *The German and Swiss Settlements of Colonial Pennsylvania.* New York, 1901.

Lecky, W. E. *History of England in the Eighteenth Century.* 7 vols., New York, 1892. Vol. III.

Lee, Jesse. *A Short History of the Methodists in the United States of America.* Baltimore, 1810.

————. *A Short Account of the Life and Death of the Reverend John Lee.* Baltimore, 1805.

————. *Memoirs.* Compiled by the Reverend Minton Thrift, 1823.

Lee, Le Roy. *The Life and Times of Jesse Lee.* Nashville, 1859.

Leland, John. *Writings.* Ed., L. F. Green. New York, 1845. Contains the valuable *Virginia Chronicle.*

Lockwood, J. P. *The Western Pioneers, or Memorials of the Lives and Labours of the Reverend Richard Boardman and the Reverend Joseph Pilmoor.* London, 1881.

MacLean, John. *History of the College of New Jersey from 1746.* 2 vols., Philadelphia, 1877.

Maddox, W. A. *The Free School Idea in Virginia Before the Civil War.* New York, 1918.

Matlack, L. C. *The Anti-Slavery Struggle and Triumph in the Methodist Episcopal Church.* New York, 1881.

————. *The History of American Slavery and Methodism from 1780 to 1849.* New York, 1849.

Maxson, C. H. *The Great Awakening in the Middle Colonies.* Chicago, 1920.

McIlwaine, H. R. *The Struggle of Protestant Dissenters for Religious Toleration in Virginia.* J. H. U. Studies, Series X. Baltimore, 1894.

McTyeire, H. N. *A History of Methodism.* Nashville, 1898.

Meade, Wm. *Old Churches, Ministers and Families of Virginia.* 2 vols. Philadelphia, 1857.

Miller, Samuel. *Life of the Reverend John Rodgers.* New York, 1829.

Minutes of the Baptist General Committee . . . Richmond, May 8, 1790. Richmond.

Minutes of the Baptist General Committee . . . County of Goochland, May 1791. Richmond

Minutes of the Baptist General Committee . . . County of Chesterfield, Virginia, May 1792. Richmond.

Minutes of the Baptist General Committee . . . Powhatan County, Virginia, May 1793. Richmond, 1793.

Minutes of the Baptist General Committee . . . Spottsylvania County, May 1799.

Minutes of the Baptist General Meeting of Correspondence . . . Chesterfield County, Virginia, October, 1808.

Minutes of the Dover Baptist Association of Virginia, 1790, 1791, 1793, 1794, 1795, 1796, 1797, 1798.

Minutes of the Goshen Baptist Association . . . Caroline County, October 1793 . . . .

Minutes of the Virginia Portsmouth Baptist Association, 1791, 1792, 1793, 1794, 1796, 1797, 1798, 1799.

Minutes of several Conversations between the Reverend Thomas Coke, the Reverend Francis Asbury and others, at a Conference begun in Baltimore . . . on Monday, the 27th of December, in the year 1784. Composing a Form of Discipline for the ٠ . . Methodist Episcopal Church in America. Philadelphia, 1785.

Minutes of the Methodist Conferences annually held in America from 1773 to 1794 inclusive. Philadelphia, 1795.

Moore, M. H. *Sketches of the Pioneers of Methodism in North Carolina and Virginia.* 1884.

Morgan, George. *The True Patrick Henry.* Philadelphia, 1907.

Morrison, A. J. (ed.). *Hampden-Sydney College Calendar of Board Minutes 1776-1876.* Richmond, 1912.

Motley, D. E. *Life of Commissary James Blair.* Baltimore, 1901.

Murphy, T. *The Presbytery of the Log College.* Philadelphia, 1889.

Nagler, A. W. *Pietism and Methodism.* Nashville, 1918.

Overton, J. H. *The Evangelical Revival in the Eighteenth Century.* London, 1886.

Patton, J. H. *The Triumph of the Presbytery of Hanover; or Separation of Church and State in Virginia.* New York (1887?).

Perry, W. S. *Historical Collections relating to the American Colonial Church.* 5 vols., Hartford, 1870-78. Vol. I, Virginia.

————. *History of the American Episcopal Church.* 2 vols., Boston, 1885.

Peyton, J. L. *History of Augusta County, Virginia,* Staunton, 1882.

Philadelphia Confession of Faith Being the London Confession of 1689, The. Philadelphia, 1907.

Phoebus, Wm. *Memoirs of the Reverend Richard Whatcoat.* New York, 1828.

Porter, J. *Revivals of Religion.* New York, 1878.

Prince, Thomas (ed.). *The Christian History* for the years 1743 and 1744. Boston.

Purefoy, G. W. *A History of the Sandy Creek Baptist Association from its organization in A.D. 1785 to A.D. 1858.* New York, 1859.

Records of the Presbyterian Church in the United States of America, etc. Philadelphia, 1841. See Engles, Wm. (ed.).

Rice, David. *Memoirs.* See under Bishop, R. H.

Rice, John H. *Memoir of Samuel Davies.* Boston, 1832. Published anonymously.

Rippon, John. *The Baptist Annual Register for 1790, 1791, 1792, and part of 1793.* London.

Robinson, Morgan P. *Virginia Counties.* Richmond, 1916. Virginia State Library Bulletin, Vol. IX.

Schuricht, H. *History of the German Element in Virginia.* Baltimore, 1898-1900.

Scott, W. W. *History of Orange County, Virginia . . . 1734-1870.* Richmond, 1907.

Semple, R. B. *A History of the Rise and Progress of the Baptists in Virginia.* 1810. G. W. Beale edition, Philadelphia, 1894.

Shadford, George. *Autobiography.* See under Jackson, Thomas (ed.).

Shepherd, Samuel. *The Statutes at Large of Virginia, 1792-1808.* Richmond, 1835-6. Continues the work of Hening.

Sherman, David. *History of the Revisions of the Discipline of the Methodist Episcopal Church.* 3rd ed. New York, 1890.

Sketches of History of the Baptist Churches, within the limits of the Rappahannock Association in Virginia. Compiled by a Committee of the Association, Richmond, 1850.

Slaughter, Philip. *A History of Bristol Parish, Virginia.* Richmond, 1879.

————. *A History of St. George's Parish.* Richmond, 1890.

————. *A History of St. Mark's Parish.* Baltimore, 1877.

————. *A History of Truro Parish.* Philadelphia, 1898.

Sprague, W. B. *Annals of the American Pulpit.* 9 vols., New York, 1857-1869.

Stevens, Abel. *History of the Religious Movement of the Eighteenth Century called Methodism.* 3 vols., New York, 1858-1861.

————. *History of the Methodist Episcopal Church in the United States of America.* 4 vols., New York, 1864-1867.

————. *Centenary of American Methodism.* New York, 1866.

Strickland, W. P. *Life and Times of Francis Asbury.* London, 1860.

Summers, L. P. *History of Southwest Virginia, 1746-1786, Washington County, 1777-1870.* Richmond, 1903.

Taylor, J. B. *Virginia Baptist Ministers.* Series I and II. New York, 1860.

Thom, W. T. *The Struggle for Religious Freedom in Virginia: The Baptists.* J. H. U. Studies, Series XVIII. Baltimore, 1900.

Thomas, David. *The Virginian Baptist.* Baltimore, 1774.

Thomson, John. *Doctrine of Conviction set in a Clear Light.* Philadelphia, 1741.

————. *The Government of the church of Christ . . . or the matter of the difference between the Synod of Philadelphia and the Protesting Brethren justly and fairly stated.* Philadelphia, 1741.

Thrift, Minton (ed.). *Memoirs of Jesse Lee.* 1823.

Tigert, J. J. *A Constitutional History of American Episcopal Methodism.* Nashville, 1904.

————. *The Making of Methodism.* Nashville, 1898.

Townsend, L. T. *The Supernatural Factor in Religious Revivals.* Boston, 1877.

Townsend, W. J., Workman, H. B., and Eayrs, George (eds.). *A New History of Methodism.* 2 vols., London, 1909.

Tracy, Joseph. *The Great Awakening: . . .* Boston, 1842.

Trostle, J. A. *Timber Ridge Presbyterian Church, Rockbridge County, Virginia.* 1906.

Tucker, J. R. *Influence of Presbyterian Polity on Civil and Religious Liberty in Virginia.* Richmond, 1889.

Tucker, R. L. *The Separation of the Methodists from the Church of England.* New York, 1918. (Ph.D. thesis Columbia Univ.)

Turner, F. J. *The Frontier in American History,* Ch. III, "The Old West." New York, 1921.

Turpin, J. B. *A Brief History of the Albemarle Baptist Association.* Richmond (1891?).

Tyerman, Luke. *The Life and Times of the Reverend John Wesley.* 3 vols., New York, 1870, London, 1872-5.

————. *The Life of the Reverend George Whitefield.* 2 vols., London, 1876-7.

Tyler, M. C. *Patrick Henry.* Boston, 1898.

Van Devanter, J. N. *History of the Augusta Church, 1737-1900.* Staunton, 1900.

Waddell, J. A. *Scotch-Irish of the Valley of Virginia.* Staunton.

————. *Annals of Augusta County Virginia from 1726 1871*. Second ed., rev. and enlarged. Staunton, 1902.

Ware, Thomas. *Sketches of the Life and Travels of*. New York, 1842.

Watters, William. *A Short Account of the Christian Experience and Ministerial Labours of . . . Drawn up by Himself*. Alexandria (preface dated 1806).

Wayland, J. W. *History of Rockingham County, Virginia*. Dayton, Va., 1912.

————. *The German Element of the Shenandoah Valley of Virginia*. Charlottesville, 1907. Also in *Va. Mag. Hist. and Biog.*, IX-X.

Webster, R. *History of the Presbyterian Church in America from its origin until the year 1760. . . .* Philadelphia, 1857.

Weeks, S. B. *Southern Quakers and Slavery. Baltimore,* 1896.

Wertenbaker, T. J. *Patrician and Plebeian in Virginia*. Charlottesville, 1910.

Wesley, John. *A Calm Address to our American Colonies*. Bristol, England, 1775.

————. *The Journal of the Reverend John Wesley, A.M.* Standard ed., 8 vols., London, 1909-1916.

Wesley, John. *Reflections on the rise and progress of the American rebellion*. London, 1780. First published anonymously.

————. *Some Account of the Late Work of God in North America, in a Sermon. . . .* London, 1778.

————. *Thoughts upon Slavery*. Philadelphia, 1774.

Whitsitt, W. H. *Life and Times of Judge Caleb Wallace*. Louisville, 1888.

Woods, Edgar. *Albemarle County in Virginia*. Charlottesville, 1901.

Woolman, John. *Journal of John Woolman*. Boston, 1871. Reprinted in the Harvard Classics series.

III. ARTICLES, LETTERS AND MATERIAL IN NEWSPAPERS, PERIODICALS, AND OTHER PUBLICATIONS

Adams, Charles. "Wesley the Catholic." *Meth. Quar. Rev.* (N. Y.), Vol. XXXII (1850).

Alexander, A. "Reverend Drury Lacy." *Watchman of the South,* January 10, 1839.

————. "New Lights." *Watchman and Observer,* March 18, 1847.

————. "Reverend William Graham." *Watchman of the South,* January 4, 1844.

Alexander, Gross. "Two Chapters from the Early History of Methodism in the South." *Meth. Rev.* (So.), Vol. XLVI (1897). Same in *Meth. Quar. Rev.,* Vol. LXIII (1914).

Alexander, J. W. "Memoir of James Waddel." *Watchman of the South,* September 19, 26, October 3, 1844.

Anthony, Joseph. "Sketch of." *Religious Herald,* August 29, 1872.

Ayers, S. G. "Francis Asbury and His Presbyterian Friends." *Meth. Rev. Quar.* (So.), Vol. LXVI (1917).

————. "Sources of American Methodist History." *Meth. Rev.* (N. Y.), Vol. XCVI (1914).

Baker, Elijah. "Sketch of." *Religious Herald,* September 12, 1872.

Baketel, O. S. "The First Educational Institutions of the Methodist Episcopal Church." *Meth. Rev.* (N. Y.), Vol. XCVII (1915).

"Baptist Ministers, Persecution of, in Chesterfield County, Virginia, 1771-1773." *Va. Mag. of Hist. and Biog.,* Vol. XI.

Bassett, J. S. "The Development of the Popular Churches after the Revolution." *Proc. Mass. Hist. Soc.,* Vol. XLVIII.

————. "Relations Between the Virginia Planter and the London Merchant." *Proc. Am. Hist. Ass'n.,* 1901, Vol. I.

Beam, J. N. "Dr. Robert Smith's Academy at Pequea, Pennsylvania." *Jour. Pres. Hist. Soc.,* VIII, 145-161.

Benson, L. F. "President Davies as a Hymn Writer." *Jour. Pres. Hist. Soc.,* II, 277 ff. and 343 ff.

"Blair, Samuel, of Fagg's Manor." *Watchman of the South,* September 28, October 5, 12, 1843.

Bond, T. E. "The Methodist Episcopal Church South." *Meth. Quar. Rev.* (N. Y.), Vol. XXXI (1849), pp. 282-302.

Bostwick, David. "Character of Samuel Davies." In Davies' *Sermons,* 4th Amer. ed., New York, 1828, I, 47-51.

Broadus, J. A. "The American Baptist Ministry 100 Years Ago." *Bap. Quar.,* IX (1875), pp. 1-20.

Brooks, E. C. "Francis Asbury an Educational Reformer." *Meth. Rev. Quar.* (So.), Vol. LXV (1916), pp. 341-362.

"Byrd Library at Westover, 1777, The." *Va. Mag. of Hist. and Biog.,* XII, 205-7.

Capers, T. S. "The Great Awakening in the Middle Colonies." *Jour. Pres. Hist. Soc.,* VIII (1916), 296-315.

Carter, Robert. "A catalogue of books in the library of, at Nomini Hall." *William and Mary Quar.,* X, 232-241, XI, 21-28.

Carter, Col. Landon. "Extracts from the Diary of." *William and Mary Quar.,* Vols. XIII-XVIII, XX-XXI.

Chiles, James. Sketch of. *Religious Herald,* August 15, 1872.

Cokesbury College, Description of. *Arminian Mag.* (Amer.), II (1790).

Conoly, W. J. "The Catholicity of Methodism." *Meth. Rev. Quar.* (So.) Vol. LXV (1916), pp. 718-28.

Courtenay, A. M. "The Reverend Devereux Jarratt." *Meth. Rev.* (So.), Vol. XLVII (1898), pp. 336-349.

Craig Lewis, Sketch of. *Religious Herald,* August 8, 1872.

Craven, E. R. "The Log College of Neshaminy and Princeton University." *Jour. Pres. Hist. Soc.,* I, 308-314.

Cronk, W. C. "Spener and Pietism." *Meth. Quar. Rev.* (So.), Vol. LXIV (1915), pp. 763-769.

Curry, D. "Reverend Jesse Lee." *Meth. Quar. Rev.* (N. Y.), Vol. XXXII (1850), pp. 58-80.

Davies, Samuel, "Memoir of." Rice's *Virginia Evangelical and Literary Magazine,* II (1819), 112, 186, 201, 329, 353, 474, 560 ff.

De Witt, J. "The Planting of Princeton." *Jour. Pres. Hist. Soc.,* VIII; also *Pres. and Reformed Rev.,* VIII; also *Princeton Sesquicentennial Celebration* volume.

Edson, H. A., "John Todd of Virginia and John Todd of Indiana." *Pres. Rev.,* VII (1886), 16-26.

"Evangelism of the Eighteenth Century." *Pres. Quar. Rev.,* IX (1860-61), 476-493.

Faulkner, J. A. "Certain Aspects of Early Methodism." *So. Meth. Rev.,* N. S. III (1887), 179-192.

Foster, F. H. "Revivals of Religion." *New Schaff-Herzog Cyc. of Religion,* X.

Finley, S. "Sermon on the Death of the Reverend Samuel Davies." Davies' *Sermons,* fourth Amer. ed., New York, 1828, Vol. I.

Garrettson, Freeborn, "Life of." *Meth. Mag. and Quar. Rev.,* XII (1830), pp. 341-60.

Garrettson, Freeborn, "Memoir of." *Meth. Mag.,* XI (1828), 92-99.

Garrettson, R. "An Account of the Revival of the Work of God at Petersburg in Virginia." (Dated February, 1788.) *Arminian Mag.* (Eng.), XIII, 1790, 300-307.

Gewehr, W. M. "Factors in the Expansion of Frontier Methodism." *Journal of Religion,* January, 1928, pp. 98-120.

Gibbons, Thos. "Divine Conduct Vindicated. . . ." (Two discourses preached in London, March 29, 1761, occasioned by the decease of Samuel Davies.) Davies' *Sermons,* 4th Amer. ed., New York, 1828, Vol. I, 31-47.

Gordon, Colonel James. "Journal." *William and Mary College Quar.,* XI, XII.

Graham, William, "Memoir of." Rice's *Virginia Evangelical and Literary Mag.,* IV (1821), 75, 150, 253, 397 ff.

――――. Sketch on his preaching by a contemporary. *Watchman of the South,* December 12, 1839.

"Great Awakening, The." *The Christian Review,* IX (1844), 372-395.

Grigsby, H. B. "The founders of Washington College." *Wash. and Lee Hist. Papers,* no. 2, 1890.

Harvey, W. P. "Reverend William Hickman." *Pubs. Ky. Bapt. Hist. Soc.,* no. 1.

Hendrix, E. R. "Jonathan Edwards and John Wesley." *Meth. Rev. Quar.,* Vol. LXII (1913), pp. 28-38.

――――. "The Evolution of the Methodist Hymnal." *Meth. Quar. Rev.* (So.), Vol. LV (1906), pp. 3-18.

――――. "The Second Rise of Methodism." *Meth. Rev.* (So.), Vol. L (1901), pp. 217-231.

Hill, William, "Life and Times of." *Pres. Quar. Rev.,* Vol. II, 41-63.
————. "Reverend Cary Allen." *Pres. Quar. Rev.,* Vol. IV, 55-79.
————. "Rev. Nash Le Grand." *Pres. Quar. Rev.,* Vol. III, 601-16.
————. "Reverend James Turner." *Pres. Quar Rev.,* Vol. III, 270-8.
Hinke, Wm. J., and Kemper, C. E. (eds.). "Moravian Diaries of Travels through Virginia." *Va. Mag. of Hist. and Biog.,* Vols. XI and XII.
Hoskins, J. P. "German Influence on Religious Life and Thought in America." *Princeton Theol. Rev.,* V (1907).
Hughes, J. G., Jr. "Samuel Davies." *J. P. Branch Historical Papers of Randolph-Macon College,* Vol. IV, no. 2 (1914).
Hunt, G. "James Madison and Religious Liberty." *Rep. Amer. Hist. Ass'n.,* 1901, Vol. I, pp. 163-172.
Ingram, G. H. "Erection of the Presbytery of New Brunswick." *Jour. Pres. Hist. Soc.,* VI, 212-233.
————. "History of the Presbytery of New Brunswick." *Jour. Pres. Hist. Soc.,* Vols. VI, VII, VIII, X. Contains the early minutes.
James, E. W. "Libraries in Colonial Virginia." *William and Mary Quar.,* Vols. II, III, IV, VI, VIII.
Jarratt, Devereux, "Review of the Life of, published in Baltimore, 1806." *Virginia Evan. and Lit. Mag.,* XI, 257-263.
————. "Testimony of, in favor of Evangelical Doctrines." *Va. Evan. and Lit. Mag.,* IV, 178-180.
Jernegan, M. W. "Religious Toleration and Freedom in Virginia, 1689-1786." Harper's *Parallel Source Problems in United States History.*
————. *Slavery and Conversion in the American Colonies.* Amer. Hist. Rev., XXI, pp. 504-527.
Kemper, Chas. E. "Early History of the Peaked Mountain Presbyterian Church, Rockingham County, Virginia." *Jour. Pres. Hist. Soc.,* X, 17-23.
————, (ed.). "Early Westward Movement of Virginia, 1722-1734." *Va. Mag. Hist. and Biog.,* Vols. XII, XIII.
Letter of Philip Bruce to Coke, March 25, 1788, describing the revivals in Virginia. *Arminian Mag.* (Amer.), II, 563-4.
Letter of Philip Cox to Coke, July, 1787, describing the revivals in Virginia. *Arminian Mag.,* II (Amer.), 91-95.
Letter of Samuel Davies to R. C. Esq. (of London), March, 1755. *Evan. and Lit. Mag.,* IV, 539-42. Another letter to the same March 2, 1756, in *ibid.,* 544-49.
Letter to Samuel Davies to Mr. Bellamy in regard to Jonathan Edward's coming to Virginia. *Pres. Mag.,* IV, 513-515.
Letter of Samuel Davies from Hanover, July 14, 1756. *Va. Evan. and Lit. Mag.,* IV, 552. Same in Gillies, *Hist. Colls.,* p. 506.
Letter of Samuel Davies in reference to his being chosen President of Princeton. *The Presbyterian* (Phila.), July 17, 1833.

Letter of Samuel Davies, June 3, 1757. *Va. Evan. and Lit. Mag.,* IV, 573-577.

Letters of Samuel Davies of a religious nature. *General Assembly's Missionary Mag. or Evangelical Intelligencer,* I (1805), 371, 425, 538, 578.

Letters of J. W. Giberne to the Irreverend Mr. James Waddell, in Lancaster (Va.). Rind's *Virginia Gazette,* August 18, 1768, Supp.

Letter of Thomas Rankin to Mr. Wesley describing the revivals (1776) in Virginia. In Jarratt's *Narrative.*

Letter of J. B. Smith, October 6, 1788, to 'A Lady in Philadelphia.' *The Presbyterian,* Vol. XV, p. 153, September 27, 1845.

Letter of Robert Smith to same in *ibid.,* describing the revival at Hampden-Sydney.

Letter of John Todd to Whitefield, June 26, 1755. *Evan. and Lit. Mag.,* IV, 550-551. Same in Gillies, *Hist. Colls.,* pp. 505-6.

Letter of John Wright to the Rev. Mr. —— in Scotland, January 20, 1757. *Evan. and Lit. Mag.,* IV, 572-3.

Letter of John Wright, August 18, 1755. *Ibid.,* 551-2. Same in Gillies, *Hist. Colls.,* p. 506.

Letter of James Waddell to Rev. Mr. W(illiam) G(iberne). Rind's *Virginia Gazette,* July 21, 1768.

Letters of Patrick Henry, Sr., Samuel Davies, James Maury, Edwin Conway, and George Trask. (From Dawson MSS.) *William and Mary College Quar.,* 2nd series I (1921), 261-281.

Lovejoy, W. P. "The Influence of Methodism." *Meth. Rev.* (So.), Vol. LI (1902), 367-382.

McCulloch, J. E. "The Place of Revivals in American History." *Meth. Rev.* (So.), Vol. LI (1902), 681-697.

McRoberts, Archibald. "Trial of, 1772-4." *Va. Mag. of Hist. and Biog.,* XI, 414.

"Methodist Hymnology." *Meth. Quar. Rev.* (N. Y.), Vol. XXX (1848), 602-13.

Mirbt, C. "Pietism." New *Schaff-Herzog Cyc. of Religion,* Vol. IX.

Mode, P. G. "Revivalism as a Phase of Frontier Life." *Journal of Religion,* July, 1921.

"Moravian Diaries of Travels in Virginia." *Va. Mag. of Hist. and Biog.,* Vols. XI and XII.

"Old Hanover Records." *Watchman and Observer,* November 6, 20, 27, December 4, 18, 1845.

"Origin of Presbyterianism in Virginia." *Evan. and Lit. Mag.,* II, 346-53. Contains Hunt's narrative of the Hanover revival.

Parham, E. P. "Jesse Lee, Methodist Historian." *Meth. Rev. Quar.* (So.), Vol. LXV (1916), 352-6.

Patton, J. H. "The Separation of Church and State in Virginia." *Pres. Rev.,* IV (1883), 20-43.

"Petition for charter of Liberty Hall Academy." *William and Mary College Quar.,* XIII, 265-266.

Pickett, John. "Sketch of." *Religious Herald,* September 5, 1872.

"Presbyterian Church in Hanover, Virginia, previous to Mr. Davies." *Watchman of the South,* June 15, 1843.

Rankin, Thomas, "Short Account of Mr., in a letter to the Reverend John Wesley." London, November 16, 1778. *Arminian Mag.* (Eng.), II (1779), 182-198.

"Reciprocal Influence of the Evangelical Denominations." *Pres. Mag.,* II (1852), pp. 1-5.

Religious Herald, The. (The great Baptist organ of Virginia which has been in existence for a century, 1828-. The Va. Bap. Hist. Soc. has the complete file.)

Rice, David. "Slavery inconsistent with Justice and Good Policy, 1792." In Bishop, *History of the Church in Kentucky,* pp. 385-418.

Sasnett, W. J. "Theory of Methodist Class Meetings." *Quar. Rev. of M. E. Church South,* V (1851), 265-284.

Smith, G. G. "Jesse Lee." *So. Meth. Rev.,* N.S. III, Vol. I (1887), pp. 80-95.

————. "The Colonial Church of Virginia." *Meth. Quar. Rev.* (So.), N.S., Vol. XIII, January, 1893, and Vol. XIV, April, 1893.

Smith, J. T. "Life and Times of the Reverend John Leland." *Bap. Quar.,* V. (1871), 230-256.

Smith, J. W. "Devereux Jarratt and the beginnings of Methodism in Virginia." *J. P. Branch Hist. Papers of Randolph-Macon College,* no. 1, June, 1901.

Smucker, J. A. "The Great Awakening." *Amer. Ant. Soc. Proc.,* 1874.

Smyth, T. "Presbyterianism, the Revolution, the Declaration and the Constitution," in *The Southern Presbyterian Review,* March, 1848, Vol. I, no. 4, pp. 33-79.

"Society in East Virginia." *William and Mary Quar.,* XXII, 221-8, 252.

Stannard, W. G. "Racing in Colonial Virginia." *Va. Mag. of Hist. and Biog.,* II, 293-305.

"The First Presbyterian Preacher in the Middle Counties of Old Virginia (William Robinson)." Contains account of the Hanover revival. *Watchman of the South,* May 25, June 1, 8, 1843.

"Thoughts on Revivals of Religion." Art. signed "Holem," *Evan. and Lit. Mag.,* V, 301-8.

Tigert, J. J. "Original Status of the M. E. Church." *So. Meth. Rev.,* N.S. II, no. 1, March, 1887.

Tyler, L. G. "Education in Colonial Virginia." *William and Mary Quar.,* Vols. V, VI, VII.

Tillett, W. F. "Methodist Hymnology." *Meth. Quar. Rev.* (So.), Vol. LII (1903), 333-348.

Tinkling Spring Church, Augusta County, Virginia. "Sketch of the History of." *Pres. Mag.,* II, 462-470.

Turner, F. J. "The Old West," in his *Frontier in American History,* New York, 1920, pp. 67-125.

Virginia Gazette (those available for the period of the Great Awakening, files very incomplete). Williamsburg and Richmond.

Virginia Gazette or American Advertizer. Richmond.

Virginia Gazette and Weekly Advertizer. Richmond.

Virginia Independent Chronicle. Richmond.

Waddell, James. "Briefs of Sermons from the original manuscripts." *Watchman of the South,* March 28, April 11, 18, 1844.

Waller, John, "Sketch of." *Religious Herald,* August 1, 1872.

Ware, Thomas. "The Christmas Conference." *Meth. Mag. and Quar. Rev.,* January, 1832, pp. 96-104.

Watchman of the South, Richmond, 1837-45. A leading Presbyterian organ for the period. Complete file in the Union Theological Seminary of Richmond.

Watchman and Observer, Richmond, 1845-65. Continues the above after union with the Charleston *Observer.*

Webber, William, "Sketch of." *Religious Herald,* August 22, 1872.

White, A. D. "Diabolism and Hysteria." *Popular Science Monthly,* XXXV, 1-16, 145-155.

Winter, L. P., "Charles Wesley in America." *Meth. Quar. Rev.* (So.), Vol. LXV (1916), 71-84.

IV. MANUSCRIPT MATERIALS

Brown, John. Memorandum book of the Pastor of the Congregations of Timber Ridge and New Providence, 1754-97. Pres. Hist. Soc., Philadelphia.

Church Books for the period in the Va. Bap. Hist. Soc.

    Albemarle Church, 1773-1811.

    Boarswamp Church, 1791-1828.

    Broad Run Church, 1762-1872.

    Morattico Church, 1778-1844.

    Upper King and Queen Church, 1774-1816.

Dawson Manuscripts, 1728-1775. Library of Congress.

Dozier, Richard. Text Book from 1771. Sermons preached from the within texts and heard by Mr. Richard Dozier, son of Thomas, in Westmoreland County, Virginia.

Dunaway, ——. History of Morattico Church. Va. Bap. Hist. Soc.

Edwards, Morgan. Materials Towards a History of the Baptists in Virginia to 1772. First 39 pages missing. Copy in Va. Bap. Hist. Soc. Original in Amer. Bap. Hist. Soc., Chester, Pa.

Hanover Presbytery Records, 1755-1795, 3 vols. Union Theological Seminary, Richmond.

Minutes of Baptist Associations. Va. Bap. Hist. Soc.

    Burrus's Meeting House, Caroline County, October 3, 1788.

Roanoke Association, 1788-1831.

Strawberry District Association, 1787-1822.

Moore, Jeremiah, Sketch of. Anon. Va. Bap. Hist. Soc.

Observations on Mr. Samuel Davies, his Letter, etc. 39 pp. Va. Religious Papers, Lib. of Cong.

Saunders, Nathaniel. Papers. Va. Bap. Hist. Soc.

Tax Lists of Virginia Counties in Va. State Library archives.

Virginia Bap. Hist. Soc. MSS. Miscellaneous letters, petitions, orders for arrest, etc., which appear in this study.

Virginia Religious Papers in Lib. of Congress contain various odds and ends dealing with the eighteenth century.

Virginia Religious Petitions. There are several hundred of these petitions to the legislature bearing on the subject matter of this study for the period from about 1770 on. They are filed in order of county or denomination and date.

Williams, John. Diary, 1771. Va. Bap. Hist. Soc.

INDEX

Abingdon, Md., seat of Cokesbury College, 233.

Act for Establishing Religious Freedom, in Virginia, 212.

"Address to the Anabaptists Imprisoned in Caroline County, August 1771," 128 n. 112 ff.

"Address to the House of Burgesses," 1751, presented by the Anglican clergy, 73.

Adopting Act, 10.

Alexander, Archibald, 182, 184 n. 81; president of Hampden-Sydney, 229 n. 46.

Alison, Francis, master of schools at New London and Philadelphia, 223 n. 17.

Allen, Cary, 178.

Amelia Circuit, revivals on, 156-7, 168-9, 171.

American Husbandry, 24.

American Revolution, *see* Revolution.

Anderson, James, Presbyterian itinerant, 43.

Anglicans, *see* Clergy, Established Church.

Antony, Joseph, Baptist preacher, arrested, 123, 127.

Apostacies, 112, 176, 181.

Appendix Proving the Right of the Synod of New York to the Religious Liberties and Immunities allowed to the Protestant Dissenters, by Samuel Davies, 75, 84.

Arminianism, 165; inroads of, upon Baptists, 254.

Asbury, Francis, in Virginia, 145; and Robert Williams, 145, 148; quoted, 145, 259; elected Bishop, 159; and ordinance controversy, 161; interest of, in education, 233 and n. 66; attitude of, in slavery, 242.

Asplund, John, *Annual Register,* Baptist, 106.

Associations, Baptist, 173, 174, 175 n. 42; political influence of, 194;

composition and powers of, 196; attitude towards slavery, 240-1. *See* Ketocton, Regular Baptist Association.

Augusta Church, 44.

Augusta County, created, 42; seminary in, 226; weakness of Established church in, 42-43.

Backcountry, settled, 25; characteristics of, 27 ff.; religious conditions in, 34 ff.

Baker, Elijah, Baptist preacher, 120.

Bands, Methodist, 7, 163-4, 198.

Baptist Annual Register, see Asplund, John, Rippon, John.

Baptists, growth in numbers, 106; Separate and Regular, 107; changed status by 1790, 116-117, 134-5, 177, 254-5; effects of American Revolution on revival, 136; post-revolutionary revival among, 173 ff.; union of Regulars and Separates, 177; and the Revolution, 188 ff.; political influence of, 193-4; church government of, 195; petitions from, 200 ff.; and Toleration Act of 1772, 202-3; war on glebes, 214; and education, 234, 256-7; and slavery, 239-41; attention of, to ministerial support, 255-6; migration of preachers to Kentucky, 255; proposal of, for a Seminary, 256; proposal of, for a history, 257; improved economic status of, 259-60; *see* General Committee, Dissenters, Petitions, Religious Liberty, Separate and Regular Baptists.

Barrow, David, Baptist preacher, 120; *Circular Letter,* 191; political philosophy of, 192; attitude of, towards slavery, 239-40; removal of, to Kentucky, 239.

Bath, parish of, revival in, 139 ff.; *see* Jarratt.

Bedford County, Presbyterian revival in, 181 ff.

[281]

"Luther," *pseud.*, attacks Hampden-Sydney College, 227-8.

Luther, Martin, influence of his *Commentary on Galatians* on Hanover revival, 47-48.

Lutherans, name of, assumed by people in Hanover revival, 49.

Mabury's (Mabry's) Chapel, meeting at, in 1776, 151; in 1787, 169.

Madison, James, champion of Baptists, 135 and n. 143; and John Leland, 189 and n. 8; enlists Baptists in favor of the Constitution, 194; and religious liberty, 203-4; leads struggle against a general assessment, 206; Memorial of, against assessment, 209.

Makemie, Francis, pioneer of Presbyterianism in Virginia, 40.

Major, Richard, Baptist minister, 114 n. 39.

Marshall, Daniel, Baptist preacher, 117.

Mash, William, Baptist preacher, imprisoned, 122.

Methodist Book Concern, 146, 165.

Methodists, in Virginia, beginning of revival, 141; first circuit in Virginia, 141, 144; membership of, in 1773-4, 145; attachment of, to Established Church, 146; evangelical views of, 146; revival of 1775-6 described, 148 ff.; membership and circuits in 1774-6, 155-6; increase in ministers among, 157; effects of the Revolutionary War upon, 158-9; recovery of, after the war, 159; controversy over ordinances, 160-162; factors in expansion of, 162-166; itinerant system among, 162-3; lay ministry among, 163; local organization of, 163-4; hymnody, 164; theology, 164-5; distribution of literature by, 165-6, 234; spared from persecution, 166; post-Revolutionary revival among, 168 ff.; increase of, after 1787, 173; a popular church, 195, 198; church government among, 198; emphasis on individual, 198; and education,

233; and slavery, 242-9; petition for emancipation of slaves, 247, 249 n. 71.

Middlesex County, court records, 128; Baptist prosecutions in, 123, 128.

Miller, Alexander, Presbyterian minister, in Augusta County, 44; joins Hanover Presbytery, 100.

Montgomery, John, assistant to Graham at Liberty Hall Academy, 230.

Moore, Jeremiah, Baptist preacher, 118.

Morattico Church, Baptist, 175, 259.

Moravian itinerants, 35.

Morris, Samuel, leader in Hanover revival, 47 ff.; his "Reading House," 48; brought to trial, 57 and n. 93; fined, 58; mentioned by Parson Henry, 59.

McCrea, James, licensed by New Brunswick Presbytery, 15.

McRoberts, Archibald, Episcopal minister, 138; associated with Jarratt's revival, 140-141; leaves the Episcopal Church, 142; his dislike of Methodists, 142-3.

Münster, Anabaptists of, 131, 257.

Negroes, and the Presbyterians, 72, 96, 236; conversion of, 169, 170; revival phenomena among, 170; received in communion by evangelicals, 235, 239 n. 20, 241 and n. 34, n. 35, 249; spiritual welfare of, emphasized, 249. *See* slavery.

New Brunswick, N. J., revival at, 5.

New Brunswick Presbytery, erected by New Side Presbyterians, in 1738, 10; purpose in erecting, 15; exclusion from Synod of Philadelphia, 17.

New Jersey, College of, *see* Princeton.

New Lights, origin of term, 45 n. 28; doctrines and methods described by Old Side wing, 16, and Parson Henry, 59-61; denounced by Anglican clergy, 73; question of whether the Toleration Act extended to, 81; the appellation re-